BIRTH AN

Martha Browning Bryant had just done what she did best—helped another woman deliver a new life into the world. Now in the early morning hours of October 9, 1992, the immensely popular young Oregon midwife was driving home to her husband in her Volkswagen Beetle. She never made it. She was found dead on the road, her body riddled with bullets. The search for a killer was on.

That search would not end until the bodies of many more women were discovered, on a trail of sickeningly savage perversity from Florida to the Pacific Northwest. Now the chilling story is told about a sexual sadist who brutalized even the woman who had loved and raised him as a child—a killer whose death toll staggered even the seasoned professionals who finally brought him to justice.

This is the riveting true-crime shocker about Jimmy Rode, alias Cesar Barone, the handsome charmer who could have had any woman he desired to love—but only desired one woman after another—to kill. . . .

DEAD OF NIGHT

Ⓢ **SIGNET**   Ⓞ **ONYX**   (0451)

TRUE-LIFE CRIME

☐ **GOTTI: RISE AND FALL by Jerry Capeci and Gene Mustain.** With 8 pages of powerful photos. By using F.B.I. tapes and a host of sources on both sides of the law, star organized-crime reporters Jerry Capeci and Gene Mustain tell the whole, true, uncensored story of John Gotti.   (406818—$6.99)

☐ **MOCKERY OF JUSTICE The True Story of the Sheppard Murder Case by Cynthia L. Cooper and Sam Reese Sheppard.** With 8 pages of haunting photos. Dr. Sam Sheppard was convicted of murdering his wife. Only after ten years of prison was Sheppard freed. His life in ruins, Sam Sheppard died tragically young. Behind him, he left a son who set out to clear his father's name and track down his mother's murderer. Now that work has been done in the headline-making book that at last names the killer who got away. "The infamous case that inspired *The Fugitive!*"—*People*   (407636—$5.99)

☐ **THE STALKING OF KRISTIN** *A Father Investigates the Murder of His Daughter* **by George Lardner, Jr..** With a special personal photo insert for this edition. When *Washington Post* reporter George Lardner learned his daughter Kristin had been shot and killed by an ex-boyfriend, his first reaction was grief. Then he set out to uncover the full truth about this monstrous crime. "A fascinating account of two short lives."—*Washington Post*   (407318—$5.99)

☐ **GOODBYE, MY LITTLE ONES The True Story of a Murderous Mother and Five Innocent Victims by Charles Hickey, Todd Lighty, and John O'Brien.** With 8 pages of photos. When Waneta Hoyt's five babies died one after another, nobody, including her husband, stopped her from having more babies to kill. For a famed medical expert had declared they died of Sudden Infant Death Syndrome. However, District Attorney Bill Fitzpatrick set out to expose the truth about a crime hard to imagine.   (406923—$5.99)

☐ **THE DEATH SHIFT:** *The True Story of Nurse Genene Jones and the Texas Baby Murders* **by Peter Elkind.** This nerve-shattering account reconstructs the chilling events that lead to the deaths of up to thirteen children, as it probes the darkest depths of criminal madness. "Shocking ... true-crime reporting at its most compelling."—*Booklist*
                    (401964—$4.95)

Prices slightly higher in Canada.

Buy them at your local bookstore or use this convenient coupon for ordering.

PENGUIN USA
P.O. Box 999 — Dept. #17109
Bergenfield, New Jersey 07621

Please send me the books I have checked above.
I am enclosing $_____ (please add $2.00 to cover postage and handling). Send check or money order (no cash or C.O.D.'s) or charge by Mastercard or VISA (with a $15.00 minimum). Prices and numbers are subject to change without notice.

Card #_____ Exp. Date _____
Signature_____
Name_____
Address_____
City _____ State _____ Zip Code _____

For faster service when ordering by credit card call **1-800-253-6476**

Allow a minimum of 4-6 weeks for delivery. This offer is subject to change without notice.

DEAD
OF
NIGHT

THE TRUE STORY
OF A SERIAL KILLER

Don Lasseter

AN ONYX BOOK

ONYX
Published by the Penguin Group
Penguin Putnam Inc., 375 Hudson Street,
New York, New York 10014, U.S.A.
Penguin Books Ltd, 27 Wrights Lane,
London W8 5TZ, England
Penguin Books Australia Ltd, Ringwood,
Victoria, Australia
Penguin Books Canada Ltd, 10 Alcorn Avenue,
Toronto, Ontario, Canada M4V 3B2
Penguin Books (N.Z.) Ltd, 182–190 Wairau Road,
Auckland 10, New Zealand

Penguin Books Ltd, Registered Offices:
Harmondsworth, Middlesex, England

First published by Onyx, an imprint of Dutton Signet,
a member of Penguin Putnam Inc.

First Printing, October, 1997
10 9 8 7 6 5 4 3 2

Copyright © Don Lasseter, 1997
All rights reserved

   REGISTERED TRADEMARK—MARCA REGISTRADA

Printed in Canada

Without limiting the rights under copyright reserved above, no part of this publica-
tion may be reproduced, stored in or introduced into a retrieval system, or transmit-
ted, in any form, or by any means (electronic, mechanical, photocopying, recording,
or otherwise), without the prior written permission of both the copyright owner
and the above publisher of this book.

BOOKS ARE AVAILABLE AT QUANTITY DISCOUNTS WHEN USED TO PROMOTE PRODUCTS OR
SERVICES. FOR INFORMATION PLEASE WRITE TO PREMIUM MARKETING DIVISION, PENGUIN
PUTNAM INC., 375 HUDSON STREET, NEW YORK, NEW YORK 10014.

If you purchased this book without a cover you should be aware that this book is
stolen property. It was reported as "unsold and destroyed" to the publisher and
neither the author nor the publisher has received any payment for this "stripped
book."

ACKNOWLEDGMENTS

Every author who writes nonfiction owes widespread debts of gratitude, particularly to the generous people who ease the long and tortuous path of research.

We are especially grateful to Sergeant Tom Robinson, Hillsboro Police Department, whose courtesy and good humor made it a pleasure to spend several days with him and his group of detectives. Captain Lila Ashenbrenner graciously made us feel welcome, unlike the intruders we really were. In the Washington County Sheriff's Office, Detective Michael O'Connell took time out of his busy schedule to spend with us. And in the Cornelius PD, Sergeant Mark Christy's help was indispensable.

Court records are a daunting mountain of material to sort, read and digest, and that task was made much easier by the exceptionally personable and efficient Kathy Meade. Pancho Hernandez came to our aid several times, along with Helen Floan. In the search warrants department, Janet Morris expedited the hunt for and reproduction of essential documents. Court reporter Nancy Walker also squeezed our needs into her jammed schedule.

It's a privilege to meet and share time with men like Chief Deputy DA Bob Hermann and DDA Roger Hanlon. Without their generous, intellectual, and entertaining help, this project wouldn't have made it.

Psychotherapist Saul Stolzberg answered our call for some expert assistance, and now we're thinking about asking for some professional help from him. His couch looked inviting as we faced our deadline.

Michaela Hamilton, vice president, Dutton Signet, provided advice and encouragement while editorial assistant Laura Turley knew how to work out all the details. Our agent, Susan Crawford, pulled it all together.

There is a great deal of quoted material in this book, largely from trial transcripts, court records, police reports, videotapes, and interviews. It was necessary to re-create some small segments of the dialogue through the use of these resources.

To the best of our knowledge, all of the events in this book took place as we have reported them. It is a factual account of brutal crimes, involving some individuals who would prefer to keep their real identities confidential. To honor that and respect the privacy of others, we have assigned the following pseudonyms: Kathi Lockhart, Lynn Kramer, Sheila Hawkins, Brenda, Gloria Thomas, Greg Thomas, Heather Crane, Andy Tremaine, Ron Price, Denise Nichols, Ray Cardenas, Matilda Gardner, Sarah Ross, Troy Masters, Karen Masters, Dave Sparks, Wayne Fallon, Bruce Dowling, Carlos Romero, Norma Thorpe, George Demory, Frank Ellison, Tony Campbell, Doug Hunter, Pam Evans, Ashley Price, and Dora Vinson.

Prologue

October 1992
Oregon

"Catching babies," she called it. Martha Browning Bryant's reputation put her at the other end of the spectrum from the childish, scatterbrained Prissy of *Gone With the Wind,* who proclaimed she didn't know "nothin' " about "birthin' no babies." Martha knew everything about bringing fresh, innocent life into the world. At age forty-one, the free-spirited Bryant practiced as a nurse-midwife with grace, good humor, and the same vibrant dedication with which she traveled her life's path. Martha's radiant grin, along with the calm faith reflected in her wide-set hazel eyes, acted as a tranquilizer for nervous expectant mothers. Skilled hands did the rest. A blend of holistic touch, psychological soothing, and expert application of delivery techniques made her one of the most requested birth coaches in Hillsboro, Oregon, a few miles west of Portland, the City of Roses.

Christina Jerome-Johnson, age nineteen, couldn't get comfortable on the delivery table in the birthing room of Tuality Community Hospital in Hillsboro. She'd put all of her faith in Healthy Start, a provider of maternity services and midwives for women with few alternatives. Christina, among the lucky ones who would be guided through the process by Martha, struggled through the perspiring, groaning throes of early labor, anxiously awaiting Martha's arrival.

Working feverishly over Christina, rookie midwife Michelle LaChance wanted to check the unborn baby's heartbeat. Helped by a maternity nurse, she probed with a fetal scalp electrode but couldn't seem to make contact with the tiny head. They needed Martha.

Just after dark, on Thursday, October 8, 1992, Martha Bryant eased her 1966 green Volkswagen Bug, affectionately named "Willy," into the hospital parking spot, killed the engine and headlights, pulled a colorful scarf tighter around her shoulders to ward off the autumn evening chill, and rushed inside. After quickly donning blue hospital scrubs, tucking her dark, shoulder-length curls into a cap, and sanitizing her hands, she entered the birthing room.

Both attendants and the patient, Christina, exhaled relief when they saw Martha stride confidently into the room.

Her expertise immediately produced results. With the same meticulous skill used by surgeons, she guided the probe to the precise spot and revealed a delightfully normal heartbeat in the tiny body nearly ready to make its debut. There should be no problems. For the next few hours, Martha and Michelle guided and soothed Christina, repositioning her for maximum comfort, and coaxed her to push and breathe properly. Shortly before 1:30 on Friday morning Christina's eight-pound baby girl exited the safety of mother's womb, and entered the dangerous world.

Sometimes, after an exhausting delivery, Martha would find an unused bed in the hospital and catch a few hours of sleep before heading home. But not this night. Too many exciting things beckoned over in Portland, where she lived. First, she anticipated spending some time with her husband before he left for work so they could put final touches on their anticipated Sunday trip a hundred miles west to the magical Pacific beaches. The remainder of Friday could be used for chores and a few hours of sleep later that night. On the next day, when the opalescent morning sun warmed the coral and yellow fall landscape, she and a few girl-friends planned a shopping spree at Portland's Saturday Market, the nation's largest open-air display of arts and crafts for sale. Martha knew how to squeeze maximum enjoyment from every minute of life.

One final bit of business remained. Five blocks from the hospital, at about 2:40 A.M., Martha used her key to let herself into Healthy Start headquarters where she filled out her time card. Now she could relax and start the thirty-minute drive to her home in Portland's Eastmoreland section. There would be no traffic at this hour. The weirdos and drunks had surely faded into their lairs or passed out somewhere. A nearly full moon lighted the way. In Martha's optimistic world, danger lurked at some remote place elsewhere.

She rolled northeast along four-lane Cornell Road, made the big sweeping eastward curve and passed through open space next to the Hillsboro airport where silvery wings of small planes reflected spears of moonlight. As Martha breezed past a towering row of cottonwood trees, then past the sprawling Intel Corporation buildings on the south side of Cornell, bright headlights of a car behind her moved into a tailgating position. The blinding beams began flashing while the car weaved from lane to lane, moving alongside the Volkswagen, then dropping back. Martha flipped on her right-turn signal and tried to pull out of the way.

From out of nowhere, thunderclaps filled the unclouded darkness.

The thud of a bullet ripping through the passenger side of the Volkswagen's metallic skin rattled Martha with fear. Another loud crash and her passenger window exploded inward, scattering a million sparkling shards throughout the car's interior. One after the other, gunshots splatted chunks of lead into the green metal and through the windows.

Martha felt a slug rip into the flesh of her back near the left shoulder blade, smash through a rib, sear a hole in her lung, and exit close to her left armpit. Despite the pain, it was not a mortal wound. She remained conscious and fought to control her slowing car. She couldn't do it. The Bug veered across two westbound lanes, narrowly missed a row of trees while bouncing over a curb, crossed a patch of grass, and thumped to a halt astraddle the sidewalk. Even though the engine stalled, the right-turn signal indicator continued to blink.

Relieved that she hadn't been injured or killed in a wreck, Martha struggled to an upright position, only to see her door suddenly jerked open.

Silhouetted against the moonlight, a male figure filled the doorway. A pair of powerful arms reached for her.

PART ONE

Trouble in Florida

Chapter 1

Florida

In the city that made spring break famous, where long spits of golden sandy beaches and clear ocean water still beckon thousands of sun-seeking college students and tourists, Adolph James Rode was delivered at Broward General Hospital on December 4, 1960. A doctor, rather than a midwife, performed the procedure.

Fort Lauderdale, in those days, enjoyed the reputation of being the Easter-vacation mecca for study-weary collegians eager to escape chilled Northern campuses. Teens and young adults migrated south, swarming Florida's Gold Coast for the purpose of shedding books, class schedules, and clothes, to party on the sand and to jam every available hotel and motel with wall-to-wall bodies. Connie Francis sang "Where The Boys Are" that year, romping across the colorful Cinemascope screen in a movie about spring break, same title. The film reflected the innocent morality of the fifties, before the storm of American involvement in southeast Asia, before drugs became epidemic, before the revolution of free sex, flower power, hippies, and a national erosion of personal responsibility. The term "serial murder" hadn't yet been coined. In faraway Tacoma, Washington, a boy named Ted Bundy had recently celebrated his fourteenth birthday.

During the first few months of Jimmy Rode's life, a long smouldering problem in America reached flash point when the embers of racial injustice ignited and flared. In March 1961, police in Jackson, Mississippi, used dogs and clubs to roust more than a hundred Negroes from a courthouse. Simmering unrest in other cities evolved into social activism. In the hottest spots, it erupted into violence. The movement spread like wildfire across the South to Raleigh, and Charlotte, then to Atlanta, Birmingham, and Little Rock.

Turbulent news, of course, didn't register on the infant, Jimmy Rode. He gurgled happily in his crib, content in the comfortable community of Lauderdale Lakes. His world consisted of a doting mother and father, and two older siblings, a brother and sister who worshiped the baby. His mother, though, sometimes seemed a little distracted.

Before Jimmy's second birthday, Martin Luther King Jr. was arrested in Georgia for leading twenty-six antisegregationists to the steps of the Albany city hall, and rioting marred the admission of James Meredith to the University of Mississippi. Several people died in the melee, causing President Kennedy to send troops to enforce federal law.

During those stormy months, Mrs. Rode's preoccupation gradually intensified. She became acutely aware of racial strife which continued to erupt, especially across the South. Martin Luther King Jr. delivered an impassioned speech before more than 200,000 peaceful demonstrators in Washington, D.C., in which he said, "I have a dream," expressing his wish that the sons of former slaves and the sons of former slave owners would sit together at the table of brotherhood. Many white Americans sympathized, while others stubbornly clung to beliefs of racial superiority, insisting on the continuance of segregation. Radicals on both sides of the fence stretched tensions to the breaking point. Jimmy's mother watched with strong personal interest.

Before Jimmy Rode could even begin to understand racial problems, a devastating trauma struck him and his siblings. Without warning, their mother ran away with another man. In view of the simmering unrest at the time, it didn't help that her lover was an African-American.

Mr. and Mrs. Rode divorced when Jimmy was four.

On the surface, the split had little effect on the lives of Jimmy and his brother, Ricky, or their sister, Debbie. Their father provided a good living and as much attention as he could spare away from his job as a carpenter. And his new girlfriend, Brenda, gave the children love and attention as if they were her own. She recognized that Jimmy seemed to have special needs, and later recalled, "I used to see him almost every evening, after I got off work, and we'd always do things on weekends . . ." But Brenda noticed an underlying tendency toward obstinate and rebellious behavior in little Jimmy. Before he reached the age of five, she felt it was serious enough to recommend to the father that Jimmy be taken for counseling. But the idea dwindled and died.

While Mr. Rode may not have taken Brenda's recommendation seriously, he put great and loving importance on the relationship with her. After a two-year courtship, they exchanged wedding vows on March 3, 1967. Now the family was whole again with a stepmother for the three children. The newlyweds purchased a house from her parents a couple of miles away, and moved in immediately. Even though Jimmy, Debbie, and Ricky would be required to change schools, the new home provided an upgraded neighborhood and their own private swimming pool. Most children could only dream of another benefit they had. Their paternal grandmother owned a ranch with horses and a special ring in which the kids could ride the ponies.

Brenda thought her relationship with the kids was "very good." She recalled that the children asked her not to reveal to their friends that she was their stepmother. "They wanted everybody to think I was their real mother."

During the first couple of years, according to Brenda, they experienced a few rough spots. Her husband worked long hours to provide enough income for a wife, three children, and a new mortgage. Sometimes, she said, "he didn't come home after work. He would stay out. And the children, most of the time, would have dinner with me and be in bed. But after two years, he was home as soon as he got off work every night."

It helped when the senior Rode became a superintendent at his workplace with a commensurate increase in salary. "Jimmy's father made exceptionally good money," said Branda. "That's when he started taking Jimmy and Ricky over to the golf course in the summer . . ."

The relationship between Jimmy, Ricky, and their father couldn't have been better. With a smile, Brenda described it. "I mean, their father coached football because they wanted to play football. Their father took them hunting. Their father took them fishing. Their father took them camping. Their father took them playing golf. Their father did everything with them for years."

As in most marriages, though, as soon as one problem is solved another one arises. Tensions developed between Brenda and her husband over spiraling misbehavior by Jimmy. "Well," she said, "it seemed like either the school was calling me, a neighbor was calling me, somehow he was getting in trouble every day for doing things. And every day when his father came home from work, I'd say, 'You've got to talk to Jimmy. . . .' It got to where his father kept thinking I was picking on him. And I tried to explain to his father—I didn't even tell him everything that Jimmy did. I only told him the things I thought were important enough for him to know."

At first, Jimmy's offbeat behavior seemed relatively harmless. In nursery school, he stole toys from other children. In kindergarten, despite a deceptively innocent appearance, he became so disruptive they expelled him. And in first grade his antisocial behavior got him ejected from the lunchroom permanently. What began as kid stuff such as smoking and ditching school spun out of control. He threatened other children with knives, and tried to injure their eyes with lit cigarettes. Away from school, he stole loose change, fought, and lifted inexpensive objects from stores.

Because she was home and heard of the infractions first, Brenda felt responsible for dealing with them. She tried lecturing, explaining right and wrong to the boy. She tried instilling values in Jimmy by stressing the importance of respect for property and the rights of others. His only answer was denial. Nothing seemed to work.

And she didn't spot the unusual way Jimmy often looked at her.

As puberty changed Jimmy Rode's voice and hormones, and his wavy dark brown hair reached shoulder length, his misdeeds escalated. Smoking cigarettes evolved to toking pot. Concealing a soft drink under his shirt at convenience stores was replaced by heisting six packs of beer. He found neighbors' homes an easy mark, especially in a mobile-home park close to the back of his parents' property. He and his friends conducted raids, frequently targeting vulnerable elderly neighbors, to steal beer and money.

Another illicit activity that seemed to fascinate Jimmy was raising unusual pets. From the not too distant swamps, he brought home prohibited snakes and alligators and put them in the backyard pool. Somehow, he acquired a sick monkey which he nursed back to health. In later years, he would brag to an acquaintance about capturing neighborhood cats and throwing them into an enclosed space with the monkey. He said he liked to watch the monkey tear the cats apart.

A boyhood pal would one day confess that he and Jimmy did drugs almost daily, including marijuana, Quaaludes, LSD, and eventually, cocaine. They were "a couple of rowdy kids," he said.

Warnings failed as did any disciplinary measures from Jimmy's parents. The stress became too much for Brenda as spats erupted more frequently over the boy's misdeeds. By the time Jimmy approached the age of twelve, she'd had all she could take. She and Jimmy's father separated, ultimately to be divorced.

Adolph "Jimmy" Rode was now accountable only to a working father who had multiple responsibilities. That left the youngster with considerably too much free rein and time on his hands. Beer became his constant companion, and trouble his avocation. He soon grew to a slim five-eight, and had features many young women considered attractive including long dark hair, a strong chin, and soulful hazel eyes. The whole package was marred only by slightly protruding upper teeth.

Though blessed with good looks, Rode was unable to take advantage of them. Something in his personal makeup drove him toward destruction. The burglaries continued. A detective would later report his personal suspicion that Rode was involved in a string of illegal entries and thefts. In one case, someone had cut the telephone lines leading into the house of a seventy-year-old widow, then entered while the woman slept. The intruder bagged his loot, then masturbated and urinated inside the home before making his escape. There wasn't enough evidence to legally tie the crime to Jimmy Rode.

At the same time, in the opposite corner of the United States, young women began to vanish around the lakes and resorts of Seattle, Washington, where Ted Bundy was a law student with what appeared to be a bright future.

Retired schoolteacher Alice Stock, seventy, lived alone in a house just a short walk from Jimmy Rode's home. She'd earned the peace and contentment of retirement after years of teaching children afflicted with physical and learning disabilities. A neighbor, Iris Linton, who often looked in on Alice, described her as "a very caring and understanding person . . . the type of work she had been involved with made her even more understanding."

When Alice broke her arm, the neighbor attended to her, brought her meals, and helped her with personal chores. On May 26, 1976, Iris attended Alice's festive birthday party and sang as the smiling woman received a white-frosted chocolate cake with two lit candles in the shape of a seven and a zero stuck in the frosting.

Nearly five months later, on the balmy evening of October 5, just after dark, Alice frantically telephoned her friend Iris, who recalled, "She was quite agitated and upset. I was very concerned about her because of her hypertension and other problems she had. And she asked me to come over to her house. Something had happened."

When Iris arrived, she found Alice bewildered, trembling, almost out of control, a complete reversal of character for the elderly woman. "What's the matter, Alice?" Iris almost shouted.

In her recollection, Iris described her friend's answer. "She told me that Jimmy had been over and had broken into her house and that he had threatened her with a knife and asked her to remove her clothing. Alice, being the type of person she was, even that statement would have upset her, because she was a very prim, proper person." The frightened woman's reluctance had evidently discouraged Jimmy Rode, who had backed out of the house and disappeared into the dark.

Iris comforted her terrified friend, calmed her down, and convinced her to call the police. While they waited for the officers to arrive, Alice showed Iris a screen that had been removed from a rear bedroom window, through which the intruder had apparently gained entry.

Alice repeated her story to sympathetic police officers. As a result, Adolph "Jimmy" Rode, at age fifteen, faced his first jail sentence. He served two months and eleven days in the Florida Department of Youth Services at the Okeechobee School for Boys. But he learned nothing from the incarceration.

The following April 1977, Detective Robert Williams of the Fort Lauderdale P.D. juvenile section, arrested Rode on suspicion of burglarizing a house one block from Alice Stock's home, on the same street, just a few houses away from Rode's own residence. At the police station, Williams read Jimmy the standard Miranda warning, then asked, "Are you willing to answer my questions?"

Rode stared at the floor, looked up, and said he would. When Williams asked Jimmy if he knew anything about the recent burglary, the youth nodded. He admitted going over to the residence with two of his friends and watching as they broke in. But his own involvement, he claimed, was minimal. He'd just stood outside on lookout. This came as no surprise to Williams, because the two accomplices had already informed him of the details and implicated Jimmy Rode.

Having easily gained the admission, Detective Williams asked Jimmy about a different theft on the same block in the residence of another elderly woman. Again Rode acknowledged his guilt. He admitted going into the residence by cutting a screen and taking a small amount of cash, approximately ten dollars.

To Williams's questions, Rode described his involvement in yet a third illegal entry of an aged woman's home, where he stole some books. Accompanied by the police, he retrieved the books from his room, and returned them to the victim. Authorities released Jimmy Rode with a sharp warning that the next time, he could face serious charges.

*   *   *

The next time came in fewer than five months. Police picked him up on August 23 on suspicion of burglary. Detectives took him to the juvenile dentention facility, where he was released on his own recognizance.

Twenty-four hours later, Detective Robert Williams knocked at the door of the Rode home. Ricky Rode led him into Jimmy's bedroom and woke up his sleeping younger brother. Williams arrested Jimmy for burglarizing a residence in the Sunset Trailer Park, one block away. Rode's fingerprints had been left at the crime scene.

In the Fort Lauderdale police station, Williams once more confronted the youth with the Miranda warning. This time, growing wiser in the ways of criminals, Jimmy Rode stated that he didn't want to talk about the case without a lawyer. Williams stopped questioning him about the Sunset Park case, but continued talking about other burglaries, hoping Rode would help clear up some unsolved cases. "We're going to check," he said. "If we find your prints or anything else on any other burglary, you're going to be charged. If you want to tell me about any other burglary, as long as there [was] no violence, no physical force used, we will be able to clear the cases." The detective suggested that if Rode provided such information, no charges would be filed. But, he warned, if any violence had taken place there would be no lenience.

Rode scratched his head, looked off into space while considering the offer, then confessed to nine trailer-park burglaries, along with a couple of entries into other residences. To verify the crimes, Williams took Rode for a little automobile trip and asked him to point out each address. Jimmy willingly complied.

True to his word, Detective Williams did not ask the district attorney to file charges on the eleven burglaries to which the youth had confessed. But they slammed barred doors on him for the Sunset Trailer Park crime.

When the case came to trial a few weeks later, he was found guilty of the single count of burglary where he'd left his fingerprints. On December 5, 1977, one day after his seventeenth birthday, Jimmy Rode heard a judge sentence him to pay the victim $130 restitution and to serve three years in the Florida State Penitentiary.

Many states would have sent Jimmy Rode to another juvenile facility, but Florida had developed a multilayer program designed specifically for youthful offenders within the state prison system. They transported Rode to Indian River Correctional Institution, about 130 miles north of Fort Lauderdale. It was a low-security lockup for first-time, nonviolent offenders under the age of twenty-four who had been sentenced to fewer than ten years. Assigned to train and work as a vocational aide, he would be subject to a review every six months to evaluate his behavior.

The Florida Parole and Probation Commission had installed at Indian River a program to motivate good behavior among the youthful inmates. If the individual performed his assigned job well and kept out of trouble, he would be eligible to enter into a "contract" with administrators that would allow departure from prison sooner than the actual end of sentence. Jimmy Rode, although sentenced to three years, had already been given a tentative parole date of December 12, 1979. If he worked it right, he could get out even sooner.

In August, Rode's behavior was evaluated with the term "good adjustment." So officials gave him the opportunity to sign a contract that would allow him to go home on April 24, 1979. The contractual conditions included satisfactory continuation in his job assignment, participation in drug rehabilitation including related academic courses, and completion of a self-betterment program called "Value Clarification." If Rode complied fully with his part of the bargain, he would be allowed to enter a community work-release program to prepare him for his April exit. And finally, he would be required to pay no less than fifteen dollars a week from the money earned in the work-release program, to pay the 130-dollar restitution fee. All of this, of course, was predicated on continuing good behavior.

It all made good sense to Jimmy Rode, so he walked a straight and narrow path for the remainder of 1978. By mid-January 1979, he happily accepted a transfer to Pompano Community Corrections Center, in Pompano Beach, just north of his home city. There, he entered the pleasant surroundings of a minimum-security facility with no fences or armed guards. Within a few days he began working as a day laborer in the community, anticipating his parole release four months hence. It wasn't to be.

Chapter 2

The work-release program at Pompano Beach provided too many temptations for Jimmy Rode. Deloye Henry, Senior Management Analyst, Florida Department of Corrections, recalled the prisoner's inability to play by the rules:

"On February 19 of '79, he [Rode] was placed in administrative confinement for unauthorized absence from his job. That led to a March 2, 1979, termination from the program for that unauthorized absence, and there was an investigation which indicated that there was some theft of monies from the employer which he had been working for."

At a subsequent "violation hearing" in March, Jimmy Rode's "contract" came to an abrupt end. The April parole date was rescinded, and officials promptly sent him back to Indian River. Conditions were not as dismal, though, as they first appeared for Rode. The parole commission granted his request for an interview on September 27, at which they set a new parole date.

Rode walked away from Indian River on November 13, 1979, with instructions to report to a parole officer in Fort Lauderdale. His family welcomed him home.

In another part of Florida, on June 23, 1979, a Miami jury deliberated only six hours before convicting Theodore Robert Bundy of two counts of first-degree murder. The notorious killer had finally been brought to justice for killing two young women, members of the Chi Omega sorority at Florida State University, Tallahassee. Suspected of killing scores of young women across the country, many of them in the state of Washington, Bundy would soon face trial again, and be convicted of killing a twelve-year-old child, Kimberly Leach.

Tallahassee had also been the site of another murder in 1973. In a motel room, John Spinkelink had ended the life of another ex-convict, and was sentenced to death for it. One month before Bundy's first conviction, Spinkelink became the first man to die in Florida's electric chair in more than a decade.

No one told Alice Stock that Jimmy Rode had returned home to Fort Lauderdale. Even if they had, she probably would have paid little mind to it, even though he'd terrified her three years earlier. To Alice, Jimmy was just a wild kid who had probably learned his lesson by being incarcerated.

Alice still lived alone, a gentle woman secure in the same tidy little home Rode had entered to steal not only her money but her sense of personal security. Now seventy-three, she'd long since put the traumatic event behind her. Blessed with reasonably good health, despite having suffered a minor heart attack and a minimal-damage stroke, Alice lived a comfortable life. Always keeping herself and her home meticulously clean and neat, she interacted frequently with friends and family. With tastefully tinted gray bangs waved to the right side of her forehead, oval-shaped horn-rimmed glasses, a quick smile, and clothing appropriate to the Florida climate, she fit the image of the ideal grandmother. Visitors were always welcome in her home, but Alice didn't mind spending most of her evenings alone, relaxing in her natty brown-fabric easy chair, wearing a simple light housedress, reading or watching television.

Six days after the 1979 Thanksgiving holiday, Patrol Officer Michael Walley, in his sixth year with the Fort Lauderdale P.D., looked forward to the end of his midnight-to-eight A.M. shift. At 6:30, as the sun rose over the coral Atlantic waters on November 29, his cruiser radio crackled, ordering him to respond to the 400 block of South West 25th Terrace. He understood the dispatcher to say someone was sick or possibly dead. Walley switched on the emergency lights and siren, hit the accelerator, and arrived at the single-family residence three minutes later.

A neighbor who'd made the telephone report directed Walley into Alice Stock's home, and led him into the back

bedroom. Someone had placed a sheet over the still figure
lying on rumpled blankets. The victim's head and arms
hung limply over one edge of the mattress. Walley gently
pulled the sheet back to check for life signs. He found
none. A sense of sadness swept over the officer as he
viewed the nude body of Alice Eloise Stock, whose happy
life had ended in brutal violence.

After putting in a call for the homicide squad and medical techs, Officer Walley made a preliminary search of the
house and yard. Outside, in the gray dawn, he spotted some
footprints in the sand below the victim's bedroom window.
Using crime scene tape, he secured the area to be certain
the prints wouldn't be disturbed. Back inside, Walley
glanced around the single bathroom and found on the floor
a pair of eyeglasses with oval lenses in the horn-rimmed
frames. Continuing the search, he glanced under the bed
and discovered a screen which had been removed from the
window through which the intruder had apparently entered.
A wadded housedress also rested under the edge of the
bed, presumably the last garment Alice Stock had ever
worn.

The odd thing, Walley noted, was that nothing appeared
to have been disarranged in the house. No signs of ransacking. No opened drawers or cabinets. Nothing broken.
The victim's purse lay undisturbed on a chair beside the
bed. This crime was definitely not the work of a burglar or
thief. But what kind of a monster would enter to kill a
helpless elderly woman? Was it an act of revenge? An insurance murder? The other alternative made Walley shud-
der. Did some vile creep enter the house for the sole
purpose of stripping and raping this poor woman? Those
questions would have to be answered by specialists.

When the detectives, criminalists, and medics arrived,
and Walley had briefed them on details he'd observed, he
"secured" and left for the station to prepare his reports.

Veteran Fort Lauderdale PD detective Phillip J. Mundy
took over the investigation. Having once worn the uniform
of New York's finest before he moved to Dade County
Sheriff's duty and then to Fort Lauderdale, Mundy had
worked everything from the mean streets to murder. He
directed a forensic technician to dust for fingerprints and

to photograph and make casts, if possible, of the footprints outside.

By questioning Alice's acquaintances and neighbors
who'd seen and talked to her in those final hours, Mundy
narrowed down the probable time of death. She'd apparently died somewhere between 6:00 the previous evening,
and 4:00 A.M.

One of the forensic specialists discovered some hairs on
the body which obviously were not from Alice Stock. Using
tweezers with cautious precision, he picked them up and
slipped them into a glassine bag.

Outside, a criminalist found that making casts of the shoe
impressions was not an easy task. Detective Thomas Hill
would later describe the problem. The sand in which the
intruder had stood was "very loose. We call it sugar sand.
You could take sugar and throw it on the ground and this
is what it looks like. It's very fine, minute sand and it's
very difficult to work with. . . ." The impressions he lifted
would be classified, at best, as partial prints.

The team of investigators worked most of the day searching for any other leads that could possibly help identify
suspects. The best information came through interviews of
friends and neighbors. Several of them remembered that
Alice had been accosted three years earlier by a young man
named Jimmy Rode.

Detective Mundy pulled Adolph "Jimmy" Rode's rap
sheet, found the details of the crime he'd committed against
Stock on October 5, 1976, and noted that Rode had been
released on parole less than two weeks ago. Checking the
suspect's address, they discovered his family had moved
from the house near Alice Stock's residence on 25th Terrace. Accompanied by Detective John Bukata, he drove to
the new location on South West Ninth Avenue, two miles
from the original home.

Jimmy Rode, still pale from his three years behind bars,
invited the detectives into the house. Mundy told him exactly what prompted the visit. Alice Stock had been murdered and the detectives wanted to know where Jimmy was
during that night.

Mundy recalled it: "His response was basically to the
effect that he didn't have anything to do with Mrs. Stock's

death, and hadn't had anything to do with her since 1976. And that, in fact, he could account for his time for Wednesday to Thursday, stating that he had been at a place called the Bristol Pub, which is a beer and wine place. He said he'd been there in the evening of Wednesday, November 28, and that he took a cab home from there and arrived home at 11:15 P.M. on the same evening."

To the detectives, Rode hadn't established a clear alibi. Glancing at the sneakers the suspect wore, Mundy asked if he could have a look at Jimmy's shoes. Rode ignored the obvious reference to the ones on his feet. "He brought out a pair of leather-type shoes and I looked at the bottoms of them. They were smooth, worn. I asked if I could see the bottoms of the sneakers he was wearing while I spoke to him."

Rode nodded and lifted his foot. Mundy thought the sole looked similar to the impressions he'd seen in the fine sand. "I'd like to take those with me, if it's okay with you," he said. Rode slipped the sneakers off and handed them to the detective.

After suggesting to Rode that he not leave town, Mundy and Bukata departed to compare the shoes to plaster casts taken in the sandy soil outside Alice Stock's bedroom window. First, though, they drove to the address of the Bristol Pub on the corner of 27th Avenue and South West fourth Place, only two hundred yards from the original Rode home. On foot, they walked the most direct route to Stock's house. Through a trailer park, over a three-foot-high chain-link fence, they found themselves almost in Stock's backyard. The walk took fewer than ten minutes.

At the autopsy of Alice Stock, performed by Dr. Keene Garvin, Phil Mundy had the unpleasant task of observing. He heard the pathologist describe "petechial hemorrhages" in the eyes, tiny broken blood vessels which always accompany death by strangling. More evidence of the brutal act showed up in bruises to the neck, plus a crushed windpipe and larynx. Sufficient pressure had been applied to her neck to cause the blood vessels in the head to "occlude" or close, shutting off blood flow to the brain. The cause of death, the doctor announced, was strangulation or asphyxia by strangulation.

Other damage to her body included bruises to the left arm and "anogenital" injuries. Phil Mundy couldn't suppress the grimace forming on his face or the tight knot in his stomach. The gentle little woman had been brutally and violently raped and sodomized.

In reference to the injuries, it would be noted that, ". . . no seminal fluid was found. This was probably a foreign object of some type . . . it could be a variety of different things. It may well even have been postmortem . . ." Because there was so little blood flow, the pathologist concluded that her heart may have been "working very little, if at all" when the injuries were inflicted.

Circumstantial evidence pointed directly to Jimmy Rode. The detectives hurried back to headquarters to examine the shoe impression casts and compare them to the sneakers acquired from Rode. They studied them for hours. Forensic specialist, Detective Tom Hill, would eventually conduct even more tests, and discuss the problems they encountered. "I had a shoe and I needed to compare it to any of the marks on the cast. I took this shoe, put it on. I made my own impression in the sand and then I poured another cast of that impression." He described his attempts to match "knobs" and "patterns."

"I was not able to find individual characteristics in this particular plaster cast because the shoes themselves didn't have anything large enough to leave a mark in the sand. There were very minute individual characteristics. I could not reproduce them in the sand though." Asked about the probability that Jimmy Rode's sneakers had made the prints in the sand, Hill said, "I feel it's a very good, strong probability that this shoe made this impression." But he stopped short of a solid affirmative answer. "The left shoe is consistent with the plaster cast . . . I cannot say that it was that particular left shoe, but it will be a left shoe of that type . . . with that same pattern in it."

Disappointed, Detective Phil Mundy presented the facts to the prosecutor's office. There just wasn't enough hard evidence to tip the scales toward bringing Rode to trial.

Jimmy Rode and his family celebrated Christmas that year unhindered by any pending legal action against him. He'd been out of prison for over a month without getting in any trouble. The visit by detectives investigating the murder of Alice Stock hadn't led to an arrest, so Jimmy assumed they had accepted his alibi. They hadn't, but a paucity of corroborating evidence had forced officials to let Jimmy Rode alone. So Christmas was a festive occasion. But the feelings of cheer changed to heartbroken mourning three days later.

Ricky Rode, Jimmy's older brother, had never been in trouble. To his father and stepmother, he was an ideal child, unlike his errant sibling. So it was a cruel and unexpected blow when Ricky was involved in a grinding auto smashup. He died instantly.

To a devastated Jimmy, it seemed like the end of the world. He'd respected and loved Ricky. It didn't seem fair that life had ended so violently and much too soon for such a good guy. Perhaps Jimmy wondered if Ricky should have survived and he, Jimmy, should have been punished by dying in retribution for his misdeeds. Their stepmother Brenda agreed. After the separation from Rode Sr., she'd moved to Hollywood, Florida, but had returned for the funeral. Jimmy drove her there. Shortly afterwards, she made her opinion painfully clear. Disconsolate, tears spilling, Brenda blurted out, "If one of you had to get killed, why did it have to be Ricky? He was so good."

Shocked at her own spontaneous outburst, Brenda felt immediately sorry, and searched her mind for some way to make amends. She'd recently bought a Cadillac from her sister, and planned to sell the classic Mustang she'd been driving. Jimmy, she knew, had no car since he'd just recently been released from prison. In an effort at reconciliation for her comment, she gave the Mustang to Jimmy. His crooked grin reflected his acceptance of her peace offering.

While other parts of the country shivered through rain and snow, Broward County, Florida, basked in typical sunshine in the first week of 1980. But there were dark places, too, with dark events and bestial inhuman acts. On January 5, a relative found Josephina Verschelden, age eighty-one,

DEAD OF NIGHT 29

in her home. She'd been beaten and stabbed. A pair of scissors had been plunged into her neck and left there. No property or money had been taken. Despite intensive police efforts, no leads turned up to help solve the crime.

Brenda's Hollywood residence was fewer than ten miles from Fort Lauderdale where Jimmy lived, so she wasn't surprised when he knocked at her door one morning in mid-January 1980, a few weeks after his nineteenth birthday. She rose from bed, put on a white dressing gown, and invited him in. He said he was still grieving over Ricky's death, and needed to talk to someone.

They both took chairs at the dining room table. Brenda thought of offering Jimmy a drink but realized she had nothing in the house. Apologizing, she offered water. He accepted. She filled a glass with ice cubes and water, put it on the table in front of him, and sat down with her back to the kitchen. They spoke softly for fifteen or twenty minutes about Ricky's death.

When Jimmy finished drinking the water, he rose, returned the glass to the kitchen, and moved to a position behind Brenda.

She recalled every detail of the event: "I was sitting in a dining room chair. He came up behind me like he was going to lean over and kiss me on the cheek, goodbye or something. He slid one arm underneath my breast and the other arm under my throat and pulled me off the chair backwards."

Describing his facial expression, she recalled that ". . . it was like somebody I'd never seen in my life."

Jimmy wrestled his ex-stepmother over to a big black double-seated contour chair and tightened both hands around her throat. Then, she said, "He drug me into the bedroom and raped me." Asked if the rape included actual penetration, she softly answered, "Yes," and added, "He also told me it was something he had dreamt about for years."

Following the sexual attack, Rode again wrapped his hands around Brenda's throat, and she felt like she was going to pass out as she heard his voice. "He told me just to lay there and relax. It wouldn't hurt. It would be just like going to sleep." She ignored his advice and struggled with every ounce of strength she could muster. He still had the look of a stranger. "Right before I got loose of him, it was like he recognized me. It was like two different, completely different people.

"I kept pushing and beating on him. I screamed at him that I was his mother. It was like he recognized me and kind of relaxed or something for a minute and . . . stood up. And I think he still had his trousers around his ankles."

With a final desperate lurch, Brenda freed herself from Jimmy's grasp. "Somehow I got loose and I got in the bathroom. I laid on the floor and put my feet against the door and my head against the tub." Jimmy slammed his fists against the bathroom door yelling at her to open up. But she flexed every muscle in her body making it a human barricade. Finally she heard him muttering and making peculiar noises, and then it became quiet. She lay there, braced solidly for what seemed like hours. At last she summoned enough nerve to peek out and see if he'd left.

Trembling, Brenda eased out of the bathroom, ready to leap back at the slightest noise. But he'd gone. She discovered that before fleeing, he'd ripped a wall phone out of the plaster. She'd nearly forgotten a recently installed extension sitting on a teacart between the dining room and kitchen. It rang, reminding her that she wasn't cut off from the world. A feeling of apprehension flooded her about answering it, but she finally picked up the receiver after the fourth ring. She heard nothing but hoarse breathing. Her pleading to the caller to say something resulted only in more silence.

Completely shattered and confused, Brenda couldn't think what to do. Would anyone believe that her nineteen-year-old stepson had raped her? Would there be accusations that she'd led him on? Who could she talk to? She just wanted to hide and never again face the world. "I went to the bedroom and I put the dresser in front of the door. That's where I stayed for three days, until I finally got up enough nerve . . ." She telephoned Jimmy's father and asked him to meet her. Trying to hold back the tears, she described every detail of the assault by Jimmy and showed his father the fingerprints and bruises on her neck.

That event ended the relationship between Jimmy and

his father. They would rarely ever speak to each other again.

Subsequently, Brenda also told Jimmy's sister, Debbie, about the rape. "I told his sister because I thought if he would do it to me, he might even do it to her."

But Brenda and Jimmy's family decided not to go to the police. Rape is a difficult thing to report and the ordeal of courtroom proceedings can be even more tormenting to endure.

Brenda would not see Jimmy Rode again for fourteen years.

Chapter 3

Even though Jimmy Rode's mother had found a new love and left home, she still maintained ties with her children. She periodically hosted visits, spent as much time as possible with all three of them until Ricky was killed, and continued to see Jimmy and Debbie. Fortunately for Jimmy, she came to his rescue in March 1980.

A few weeks after Brenda endured the trauma of rape, Jimmy found himself again in the Fort Lauderdale jail, accused of attempted burglary and possession of burglary tools. Both infractions violated conditions of his parole. Witnesses had seen him use a hammer to break the window of a new Corvette, then climb inside to steal what he could. They called police, who arrested him on the spot. Rode's mother posted $200 bail to arrange for his release. While waiting for trial on those charges, he lost control of his temper again.

On the night of April 12, at 9:30, the neighbors of seventy-year-old Mattie Marino found her lying on her blood-stained kitchen floor half-conscious, her face marred with purpling bruises, eyes swollen, and bleeding from the mouth. Horrified, they summoned the police and paramedics. A patrol car arrived within minutes, along with emergency medical personnel who treated the woman before transporting her to the hospital. When she was able, Mattie answered a detective's questions. Her assailant, she said, came into her apartment to borrow a spool of white thread. She recalled that he smiled affectionately, kissed her cheek and asked permission to use her phone. Without warning, his face turned angry, his eyes glaring hatred. In a frenzy, he began slugging her, then grabbed a rolling pin from her kitchen counter and struck her several times with it. He finished by encircling her neck with his powerful hands and choking her until she fell to the floor. While she lay there stunned and bleeding, he snatched a checkbook and ten dollars from her purse then fled from the apartment.

"Had you ever seen the man before?" Detective Tony Fantigrassi asked.

"Of course I have," Mattie responded. "He's my grandson, Jimmy Rode." She added that her daughter was Jimmie's mother. "He drinks a lot of beer," she said. "He's carrying a can of beer with him all the time."

The police knew Jimmy Rode quite well and had no trouble rounding him up.

At the subsequent trial for attempted murder, Mattie Marino answered the questions of defense attorney Bruce Lincoln, who wanted to know if she was absolutely sure that Jimmy Rode was her assailant. "I know my grandson," Mattie said with strained patience. "He was smiling at me all the time. All the time he was choking me." In Rode's defense, she added, "Something had to snap in Jimmy because he wouldn't have put his hands on me otherwise."

Mattie had pleaded with her grandson not to hit her. When that failed, she prayed. "I said, 'Oh dear God, please help me because Jimmy might do it to someone else.' " At that time, she wasn't aware that he'd already vented his rage on other women. The vicious attack strained Mattie's emotional health and left her in fragile condition. During her testimony, she seemed shaken, and defeated.

The defendant, Adolph "Jimmy" Rode, took the witness stand in his own defense. He admitted that he'd gone to Mattie Marino's apartment, but claimed that he'd borrowed the thread and promptly left.

Defense attorney Lincoln pointed out to the jury that Mrs. Marino had been the victim of a burglary ten days before the attack. Possibly, he argued, the same intruder returned to finish the job and had physically assaulted her. She must have been confused.

The prosecutor, Assistant State's attorney Mark Springer, worried about the persuasive skills of Mr. Lincoln, and wondered if the jurors would even consider the possibility

that any grandson could be capable of such abhorrent behavior toward his own elderly grandmother.

The concerns turned out to be valid. The jury found
Jimmy Rode not guilty.

But exoneration on the attempted murder charge did not
keep Rode out of prison. The burglary arrest for which his
mother had bailed him out had put him in violation of his
parole from the previous November. On March 25, a judge
issued a warrant for the arrest of Jimmy Rode. He waited
in jail until he faced trial in August on the burglary charges.
This time, the jury exhibited no sympathy for Rode. They
deliberated just a few hours before finding him guilty. He
hung his head as the harsh sentence was pronounced sending him back to prison for five years.

After being processed at the North Florida Reception
Center, Rode realized that he would no longer be eligible
to serve his time at the Indian River youthful offender facility. He faced hard time in a major prison. Rode landed
in Baker Correctional Institution, near Jacksonville, which
housed three classifications of adult inmates: convicts requiring close supervision, medium security, and those who
warranted only minimum attention of correction officers.
Jimmy Rode had been classified as a medium-security
inmate.

A bit of good luck came his way immediately. In May,
the Florida Parole and Probation Commission set a parole
date of March 30, 1982, for Rode, virtually ignoring the
new conviction. With good behavior, he could walk out in
less than two years instead of five.

Some people know how to take advantage of good for-
tune. Jimmy Rode hadn't been blessed with that knowledge, or even a reasonable amount of common sense. At
the first opportunity, he blew his chance for early release.

Assigned to a work detail along a Florida state highway
on July 9, 1981, helping to fill a hole in the pavement, Rode
simply wandered away. When his two workmates reported to
the correctional officer following completion of the task, it
became obvious that one of the work trio was missing.
Within a few hours, searchers found Rode who made little
attempt to hide, and hustled him back to the lockup.

Maybe the incident would have been overlooked if Rode

could have stayed out of trouble. But nine days later he decided the food served to him was inedible. Loudly announcing that he was a vegetarian, he refused to eat the meat dish. When ordered to hand over the tray, he mouthed a few obscenities and refused. The officer on duty wrote up a disciplinary report citing Jimmy Rode for disorderly conduct.

The incident irritated Rode, who considered it unfair. He'd also been refused permission to make a phone call, which made him even crankier, so he retaliated by refusing to shave for several days. When ordered to get rid of the beard, he again refused and received another report for disobeying a verbal order.

The series of violations earned him a trip to another prison. Sumpter Correctional Institution specialized in confining inmates who have escaped. An official explained, "We don't normally leave inmates at the facility from which they escaped because of their familiarity with the institution and the likelihood that the chance might again present itself. And to prevent the escape, we did move him over to Sumpter."

The change of location, however, was not the only sanction imposed. On August 27, officials held a hearing at which they convicted Jimmy Rode of escape and sentenced him to one additional year of imprisonment.

Rode's stay at Sumpter would also be relatively short. He arrived in August, faced conviction in early October, and boarded a bus headed to the North Florida Reception Center before the month ended, to be reclassified.

At the reception center, officers conducted a battery of tests and interviews, giving Rode the opportunity to describe his own history. A report prepared by the officials reflects what he said: "Subject indicated he completed 12th grade at Dillard High School in Fort Lauderdale, Florida, in 1976." It apparently didn't occur to the interviewer that Jimmy Rode was only fifteen until December 1976, and had not worked very hard in school. "Completed" didn't necessarily mean graduated. Investigation would have revealed that he actually obtained a general equivalency diploma, GED, equal to high school graduation, in 1978. An even more questionable entry followed. "The subject also indicated he had attended Indian River Community College and received his degree at Milan University in Italy, majoring in criminal justice, receiving an associate's arts degree." Rode had, indeed, been at Indian River, at the correctional institution from January 5, 1978, when he was barely seventeen, until mid-January 1979, not exactly a community college. He may have enrolled in a few extension courses provided by the college, but no records existed to support that. And Milan University in Italy? Jimmy Rode had never been out of the state of Florida.

On the same report, another entry might have raised some serious questions. "The subject states that his wife was killed in 1981, in the month of July, in Miami, Florida." Jimmy Rode truly had a wild imagination. Under the heading RELEASE PLAN, Rode had presented an ambitious goal. "Subject states he plans to return to Italy upon release from prison." It sounded good to officials. They completed the classification process and picked a facility where Rode would be confined.

On December 10, guards led Jimmy Rode into the Marion Correctional Institution. It didn't take him long to land in the spotlight at his new home. On January 20, 1982, Rode received a disciplinary report for "possession of an unauthorized beverage." That meant he'd somehow obtained and concealed two gallons of homemade wine, or "buck" in prison vernacular. Exactly two months later, he subjected himself to another rap for "unauthorized absence" from his assigned area. He belonged in the kitchen at the time, but had found reason to be elsewhere.

Once more the Parole and Probation Commission tackled the job of trying to establish a new "presumptive release date" for Rode. Because he'd been convicted of an escape, they were required to take the additional infractions into consideration. The string of disobedient acts made it impossible for the commission to set a new parole date, since state law required a discipline-free period of ninety days before such a date can be affirmed.

That didn't seem to bother Jimmy Rode. On May 25, officers again wrote him up for fighting with another inmate, which Jimmy claimed was nothing but horseplay. On

June 1, he deemed it a good idea to make "obscene comments and profane gestures" to a medical staff member. By that time, he'd earned the classification of a "close custody" inmate. A progress report near the end of June indicated that his adjustment progress was "poor."

Officials at Marion made a decision to reshuffle the cards. They included Jimmy Rode's name on a list of five inmates to be traded to another institution with the hope that a change might put him on a better path to rehabilitation. On October 6, he was sent to Cross City Correctional Institution, another facility housing all three categories of convicts: close, medium, and minimum-security. Prison authorities still regarded Rode as an inmate who required close supervision.

The change seemed to work, at least temporarily. Jimmy Rode received no disciplinary reports for six months, earning him a presumptive parole release date of October 6, 1986. Maybe the prospect of three more years in prison depressed Rode, because he slipped again. In May, he disobeyed another verbal order. He'd managed to carry a container of coffee away from the chow hall. When ordered to take it back, he refused.

It seemed that Rode wanted to test just how much he could get away with. In June, he refused a direct order to move a food serving cart, and took another disciplinary report.

A cellmate would later confess to some activities he shared with Jimmy Rode that would have put them both in hot water if they'd been caught. At night, they'd exchanged talk about women, sex, and the need for sexual relief. According to the cellmate, they engaged in oral sex together.

If such nocturnal activities did, indeed, take place, not being discovered may have encouraged Rode to see what else he could get away with. Whatever small infractions of the rules he chose to attempt, he saved the biggest caper for August of 1983.

Corrections Officer Gladys Dean, an experienced veteran of the Florida prison system at age fifty-nine, worked the afternoon shift in the Cross City facility kitchen, charged with overseeing food preparation and cleanup duties. A broad array of inmate duties under her supervision kept her busy. She described what the men did: "Well, some were assigned to the cooking area where they had to prepare the food and get it ready for the serving lines. Some were in charge of cleanup duty from the serving lines after the meals were over. Some were assigned to the bake shop to do bread, you know, for the meals. And some were assigned to cleanup duty on floors and the garbage room . . ."

Jimmy Rode had drawn garbage duty, making him responsible for cleaning the room in which garbage was piled and to hose down the floor. Gladys Dean knew him only by his last name and reputation. But she hadn't personally experienced any problems with him. "I would tell him to get his duties done that he was assigned to. Sometimes he'd be a little slow, dragging around, not getting them done on time." But no serious problems had occurred.

Ordinarily, Officer Dean avoided chewing out anyone in the presence of other inmates. But late one afternoon, she heard Jimmy Rode speaking in profane, derogatory terms about women in general. Hoping she could make him see how disrespectful he sounded, and feeling somewhat defensive about the denigrating comments, Dean turned to Rode. "You should be ashamed to talk like that because your mother is a woman." His only response was a churlish look in Dean's direction.

A few days later, on August 23, the officer working with Dean had stepped into another room for a break while Dean entered the bake shop to verify that the oven and fan had been switched off for the night. She also needed to secure the room because it contained sugar, yeast and fruit, the ingredients for "pruno" or "buck," the home-brewed alcoholic beverage prized by inmates. Jimmy Rode, having completed his garbage room detail, stood near the door. Dean turned to him and asked, "Will you reach that switch up there over the table and turn the fan off for me?"

While Rode moved toward the table, Gladys faced the oven. With her back toward Rode, she had just reached for the controls when she felt a hand grab her neck and a muscular forearm grip her across the face. Her glasses fell to the floor. The powerful assailant pinned her arms to her sides and dragged her into an obscure area between the door and the oven, next to some scales.

Gladys recalled her helplessness. "When somebody grabs you from behind and gets you to where you don't have any control of your arms, you don't have much chance. You can kick all you want to, but you know, it doesn't do any good. Then you're just lost. You've got to take the consequences."

The man let go of Dean's head and threw her to the floor. "My head hit the scales . . . He was trying to unbutton my shirt collar or get his hand inside. I'd buttoned up the collar with a tie on." Unable to tear the clothing loose, the hands closed again around Dean's throat. She felt the wooziness that precedes a total blackout. But she could still hear the man threatening to kill her if she ever told anyone about the attack.

"I was scared . . . really afraid. I didn't know what he intended to do, and I had no time to think. About the time I thought I was going to black out, something told me to do what you've always been told to do if you're caught in a situation: grab a man where it hurts the worst. And that's what I did. And when I did and twisted down on him, he left and ran to the dorm."

Before he fled, though, Jimmy Rode pushed the door closed and slammed home a large locking dead bolt.

Choking for breath and trying to recover, Gladys picked up a milk crate to bang on the door hoping to summon help. At last, another officer heard and released the gasping, frightened and injured woman.

Rode sprinted back to his cell and hoarsely whispered to his cellmate, "I think somebody is going to say I tried to rape her." Shortly, officers arrived to seize Rode and ask him about the incident with Gladys Dean. During a strip search, they saw what appeared to be a bite mark on Rode's shoulder standing out like a strawberry in a bowl of milk. They asked him about it, and he shrugged it off as the result of wrestling around that morning with his cellmate.

Once more called to answer for his fractious behavior, Jimmy Rode probably deserved far more punishment than he received. They let him off with another DR, a disciplinary report. A hearing would be scheduled to determine the necessity of any additional measures.

He still hadn't learned his lesson, though. On October 17, a search of Rode's cell uncovered two pieces of hacksaw blades he'd concealed. Another disciplinary report followed, but it was one too many. Administrators had tolerated Rode's behavior long enough.

Nine days after that final infraction, Jimmy Rode was treated to another bus trip. The destination this time was Florida State Prison in Starke. Located thirty miles south of the Georgia border, and fifty miles west of the Atlantic beaches at St. Augustine, the state prison there is for hard-time inmates. A forbidding institution utilizing maximum-security measures, called level seven security, it also housed death row and "Old Sparky," the electric chair. Some of the inmates are held twenty-four hours a day in single-cell confinement, broken only by brief exercise periods.

It didn't take long, even in the tough surroundings of Florida State Prison at Starke, for Jimmy Rode to let his presence be known. One month after his arrival, he received a DR for disobeying a verbal order. He'd been observed using a piece of string to lower something to the cellblock below his floor. Ordered to hand over the string, he refused. A person living in freedom could see the foolishness of such behavior. The string was going to be confiscated anyway. Why didn't he just obey and give it up? But Jimmy Rode had his own agenda and system of reasoning. Another DR thickened his dossier.

In January 1984, officials met for the hearing regarding Rode's attack on Corrections Officer Gladys Dean. They convicted him of battery on a law enforcement officer and sentenced him to an additional three years in state prison. This would be added to his original sentence of five years and the one year tacked on for escape. He was looking at nine more years behind bars.

Rode had landed in prison on March 9, 1981. With good behavior, he could have been paroled at the end of March 1982. Now, after having already served nearly three years, he faced the probability of remaining in prison until 1993. It seemed to be time to pause, assess the results of temper tantrums and disobeying rules, and set a course toward eventual release. Maybe Rode did just that, because the chain of disciplinary reports stopped. By August 1984, Rode received a progress report stating that his adjustment was "satisfactory." He would still be regarded as a "close management" inmate, but at least he had improved. Within three months, the Probation and Parole Commission considered his case again and recommended a parole date of April 16, 1991.

The disciplinary reports did not stop entirely. Midway through 1985, his grudge against another inmate got the best of him. He waited for the man to pass in the chow hall and doused him with hot water. The DR cited Rode for unarmed assault. In December, three days before his twenty-fourth birthday, Rode's anger at some real or imagined slight took the form of banging his shoes on his cell door, earning him a DR for disorderly conduct.

At his biannual review in June 1986, officials weighed the possibility of extending his parole date, but gave Rode the benefit of the doubt and let the date of April 16, 1991 stand intact.

Another inmate at Florida State Prison–Starke had become a notorious celebrity. Ted Bundy occupied a cell on death row. Reporters and authors clamored to interview him. Law enforcement officers from several states worked feverishly to see if any unsolved murders, especially those of pretty young women with long, straight hair, might be attributed to Bundy.

Jimmy Rode couldn't help but be awed by the world-famous convict he sometimes passed while performing deliveries or serving food in the cellblock. A guard overheard Rode initiating conversation with Bundy as often as possible. According to some associates, Rode would later tell them that Ted had whispered to him how easy it is to kill women and hide the evidence.

One afternoon, Ted Bundy completed reading a newspaper from his home area, Seattle, Washington, the region where his bloody spree of murdering young women had started. Finished with the paper, he reportedly slipped it to Jimmy Rode.

It would be a good idea, Rode figured, to read it carefully. Maybe there would be something in there to establish some common ground with Bundy, something he could talk about with the notorious convict.

PART TWO

Death in
The Northwest

Chapter 4

In Seattle, Washington, Kathi Lockhart wanted to meet the right man. Her previous relationships had been unsatisfactory and she wondered where all the nice guys were. Surely there were some decent, eligible men out there with whom she had interests in common. At age thirty-two, she didn't want to delay marriage much longer because her biological clock was ticking away toward the autumn of childbearing age.

Kathi certainly attracted her share of men. Her oval face, framed by dark brown hair cut in a pixie style, blue eyes, a bright smile that displayed dazzling white teeth and a slight overbite (after all, didn't actor Kirk Douglas once say an overbite made him fall in love?) gave Kathi a sweet appearance that would appeal to most men. So why hadn't she found the right one yet?

No one could classify her as an airhead; she worked for a prestigious firm in Seattle processing documents and interfacing with clients, and could hold her own in any intelligent conversation. Blessed with an easy laugh and a great sense of humor, Kathi wanted to meet someone with similar attributes. She hated the bar scene. All she could meet in those smoke-filled joints were lounge lizards or married men looking for a one-night stand. And that just didn't interest her.

A friend once suggested she could meet a nice guy by placing an ad in a weekly newspaper listing people interested in finding new relationships. Kathi had rejected the idea, but now started to wonder just what kind of responses she would get.

Just for fun, she drafted her self-description, her interests, and what she was looking for, then jammed it in her purse for a couple of days. At last, she called the newspaper.

She placed the ad in early summer. Summers are glorious around Seattle. The waters of Puget sound sparkle under bright warm skies and Mount Rainier towers in magnificent reign over the state. It's a perfect time to meet someone new, because there are so many things to share in the Pacific Northwest summers. Visit the glaciers on Mount Rainier, drive through the rain forest on the Olympic Peninsula, watch the spectacular Pacific waves batter the shore from Neah Bay to Long Beach, or maybe take a ferry ride across Puget Sound. Kathi placed the ad and waited. In the first week of July, she read a few answers, and tossed most of them. One of them, from distant Florida, dated July 7, 1986, caught her interest: *"Hi, how are you doing? I hope this letter finds you in the best of health and spirits. I saw your ad in the Weekly. I've never written to anyone before, but I was feeling kind of lonely today, so thought I'd write you a few lines."* The writer speculated that Kathi had received a large response to her ad, but expressed the hope that she would find his letter the most interesting. He continued by describing himself as 33, an Italian national, 5'10", 173 pounds, with black hair and hazel eyes. He was a native of Milan, he wrote, and had been in the United States since 1983. His extensive education included attending school in Italy, France, and England, where he had majored in languages. He had recently completed eight years in the "Italian Special Forces".

Following that remarkable and romantic self-portrait, he disclosed a minor negative fact. *"I would like for you to know that I'm in prison. I've not been here long, not much time before I am released. I won't go into why I am here in this letter, although it was nothing spectacular."*

The writer revealed that he was an incurable romantic, who loved to spend quiet evenings with an attractive lady. In his conclusion, he deeply hoped that Kathi would write to him. If she would, he promised, he would tell her more about himself. Expressing hope that hadn't bored her, he ended by saying, *"If you feel that you and I have a chance of hitting it off together, as I do, I'll send a photo of myself in my next letter. Take care."* He signed it, *"Jimmy."*

*   *   *

At the bottom of the letter, neatly printed, Kathi read the full name, JIMMY RODE, along with his prison number, and the post office box in Starke, Florida.

Well, she figured, what did she have to lose? The guy was certainly a GU in singles slang, meaning geographically undesirable. Florida was only about 3,000 miles away. So what would it hurt to correspond with him, even though he was in prison? At least he was honest about it.

Kathi had no way of knowing the "honesty" wasn't exactly true, that the letter overflowed with lies and exaggerations. So she replied with an equally cheerful, upbeat letter encouraging continuance of the exchanged messages.

In his third letter, Jimmy "explained" to Kathi about his incarceration. She later told the story he'd given her: "He said that he had been stopped while driving one night, that his car looked identical to one that had just been involved in a robbery, which is why the police stopped him, and that they found a large amount of marijuana in the glove compartment and that's why he had been arrested." Jimmy had added that he'd served just a few months in prison, and that he'd made arrangements to have the conviction expunged.

After a few months, Jimmy began signing his letters with a new name, Cesar Barone. He explained to Kathi that Barone was the name of the family who had raised him, and asked her advice on legally changing his name to Cesar Barone. She'd be glad to help, she wrote.

Kathi and Jimmy Rode, aka Cesar Barone, corresponded for nearly a year, until May 1987.

Jimmy Rode felt pleasantly surprised when Kathi Lockhart answered his letter. He planned to continue the relationship by mail as long as possible. He received an even better surprise in January 1987. Officials notified him that he would soon be transferred to the Union Correctional Institution to await his imminent release from prison!

Administrators had decided that Adolph "Jimmy" Rode had served his full sentence. The time tacked on for infractions during his imprisonment would be considered as concurrently served with the original sentence. He also learned that according to policy, no one is released directly from Florida State Prison at Starke. Thus the transfer.

After arriving at Union in February, Rode received yet another DR for fighting, but it had no effect on the decision to release him. So, on April 22, 1987, they put him on a bus back to Broward County, a free man, not even under parole supervision. With a few limitations applying to felons, such as prohibition against owning a gun, he could do anything he wanted or travel anywhere in the country.

Seattle, Washington, seemed as good a destination as any.

Within a month of his release, Jimmy Rode made his way to Seattle. The long correspondence with Kathi had influenced his decision along with the desire to escape the scene of all his trouble. If things worked out between them, he planned to start a new life with her. He'd also made up his mind to legally change his name. Fully aware of the stigma borne by ex-cons, he hoped that adopting the identity of Cesar Barone would conceal his past and let him start with a clean slate. For all intents and purposes, Adolph "Jimmy" Rode would die and his memory would fade into oblivion.

When he met Kathi Lockhart face to face, the mutual feelings established by mail translated to physical attraction. He complimented her femininity and sweet look, while she fell for his macho appearance and soft Southern drawl.

Cesar Barone adjusted quickly to the beautiful Pacific Northwest, Ted Bundy's old killing grounds, despite the sharp contrast with the balmy semitropic atmosphere of Florida. The winters would be much colder, but he could handle that. Best of all, he and Kathi seemed to have a solid future together.

During their first few months of dating, Barone took a job in a large car wash while Kathi continued her professional career. He eventually found work as a cabinetmaker. In September, he felt the time had come to legalize the name change. Kathi found the correct form and filled it out for him. When she came to the blank space in which to enter reasons, she asked, "What do you want me to put down?"

"Oh, just put personal reasons," Cesar replied.

Correctly assuming that something more specific was needed, and recalling his early letters, she suggested, "Why don't you say that you want to take the name of the family who helped you?"

"Okay, fine," he agreed.

So Kathi typed on the form, "Wishes to take family name of relatives who raised him." The name change became official on September 22, 1987.

As the summer of 1987 faded into early autumn, Kathi and Cesar decided to make the relationship permanent. They exchanged wedding vows in a private ceremony on October 27. Kathi's mother, Joyce Marie Scarbrough, owned a roomy, comfortable home in Hillsboro, Oregon, seventeen miles west of Portland. It would be financially easier, the newlyweds figured, to move in with Joyce temporarily until they could find a place of their own. One month into their marriage, they arrived at Mrs. Scarbrough's single-story home in a quiet cul-de-sac on the western edge of Hillsboro. Two towering birch trees decorated the expansive lawn in the well-manicured front yard. With the attractive landscaping, a house that included a fireplace and a recreation room with a pool table, Cesar Barone had no trouble at all making himself at home.

Kathi transferred to her firm's Portland office while Cesar soon found another cabinetmaking job. They paid their share of expenses, while she tried to save any extra money for a down payment on their own place.

Kathi and Cesar couldn't have picked a town with a better future than Hillsboro, the seat of Washington County. The community had been an agricultural center for decades, but recently a number of high-tech industries had selected the rolling hills and valleys on which to erect sprawling warehouses and factories. Washington County's economy boomed and property values skyrocketed.

Originally called East Tualatin Plains, the town became Hillsborough (later shortened) in 1850, named after David

Hill. He came west on the Oregon Trail, acquired some
land in the fertile Tualatin Valley and eventually became
provisional governor and a member of the state legislature.
He donated a large land parcel as a site for the courthouse
that still stands in the center of a forested block. In 1880,
a pioneer nurseryman, John Porter, who'd participated in
the California gold rush, brought six seedling Sequoia trees
from the Sierra Nevada mountains and planted them on
the south side of the courthouse. Five of them still tower
over 150 feet into the clean air, and a sixth replacement
tree is trying to catch up. U.S. Federal Highway 26 connects
the picturesque coastal towns of Seaside and Cannon Beach
to Portland. Called the Sunset Highway, it is a four-lane
freeway from the northern city limits of Hillsboro to the
city, which enables commuters to cover the fifteen miles in
a short time.

By the time Kathi and Cesar settled into the town in
1987, urban growth had already expanded the population
from fewer than 15,000 in the sixties, to over 40,000. New
shopping centers on the perimeter acted as a magnet to the
large department and chain stores, which moved from the
town center. Both motion picture theaters, the Town and
a smaller one on 2nd Street near Main, closed. But local
business executives refused to let the shops along Main
Street wither and die. The ambitious, civic-minded men attracted a variety of commercial enterprises, including restaurants, gift shops, and clothing stores, made intelligent
changes to meet other needs of citizens, and kept the downtown section healthy. The courthouse expanded with modern annexes, also accommodating the Washington County
sheriff's department and the county jail.

On the outskirts, the county fair grounds were upgraded
to improve and expand the annual celebration, and the
Hillsboro airport thrived with traveling executives of the
burgeoning high-tech businesses moving in. The county
would soon gain the distinction of being the fastest growing
area in the entire state.

The stay by Cesar and Kathi with her mother, as
planned, was for a short duration. After two months of
sharing the home, Cesar and Kathi moved to a modest
rented house on 10th Street in Hillsboro. After seven

months they saved enough for a down payment on their own home. They selected an attractive single-story house painted white and trimmed in blue, with a perfectly landscaped yard in a well-maintained neighborhood.

Plentiful jobs afforded Cesar Barone with ample opportunity to work, but he couldn't seem to find any place he wanted to stay very long. For most of 1988, he bounced from job to job, sometimes as a cabinetmaker, then as a craftsman for a hotel supply company and for a promotional products firm building exhibit displays. By their first wedding anniversary, he'd worked six different jobs. Restless, Cesar finally announced to Kathi that he'd made an important decision. He wanted to join the U.S. Army.

Kathi wanted to know why. Cesar told her it was something he'd been thinking about for a long time, that he'd always wanted to be a soldier. He showed her a stack of magazines he'd saved and read repeatedly, featuring vivid accounts of military adventures and war. "I've finally decided to do it," he said, leaving no room for argument.

And he did. During the enlistment interview, he gave the sergeant the same information he dreamed up while being processed into the Florida penitentiary system. Barone said he'd studied two years at Indian River Community College, and that he'd never been convicted of a felony. As Cesar Barone, he hadn't, and in his own view, Jimmy Rode no longer existed. In January 1989, a few weeks past his twenty-eighth birthday, he boarded a plane bound for Fort Benning, Georgia.

In that same month, on the twenty-ninth, a convict in Florida who may have had a significant influence on Barone's life, sat down to a breakfast of eggs, steak, hash browns, and coffee. But he couldn't eat a bite. Ted Bundy had spent a portion of the previous evening videotaping his verbal harangue against pornography, claiming it had put him on the path of destruction. Dressed in blue pants and a lighter colored shirt, Bundy sat still while a barber shaved his head and right calf. At about 7:00 A.M., two guards led him toward a solid, simple oak chair bedecked with straps. Looking gaunt, weak-kneed and older than his forty-two years, Bundy slumped into "Old Sparky." Attendants buckled the leather straps down and attached electrodes to his head and calf. At 7:16, his life was over. He'd never kill again.

In Fort Benning, Barone completed basic training and qualified as a sharpshooter with an M-16 on the rifle range. After the completion of basic, Barone advanced to airborne school where he earned his parachute badge. A few weeks later, he graduated from emergency medical technician training.

Kathy stayed in the house but spent much of her time with her mother in those lonely months. She jumped with glee when Cesar told her he'd been assigned to Fort Lewis, Washington, only 120 miles north of Portland, as a member of the 75th Ranger Regiment, 2nd Battalion. He could wear a beret and bloused boots, commanding the respect of ordinary infantry soldiers. Rangers, a recruiter would say, are "one of the Army's most elite fighting units, who live a rougher, tougher life than the average infantryman." In their creed, they vow to move farther, faster, and fight harder than other soldiers and set an example for them to follow. Rangers must also be more physically fit than the average soldier, and must possess certain personal characteristics that set them apart. A high level of discipline and mental toughness is a requirement. Cesar Barone and his wife had good reason to be proud.

The couple gave up their home and found a small rental house in Lacey, near Olympia, the capital of Washington, a few miles south of the main entrance to Fort Lewis. Cesar Barone seemed content with his military experience. Duty in the peacetime army isn't bad even if it's often dull and routine. Rain falls incessantly around Fort Lewis in December, soaking the pine-needle-carpeted ground, dripping from trees, and occasionally changing to sleet or light snow. The chilly dampness creeps right through to the bones of young troopers from sunnier regions of the country. Constantly gray skies can be depressing, sending soldiers into daydreams of tropical climates. If Cesar Barone was bored, the problem came to a jolting end in December 1989.

Members of Company B, 2nd Battalion, 75th Rangers,

including Cesar Barone, had their dreams of warmer climates come true most unexpectedly.

In mid-December, the outfit had been activated in a rapid deployment exercise when the word came to pack up and be ready to move out within eighteen hours.

Tensions had been building in Central America, especially in the hotspot of Panama, during the last two months of 1989. Focusing on issues of democracy in the tiny country and the headache of free-flowing drugs, the problems were a festering thorn in Uncle Sam's side. The petulant leader of Panama, General Manuel Antonio Noriega, had evaded every attempt, subtle or overt, by the U.S. to pry him from his seat of power. He ran a military dictatorship and refused to accept the results of a May election in which countryman Guillermo Endara apparently won the presidency. Short, stocky, with a pockmarked face expressing defiance toward his agitated northern neighbor, Noriega had appointed a 510-member National Assembly of Representatives as his puppet legislature. In turn, they voted to name him head of the government and "maximum leader of the struggle for national liberation." They also resolved that their country was "in a state of war" with the United States.

On December 16, a group of U.S. military officers traveling in a civilian car pulled up at a roadblock manned by soldiers of the PDF, Panamanian Defense Forces, outside Panama City. In the ensuing confusion, a Marine, Lieutenant Robert Paz, age twenty-five, fell mortally wounded by gunfire. From a nearby vantage point, a U.S. Navy lieutenant and his wife watched in horror as the bloody events developed. They were captured and interrogated by the PDF, and later reported that the troops had beaten him and sexually threatened the woman.

President George Bush called for a "delta" alert of the American military, resulting in the 75th Ranger Regiment embarking on a rapid deployment exercise. Of course, the detailed reasons for the surge of activity were not passed on to Private 2 Cesar Barone or his comrades in Company B.

Outraged at the Marine's death, Bush announced to the world at 7:00 A.M., EST, on December 20, that Noriega,

"an indicted drug trafficker," had rejected all diplomatic
and peaceful attempts to resolve the crisis. "General Noriega's reckless threats and attacks on Americans in Panama,"
Bush said, "created an imminent danger to 35,000 American citizens" in that country. As a result, the president had
decided to launch a force of 12,000 troops from all branches
of the American military to join an equal number already
stationed in Panama, to overthrow Noriega's government
and to capture the defiant leader. Dubbed Operation Just
Cause, the invasion would meet all of its goals except one.
Manuel Noriega escaped. But his freedom was only temporary. Before Noriega was eventually taken into custody and
shipped to Florida to face trial, California's Governor Pete
Wilson summed up the attitude of most Americans when
he said, "Noriega is a murderous thug who is up to his
eyeballs in the drug trade. Obviously, he was not going to
be removed by any means but force."

Cesar Barone's outfit was among the military force of
12,000 troops sent to Panama. In the battle of "Just Cause,"
another member of the 75th Rangers, Sergeant First Class
David DeBaere, recalled their participation. He expressed
pride about his unit's involvement in seizing and securing
a key airfield. DeBaere would be quoted as saying that the
Rangers "are always in a trigger-pulling mode" with their
9 mm pistols and M-16 rifles.

An associate of Cesar Barone would one day divulge that
Barone bragged to him of killing several Panamanians. If
that truly happened, Barone included not only PDF soldiers
as targets, but also a few civilians, including a couple of
women. Records cannot verify the claim.

What can be verified is that Kathi received a surprise
package through the military mail from Panama while
Cesar was there. She recognized his return address and
handwriting. Curious, she tore it open and found a Browning 9 mm pistol wrapped in two T-shirts. Somewhat disappointed and more than a little perplexed, she carefully
replaced the box top and shoved the package onto a top
closet shelf to wait for the return of Ranger Cesar Barone.

Chapter 5

Life for Kathi Barone settled into a relatively smooth pattern after Cesar returned from Operation Just Cause in Panama. American troops had sustained casualties in the conflict, including 23 deaths, and Kathi felt grateful that her husband had avoided injury. On the home front, she'd been lucky enough to land a new job with a firm in Tacoma, just north of Fort Lewis. In the spring Kathi celebrated something she'd always anticipated, delighted to discover that she was pregnant. She calculated that the baby should be born in the third week of January 1991, so she informed her bosses at the office, started buying maternity smocks and baby garments, and mulled over an endless list of potential names for the child.

A confusing telephone call interrupted the pleasant routine in early October and sent a rush of alarm racing through Kath's already overburdened system.

"I received a phone call at work one day," she recalled, "from . . . a police officer, saying that there had been a complaint by an elderly woman. This woman said a man had been showing up at her house continually and was scaring her." The odd visitor, Kathi learned, told the aged woman he was with the Rangers at Fort Lewis and described where his pregnant wife worked in Tacoma. It hadn't taken investigators long, by contacting her employer and using a process of elimination, to zero in on Kathi Barone. "With that information," she said, "they tracked me down and called to ask my husband's name and whether he was in the Rangers."

The questioning officer didn't reveal to Kathi that the frightened woman was eighty years old and that the man lurking about had exposed himself to her and attempted to fondle her.

The victim, Dora Vinson, had told police that one afternoon in September, on her rural farmhouse property, she saw a soldier who appeared to be searching for something. When she asked him about it, he glanced around and said that a little white poodle belonging to his wife had leaped out of his car window and disappeared into the trees. With a worried expression, he stressed the importance of finding it and how heartbroken his poor wife would be. Dora helped search for the pet, and when no dog turned up, she agreed to keep a sharp lookout for it. He thanked her and left.

In the following week, the soldier showed up again several times, acting friendly to the woman who lived alone at a considerable distance from the closest neighbor. While she didn't mind the company, she became troubled at the man's tendency to be pushy about coming into her home. He seemed very distracted during one visit when he sat on her couch stroking and kneading a pillow. She felt the first real sense of danger. On the next visit, the soldier led her to a chair with more force than she thought necessary, began rubbing her neck and shoulders exactly as he had stroked the pillow, then tried to grope her under her blouse. She asked him to stop, and he complied.

Dora's apprehension grew when he showed up again the next day. This time, he wanted to demonstrate Army techniques for edging forward while belly down on the floor. Reluctantly, she humored him. As he crept closer to her, he grabbed her leg. Desperately hoping that he meant no harm, she again pled in a friendly way for him not to touch her. Once more, he backed off.

Hoping that the young man was simply a lonely soul who needed company, but sensing that he represented a serious threat to her, Dora at last decided she'd better talk to someone about it. She described the episodes to her son. Astonished and angry, he arranged for his mother to stay with family members, and called the police.

Dismayed and bewildered, Kathi couldn't accept the possibility that Cesar would abuse a helpless elderly woman.

"No!" she gasped into the phone. "There must be some mistake. That couldn't possibly be my husband." Absolutely convinced of Cesar's innocence in the matter, she gave the officer a phone number where he could be reached at Fort Lewis.

A soon as she disconnected from the distressing conversation, she telephoned Cesar at the base and told him of the police inquiry. His reaction contrasted starkly with hers, showing no concern at all. "It must have been somebody else," he said. What a coincidence that another man in uniform, identified as a Ranger, also had a pregnant wife working for the same Tacoma firm. Cesar chose to be reticent, and not discuss the matter any further.

The consequences of the ensuing investigation hit Cesar Barone within days after the police called Kathi. While it was questionable whether he'd committed a crime or not, he wouldn't be arrested but he must have known he was in trouble. The police informed Army officials of their discoveries: That Cesar Barone had been known as Adolph Rode in Florida and that he'd served several years in prison for felony convictions.

The puzzled Army couldn't explain how Barone had slipped through their screening process, but they acknowledged accepting his enlistment under fraudulent conditions. They promptly mustered him out with a general discharge, effective immediately, on October 5, 1990.

Cesar's explanation to Kathi for his sudden departure from military service omitted any reference to the elderly woman. He said the Army had discovered some minor discrepancies in his original application to join, so they ended his tour of duty. When Kathi was later asked about Cesar's reaction to being discharged, she said, "He seemed to be almost relieved to be getting out of the Army. It didn't seem to bother him at all."

Now unemployed, Barone made several attempts to find work, but had little success. They lived on her income plus their savings. Cesar had leisure time on his hands, much of it spent with his dog, a female black Labrador retriever.

Even though expenses strained their budget, they managed a nice Christmas with a pile of gaily wrapped presents under a brightly ornamented tree. Kathi snapped a photo of Cesar playing with the Lab next to the tree, in which he appeared relaxed and happy. As the year ended, Kathi ballooned into the final months of pregnancy, and their son was born on the third week of January 1991.

Both parents beamed at the beautiful little boy, but worried about finances. Finally, in March, Cesar contacted a cabinetmaking company in Forest Grove, next to Hillsboro, where he'd worked before. The manager agreed to rehire him.

Of course, his new job required they move back to Hillsboro. Kathi needed to give her employer in Tacoma at least thirty days' notice and to forewarn their landlord one month in advance that they planned to move out. The couple agreed that Kathi would remain in the house four more weeks, with the child, while Cesar could once again stay with Kathi's mother and take the Forest Grove job. In mid-March, he drove down to Hillsboro, alone.

Margaret Schmidt, at sixty-one years of age, loved sitting on either of the two covered porches of her pale pink two-story home located at the corner of Walnut and Fourth Streets in Hillsboro, just a few blocks from the town center. She especially enjoyed spring days, when the sun reflected from the new leaves of her copper beech tree, shrubs inside the hedged yard sparkled with fresh green growth, and flower buds threatened colorful explosions. Over the neatly trimmed hedge she could see frolicking children in the playground of David Hill Elementary School across the street. Their happy shrieks warmed her heart with nostalgia. Some of kids would smile and wave at the pleasant woman, and she'd wave back.

Dangerously overweight and crippled from having broken a leg several months earlier, Margaret required the use of a walker to get around. But that didn't keep her from frequently visiting nearby friends or the neighboring Community-Senior center. On her most recent trip there, she'd proudly told of selling some antiques and reaping substantial profits. To prove it, she pulled a big wad of bills from her purse and showed it to several people.

Margaret had lived in Hillsboro most of her life, watching it grow from a sleepy little farming town to a bustling high-tech industrial center. She'd graduated from Hillsboro High School soon after World War II ended, and had learned skills that qualified her to work in a nursing home. In later years, she supplemented her income by cleaning homes of prominent Hillsboro citizens. She never married and never had children but seemed contented, happy, and uncomplaining, always ready with a word of cheer. Neighboring visitors often dropped in to pass the time of day and play with her live-in companions, three cats she adored.

Always safety conscious, Margaret kept doors and windows protected from intruders with locks. On the interior frame of a small window in the bathroom, she'd hammered two nails into the wood to limit the swing of the hinged window to only a few inches, thus allowing the cats to go in or out at their leisure while still maintaining security. Sometimes, she put a can of talcum powder on the sill.

On Thursday evening, April 18, 1991, Margaret's friend Kathy Ackerman stopped by to chat and share some pizza. April showers threatened at dusk on that spring day, so Kathy said good night to Margaret at 7:00 P.M., and hurried home.

The next visitor arrived thirteen hours later on a drizzly Friday morning. Dorothy Baber, an in-home caretaker, paid calls to Margaret three times each week, Mondays, Wednesdays, and Fridays, to assist her with cleaning, laundry, and other housekeeping chores.

As Dorothy opened the picketed gate between two ends of hedges on the 4th Street side of the house, she instantly sensed something wrong. The porch light, always kept on by Margaret, was dark. Maybe it had just burned out, Dorothy hoped. She knocked once, and then again. No response. She put her hand to the glass window of the door and it felt cold to the touch. The heater inside hadn't warmed the house for hours.

Alarmed, Dorothy rushed back out to her car at the curb, fished a spare key to Margaret's house from the glove box, and returned to the porch. She didn't know whether she could gain entry into the house or not, because her key fit only the door lock, not the deadbolt always set by Margaret at night. Dorothy's apprehension grew when she twisted the key and the door swung open.

Stepping quietly into the chilled house, she called out Margaret's name, but heard no answer. Heading directly toward her friend's bedroom, she noticed the door standing slightly ajar. Now frightened of what she might see, Dorothy pulled the door open, and froze.

Margaret Schmidt lay supine and motionless on the bed, nude with the exception of a few shreds of a nightgown clinging to her shoulders and neck. She reposed with her legs in a spread-eagled position, one foot hanging limply off the side of the bed, her face covered with a pillow. Blood stained the pillowcase and the remnants of the nightgown at her throat.

Horrified, Dorothy struggled to maintain her composure, rushed to a phone in another room, and telephoned the emergency number to request medical help and the police. The Hillsboro Police and Fire Departments shared a two-story brick building on 2nd Street, just two blocks away, so they arrived within a couple of minutes.

A pair of emergency medical technicians hurried into the bedroom and lifted the bloody pillow from Margaret's face. Her head, which was twisted sideways, rested on another blood-soaked pillow. They checked her wrists for a radial pulse, but found none. They felt her skin, cold to the touch. No earthly help would be of any value to Margaret Schmidt, ever again. The EMTs backed carefully out of the room, being careful not to disturb any potential evidence of the obvious homicide.

Lieutenant Lila Ashenbrenner arrived simultaneously with the medical techs along with Detective Larry Harris. Ashenbrenner, vivacious, bright, with curly dark hair, and a disarming smile, had won the respect of her fellow Hillsboro PD officers through tenacious grit, a quick sense of humor, and exceptional intelligence. She could banter with tough-talking cops, steel herself at grim sights of gruesome crime scenes, yet maintain the dignity, charm and grace of a social hostess or chief executive.

While Harris attended to examining the body and bedroom for any trace evidence, Ashenbrenner looked around the rest of the house. In the bathroom, with Dorothy Baber, she studied a negative shoeprint on the floor left in a fresh spill of talcum powder. The pattern of the shoe sole had picked up the powder, thus leaving dark blanks in the white spill. Ashenbrenner followed specks of the powder to the kitchen, where a positive print had been made, that is, white tracks on the darker linoleum floor. Clearly the same shoe. She arranged for both prints to be extensively photographed.

When the investigators later interviewed Kathy Ackerman, who'd shared pizza with Margaret and was the last person to see her alive, they learned the talcum powder had not been on the floor when Ackerman left. As a matter of fact, the container had been on the window sill where the two nails limited the swing of the hinged window, and had apparently been knocked off when someone pushed the window from the outside.

In some cities across the country, communications between law enforcement agencies suffer because of jurisdictional barriers. Not so in Hillsboro or Washington County. Lila Ashenbrenner and the whole team of HPD detectives interacted enthusiastically and effectively with the county sheriff's office. She didn't even think twice about summoning Detective Michael O'Connell from that agency to add his welcome skills in the search for leads.

O'Connell's thirteen years with WCSD belied his youthful appearance and clean-cut good looks. A native of Washington County, his father owned a service station in North Plains, but he spent a great deal of his youth playing and working on farms owned by two uncles. While in Hillsboro High School, Michael joined the Special Interest Explorers chartered by the Boy Scouts of America and sponsored by the county sheriff. He actually rode with deputies twice a week, wearing a uniform similar to theirs, and nurturing the deep roots of his interest in law enforcement. At Southern Oregon College in Ashland, O'Connell earned two degrees,

one in criminology, then returned to Hillsboro in 1980 to
join the Washington County Sheriff's Department as a patrol officer. Seven years later, he donned white shirt and tie
as a detective, graduated from the Southern Police Institute
School of Homicide Investigation (affiliated with the University of Louisville in Kentucky) and began investigating
homicides in 1987. A completely dedicated cop, O' Connell
still found time for fishing, bicycling over the rolling Northwest terrain, reading great literature such as William Faulk-
ner, and to enjoy the company of his wife, daughter, and
two sons.

Something caught Michael O'Connell's eye shortly after
his arrival at Margaret Schmidt's home that morning. The
gate to a shed on the north side of the house gapped open
about a foot. By twisting sideways and sucking in his already flat stomach, O'Connell found he could squeeze
through the narrow opening. It gave him a straight shot
through a storage area, past a roll of vinyl with a new clean
streak on the dusty surface, and into the kitchen. He and
Lila Ashenbrenner agreed that the killer had used the
same route.

Together, they examined the shoeprints in talcum powder, and by looking closely, could make out the word REE-
BOK. O'Connell stared for a long time at those impressions,
branding every detail of the pattern in his mind. He
planned to grab copies of the photos as soon as they were
printed and start searching for those Reeboks while the
trail remained fresh.

In the bedroom where the body lay, the investigators
noted that the victim's torn nightgown and underpants had
been placed on the sheet to the right side of her head.
While collecting them for future examination, they also
placed bags over Margaret's hands to preserve any hairs or
skin under her fingernails she might have scratched from
the killer. With meticulous care, they scoured the room for
any other usable evidence. Outside, they noted that the
porch light bulb had been removed. At the bathroom window which had been pushed, toppling the talcum powder
can, they found the light bulb lying in the damp grass.
O'Connell moved on around the house and stopped at Margaret's bedroom window. In his low-key manner, he sum-

moned Ashenbrenner and Harris to show them something else. Someone had sliced a rectangular section from the screen and dropped the cutting to the ground, making the window glass accessible. Smudge marks in a thin layer of dust on the glass evoked a picture of an intruder grunting, struggling to pry the window open. He'd failed because thick dried paint inside held the window solidly closed as if it had been nailed shut.

Another shoeprint the team found in mud near a shed door proved unusable. It contained insufficient detail for casting or identifying the type of shoe.

The talcum powder prints, they realized, provided the only solid lead they had. That same afternoon, with the help of more officers, they canvassed every block surrounding the crime scene in a meticulous hunt for a size eight and one-half Reebok shoe.

The search for the Reeboks became a near obsession for Michael O'Connell. The next morning he began visiting local retail stores trying to find information abut the pattern or leads to customers who had bought that type of shoe. He learned of a regional shoe purchasing agent for a big company, who worked out of Wilsonville, twenty miles down I-5 from Portland. By providing the agent with details of the shoe prints, along with photographs, O' Connell learned that the print was left by either a Reebok ERS (Energy Returned System) 2000, or ERS Blaze, both made specifically for running. He hurried to a retail outlet that handled both types, and snapped a series of photographs. By close examination of the new samples in the store, O'Connell ruled out the ERS Blaze type. Now he could narrow the search to one single type of Reebok running shoes, the ERS 2000.

Of course, the remote possibility existed that a woman, wearing the distaff size ten, had murdered Margaret Schmidt. But O'Connell knew, from the type of damage perpetrated against the victim's body, that he was searching for a man who owned size eight and one-half Reeboks.

Back in Hillsboro, he arranged for copies of the photos to be distributed in the jailhouse with instructions to examine the footwear of every person brought in. At briefing sessions for all shifts of patrol officers and deputies, sergeants told them to be on the lookout for the shoes. "When you're talking to people, issuing traffic citations, making any arrest, look for the Reeboks." But O'Connell deliberately avoided passing out any information that would relate the shoe search to any specific crime. He explained the reasons. "If we announced that Margaret Schmidt's killer left shoe prints at the scene from those shoes, there would be a great likelihood of the shoes being destroyed before we got our hands on them."

Dr. Larry Lewman, state medical examiner, performed the autopsy on Margaret Schmidt and concluded that she'd died from asphyxiation by smothering and compression of the neck. The pillow had been pressed into her face so hard that she couldn't breathe, and pressure applied to her throat as well. She'd bled profusely from the mouth and nose in the course of the savage murder. Lewman also stated that Margaret had been sexually assaulted.

Lieutenant Lila Ashenbrenner hoped that the variety of hairs collected from the blankets and sheets and on the bedroom carpet would point to a suspect. But they turned out to be from Margaret's three cats.

One single lead remained. That week Michael O'Connell started a habit of glancing at shoes everywhere he went.

Chapter 6

As they'd agreed, Kathi Barone spent a month in the apartment near Olympia, then followed her husband to Hillsboro on April 20, 1991, one day after Margaret Schmidt died.

Cesar worked at the Forest Grove cabinet shop until July. His supervisor described Barone's performance as "just average," adding that there'd been no specific problems during his short tenure at the shop. Barone resigned without explanation.

In an August application for employment in a Forest Grove nursing home, Barone cited the emergency medical-technician training he'd received in the Army. He'd also managed to wangle a certification as a nursing assistant, so they hired him. Supervisors at the home observed that he seemed to adapt quickly to helping care for elderly patients. After two months on the new job, Barone took the career a step farther by applying for an Oregon state license as an EMT. For some reason, he stated that he'd served in the Army from January 1988 to April 1991 instead of the actual period, April 1989 to October 1990. He also entered on the application form that he'd taken an EMT course at Pierce College in Tacoma. Perhaps realizing that the false information would probably be discovered, Barone never showed up to take the final certification examination. But he continued to work at the nursing home.

Gregarious and talkative, especially to female coworkers, Barone expanded his circle of friends and acquaintances.

Kathi hoped the new job and Cesar's role as a father would quiet the sense of unrest which had been nagging at her since they'd moved back to Hillsboro. It hurt her when Cesar frequently found reasons to be absent from the home and she began to wonder if he had interests in other women. "He would come home from work, change clothes, sometimes stay for an hour or so, and then [he'd say] 'Oh, I have to go back to work tonight . . .' Or he would be going out to play pool with someone, or to have coffee with someone, you know. [He'd] leave and say, 'I'll be back in a couple of hours' and then show up maybe three in the morning." She didn't mind too much that he drank beer steadily, even though they were often short of cash.

One of Kathi's uncles got along very well with Cesar, characterizing him as a likable guy who was "kind of comical." Even though the relative expressed suspicion that Barone was unfaithful to Kathi, he said, "I have to admit, I liked the guy."

Cesar seemed to love their little son, especially when other people were watching, Kathi thought, and she couldn't understand why he didn't want to spend as much time as possible with her and the child. In October, she snapped a photograph of Cesar, sitting on a couch, laughing as the little boy took some of his first steps.

On the seventh day of that same month, on the Warm Springs Indian Reservation about ninety miles southeast of Hillsboro, a woodcutter discovered the dead body of a homeless man from Portland. A few weeks later another body was found, and then a third and fourth. All four of the men had been executed with close-range gunshots to the head. Oddly, autopsies revealed that all four had recently dined on hamburgers and french fries. On October 27, police arrested Douglas F. "the Animal" Wright, an ex-con who'd once been arrested in Washington County for two other murders. While in prison, Wright won weight lifting competitions. He would be convicted in three of the four Warm Springs murders, and sentenced to death. But Oregon hadn't executed anyone since 1962, so Wright didn't appear to be in much danger.

Instead of improvements in the bonds of marriage that Kathi hoped for, conditions deteriorated. Financial problems worsened, and they received a letter from the manager of their bank informing them of an overdrawn account. By

the child's first birthday, in January 1992, Kathi realized it
was hopeless. She and Cesar agreed to separate and file for
a divorce based on irreconcilable differences. Kathi and her
son moved back in with her mother, Joyce Scarbrough.

Cesar packed his bags and moved into the ground floor
of a charming two-story turn-of-the-century-style house on
4th Street in Cornelius, two miles west of the Hillsboro city
limits. Upstairs, a fifty-one-year-old woman, living alone,
watched as Cesar Barone unloaded his belongings and settled in. Matilda Gardner thought he looked like a nice
young man, and wasn't surprised when an attractive woman
moved in with him before January ended.

At the Forest Grove nursing home where he continued
to work, Cesar befriended a young man named Len Darcell, and met several women. An attractive young cherubic-
faced blonde came to work at the home in February 1992.
They never became any more than coworkers who would
greet each other in passing, but Christina Jerome-Johnson
would always remember Cesar Barone. Another woman,
Lynn Kramer, also worked there as a certified nursing assistant (CNA) with Barone and his pal, Len Darcell. She
formed some personal opinions about both of them. Cesar,
she said, was a "gigolo," a real ladies' man. She would
report that Cesar lived with a woman for a while, who
finally moved away to California. Then, she said, he had
an affair with a married fellow employee before he met
another coworker with whom he had a serious relationship,
Sheila Hawkins, also a CNA. By the end of January, Sheila
shared quarters with Cesar in the ground floor of the old
house in Cornelius. Kramer laughed as she recalled that
Cesar once went after Sheila Hawkins's ex-husband with
a gun.

When Cesar and Kathi's divorce became final in May,
Cesar also gave up his job at the nursing home. His nursing
assistant certification wouldn't expire until the end of the
year, but he chose to leave anyway. He never applied for
the certification to be reinstated.

By working sporadically at various jobs, Cesar managed
to keep financially afloat. He'd been collecting a Veteran's
Administration disability check for $300 each month, but
Kathi persuaded him to allow continued delivery of the

check to her residence as a form of child support. Even
though she figured the payment was about fifty dollars less
than the amount a court would probably award her, she
decided to accept it. She explained, "Because knowing his
work history and having seen the way he handles money,
I honestly felt that there wasn't a chance in the world that
I would ever get a penny otherwise." To be certain he
wouldn't play games with it, she obtained a power of attorney from Cesar which would allow her to legally cash the
checks.

Single again, Cesar found even more time to spend with
his friends. One of them, Leonard Benjamin "Len" Darcell
III, at age twenty-four was Barone's junior by seven years.
Nevertheless, they seemed to have a lot in common. Hillsboro and Cornelius police knew Darcell quite well, too.
He'd been picked up several times on drug-related charges.
Called "Germ" by street people who regarded bizarre nick-
names as desirable symbols of nonconformance, Darcell
had worked now and then as a chain-saw operator in the
lumber industry. A cutback in logging had ended that career, so he found employment in the same nursing home
where Cesar Barone worked.

Tall with a medium build, dark eyes and hair, a noticeable bump in his high-bridged nose, a thick neck, and scattered blemishes on his high, round cheekbones, Darcell
sometimes clipped sections of his scalp into punk-rocker
styles and wore a pencil-thin mustache. More recently
though, he'd shaved the narrow space between his nose and
full lips and wore a modified Dutch boy hair style. He was
also a chain smoker and could converse with reasonable
intelligence in a somewhat whiny twang.

Darcell and Barone hit it off so well, Barone allowed
his pal to join him and Sheila in the Cornelius house on
4th Street.

The rap sheet on Len Darcell revealed a checkered past.
In 1987, he and a friend were caught removing parts from
an old car being held in the Clark County impound yard.
Not a wise place to select for criminal activity. He was
convicted on a charge of second-degree burglary. Five other

felony arrests for a series of small-time crimes gave him a reputation worthy of police attention.

In 1991, Darcell was charged with "indecent liberties and unlawful imprisonment," involving a sixteen-year-old girl. Darcell's attorney convinced the prosecutor to dismiss the charges by presenting evidence that the "victim" had habitually and falsely accused numerous other people of similar behavior.

Elizabeth Wasson had the euphonious birth date of 9/9/ 09. In September 1992, she celebrated her eighty-third birthday in her modest little home in the 2100 block of Brookwood Street, Hillsboro. Elizabeth lived alone, nearly surrounded by towering pines and cedars, which scented her yard with pleasant aromas.

Exactly two weeks after her birthday, Wasson's horrified daughter and her husband summoned help to Elizabeth's little house. They had let themselves in with a spare key a few minutes after nine that evening after she failed to answer the door. In a rear bedroom, they found the little woman lying in deathly stillness. Police and medical techs examined the body. She'd been smothered with a pillow and stabbed twice in the neck. Heartbroken neighbors told investigators that Wasson often left her door unlocked when she went grocery shopping. She trusted everyone, they said, probably because she'd once been a missionary.

One witness had driven his car past the house at about the time the sun was setting, around 7:00 P.M., and seen a man whom he described as about 5' 11", Caucasian, around 170 pounds, and wearing dark-colored clothing. The stranger had been standing at Wasson's door, with his back to the street, so the motorist couldn't see his face. Some of the victim's neighbors had noticed a small foreign car in the area recently, but none had thought to jot down the license number. There were no signs of forced entry into the house, no ransacking, no sexual assault, and nothing stolen. Everyone was at a complete loss to explain why Elizabeth had been killed.

A good friend of Barone's faced some trouble over some drug charges. Before surrendering to the police, Carlos Ro-

mero arranged for Barone to safekeep an item for him, a
little .22 revolver. In mid-September, the judge handling
Romero's case received a letter regarding the inmate. It
stated that Mr. Carlos Romero had sought counseling from
the writer in June through August 1992. The sessions had
been conducted twice each week. According to the letter's
author, Romero had made progress in the area of personal
development, and was encouraged to seek counseling on a
regular basis. The "counselor" generously offered to continue seeing Mr. Romero "during his incarceration" and
upon subsequent release. It was signed: Cesar F. Barone,
Social Services Technician, Drug & Alcohol Treatment.

Attached to the letter were three receipts, each made out
for $120, signed by Cesar F. Barone, payment made by
Carlos Romero.

The exact purpose of the letter was never clear. Perhaps
it was meant to sway the judge in favor of a lighter sentence
in view of Romero's having received "counseling" for his
drug problems. The judge reviewed it and handed it to his
clerk to file.

Even though Kathi and Cesar had divorced and he was
living with another woman, he visited his ex-wife and his
son frequently. Cesar regularly drove to the day care center
where Kathi left the child while she worked and gave the
child a lift over to the Scarbrough residence. He often
stayed to visit with Kathi's mother, Joyce, and other family
members, who generally addressed him as "C." There was
no talk, however, of resuming the marriage.

Barone certainly wasn't lacking for female companionship. He and Sheila Hawkins spent most evenings together,
along with her daughter, age eleven. Gradually, Sheila
began to notice troubling aspects about her lover. She knew
that he sometimes used crank, or methamphetamine, and
suspected his use was far greater than he admitted. And
she didn't like it that he periodically carried the Browning
9 mm semiautomatic pistol and kept a .22 revolver concealed inside a green glove in the top shelf of a closet. It
also bothered her when he'd disappear and stay away all
night. Cesar would always have an explanation, usually that
he'd been fishing with a buddy. But when Sheila would ask

the buddy, she'd see a blank look or hear an outright denial.

Those concerns paled in comparison to a bigger worry she would later reveal. Sheila developed a growing suspicion that Cesar was abusing her pubescent daughter. She never found any positive proof, but early in the relationship she began a practice of never leaving them alone together.

Living below another tenant in a two-story house, it was natural that Cesar would become acquainted with the woman upstairs. He and Matilda Gardner had often nodded and said "Hi," then gradually engaged in brief conversations. Her daughter, who occasionally spent some time with Matilda, was afflicted with epilepsy. One afternoon, Cesar heard a commotion upstairs and went to see if he could help. The girl was in the full grip of a seizure. Using his Army medical training while waiting for an ambulance, Cesar made sure she couldn't swallow her tongue. Matilda thanked him for his compassion and help.

Not long afterwards, he decided to dispose of an extra sofa. Matilda said she'd like to have it, so he carried it upstairs for her. Again, she smiled gratefully and thanked her downstairs neighbor.

Detective Michael O'Connell had kept his eyes peeled for over a month, hoping to spot a pair of Reebok running shoes, size eight and one-half, on some tattooed ex-con hiking along Main Street. He wrestled with a crucial decision, wondering whether to keep the search under wraps, or publicize it in the news media. If he chose to go public, a responsible citizen might come forward and say, "I know someone who has shoes just like that." Or, conversely, spreading the news might have a disastrous effect. The killer would no doubt realize the shoes linked him to a crime that could land him on death row, so he'd make sure they never fell into the investigators' hands. Toss them in the Columbia or Willamette Rivers. Burn them to ashes. Bury them in the wet forest in rural Washington County. It would be easy to dispose of them forever. O'Connell and his peers made the decision to keep the Reeboks a secret, along with the fact that Margaret Schmidt had been sexually assaulted. That way, if they ever nailed a suspect in possession of the Reeboks, or heard mention of the molestation during an interview, the investigators would know they were on the right track.

All experienced law enforcement personnel realize that withholding key information can also help eliminate wackos who step forward and confess to heinous crimes so they can enjoy their fifteen minutes of Warhol fame. If the phony confessor isn't able to answer questions revolving around the confidential facts, he can be given a quick boot out the front door, or into a rubber room somewhere.

If O'Connell had been looking for a female suspect, his heart would have accelerated to a dangerous rate a few weeks into the search. He spotted a pair of Reebok ERS 2000 running shoes right in Hillsboro. Trouble was, they belonged to a young kindergarten teacher who was the least likely suspect in the world. It had taken weeks to see just one pair of the rare shoes. Well, at least they weren't being worn by every other person ambling along downtown sidewalks or in Hillsboro's shopping malls. That would have been even worse.

Chapter 7

The roughly 20,000 people who reside in Fredericksburg, Virginia, live only sixty-one feet above sea level, about fifty miles down I-95 from Washington, D.C., in the heartland of American history. The town served as a commercial center prior to the American Revolution due to the easily accessible ports on the Rappahannock and Potomac rivers. Convenient water routes, plus the equidistance between D.C. and Richmond, made Fredericksburg strategically valuable to both sides in the Civil War, so four ravaging battles ripped through the town, during which it changed hands no less than seven times. Yet a number of structures dating back to 1775 still stand, giving Fredericksburg a patina of historic charm.

Being one of the first of the settlements to declare independence from England, there's an inbred, perhaps inherited spunkiness among the people there, a tendency to resist mindless conformity to the establishment.

Martha Bryant came into the world in Fredericksburg on September 11, 1951, blessed with a nonconforming emancipation of the mind. She arrived at a historic juncture in an era of wars. Three days before Martha's birth, while the Korean conflict raged at full scale, the United States signed a peace treaty with Japan closing the final curtain on World War II. And on Martha's second day of life, a French general visited Washington to urge U.S. support in Vietnam. Perhaps it was predestined that Martha Bryant would one day become a vociferous activist against that spiraling mire of destruction in Southeast Asia.

First though, she had to fight some battles of her own. At age twelve, her body was racked with scoliosis, a debilitating deformity of the spine requiring long-term wearing

of a heavy brace to correct the curvature. Uncomplaining,
Martha ignored the affliction and went about childhood activities with her one brother and two sisters just as if nothing was wrong. As a teenager, she empathized with the
growing movement of counterculture youth who wore colorful tie-dyed and patched clothing to symbolize rebellion
against government, bureaucracy, and the military-indus-
trial complex. They preached "flower power" and "make
love, not war." They drove battered old VW vans and
buses painted in wild colors and decorated with peace symbols. At massive concerts like Woodstock, they reveled in
sexual freedom and music. With Martha's hatred of violence and dedication to protecting the environment, she
easily fell in line with the movement.

Martha also discovered though, that "hippies" often lived
on the edge of poverty with no jobs to provide income.
Her strong sense of personal responsibility rebelled against
that idea, so following high school graduation, she enrolled
in a Washington, D.C., college to obtain a degree in the
nursing profession. To cope with financial problems she
worked part time for the U.S. Post Office. While living in
D.C., for twelve years, she became romantically involved
with several different men, including two serious relationships. The men in both cases had a difficult time letting
go and one of the partings would later be described as
"very unfriendly."

One summer, Martha traveled to Anchorage, Alaska,
and stayed for three months working for a Native American health program.

Babies would eventually become an important part of
Martha Bryant's life, but she decided early on that she personally did not wish to become a mother. She had her fallo-
pian tubes tied when she was twenty-five.

By 1988, Martha wanted to upgrade her medical skills.
She'd heard of an attractive program at Oregon Health
Sciences University in Portland OHSU, so she migrated to
the Pacific Northwest and enrolled in the nurse-midwife
curriculum.

Some women have the classic elegance of Grace Kelly,
or the sensual beauty of Marilyn Monroe. Martha Bryant's
beauty came from her charismatic humor, sensitivity, spar-

kling hazel eyes, and a contagious smile, all combining into
a splendid earthiness. Standing about five-six, she never
gained weight despite a voracious appetite, albeit mostly
for health foods. Her hips retained the same dimensions of
her teenage years. Still wearing large floppy hats over her
long dark hair that curled over both shoulders in ringlets,
and sweatshirts, jeans, scarves, or swirling skirts with boots,
she was reluctant to discard the apparel of her "hippy"
days.

Not long after her arrival in Portland, while standing in
a cafeteria line and planning a trip back to Virginia, Martha
asked a stranger how long it would take to drive to the
airport. Another man in line heard the low, sexy voice of
Martha, and seized the opportunity to answer in order to
strike up a conversation with her. They became friends,
then lovers, but the romance didn't last, even though the
friendship survived long after the man became a successful
attorney. Another fling followed, this one with a singer-
actor, but it also fell apart.

Martha's friendships were not restricted to men. She met
a number of fellow nursing students. Among them, she developed an acquaintance with a quiet young woman named
Vickie Cutsworth.

The next year, homesick for Virginia, Martha attended a
college concert-dance featuring a group from Washington,
D.C., and spotted a kindred soul. After discreetly letting
her interest show, she learned that the bright-eyed, pony-
tailed, red-bearded young man named Rob also hailed from
Virginia, over in Roanoke. It didn't matter that Rob was
six years her junior. A deep love developed during a year
of dating, attending concerts, discussing their mutual "dead-
heading" interests in Jerry Garcia and the Grateful Dead,
searching flea markets and antique stores for fifties-style
blond furniture, and driving over to the spectacular beaches
for glorious weekends.

By the time Martha earned her Master of Science degree
in nursing, in 1990, she and Rob were living together. Now
ready to reenter the job market, she followed one of her
college instructors, Nancy Sullivan, seventeen miles west to
the town of Hillsboro.

Sullivan left the university to accept a job with Healthy

Start as clinical director. The firm had opened its doors just one year earlier, to provide maternity care services to disadvantaged pregnant women in Washington County. Employing nurse-midwives and other health care professionals with expertise in prenatal care, social services, educational programs, and postpartum care, the nonprofit organization offered hospital-based deliveries aided by qualified midwives, all financed through private contributions and federal funding.

Martha Bryant had found her calling delivering innocent babies into the world. She soon gained a reputation for excellence in her work, in which she used an almost hypnotic flow of supportive words to ease the birth process for young mothers. She would often telephone her own mother in Fredericksburg and proudly tell of "catching more babies today."

The rapport with Rob, who'd taken a job with the public works department in nearby Tigard, grew even stronger. Marriage followed in July 1991. Typical of Martha's strong independence, though, she retained her own last name. After the civil ceremony they celebrated with an expensive meal in an upscale restaurant, the Couch Street Fish House, located in a section of town still in the process of rehabilitation after it had fallen into disrepair. The neighborhood, called Old Town, still attracted homeless wanderers and the alternate-lifestyle crowd who congregated in scattered offbeat nightclubs.

A few blocks from that section stands one of the largest bookstores in the nation, Powell's. In the autumn of 1991, Rob and Martha paid a visit to the store to gaze on visiting author Ken Kesey. They posed in front of a replica of Kesey's multicolored bus, Rob wearing a battered hat, red-plaid shirt with a gray coat and clutching a handful of books, Martha in an Indiana Jones-style floppy hat, blue sweatshirt and denim jacket. They both wore shining, happy smiles clearly reflecting the happiness they felt.

Continuing with Healthy Start, Martha caught babies in 1991 from over 100 mothers who praised her in glowing terms. Sometimes, Martha also counseled women who'd been battered and bruised, telling them how to pull themselves out of rocky relationships, suggesting they dump boyfriends or lovers who were potentially harmful to the child or abusive to the mother. One of her patients, Lynn Kramer, mentioned being slugged, not by her mate but by a coworker.

Kramer worked in a nursing home herself, and counted among her fellow employees a woman named Sheila Hawkins, and a couple of guys, Cesar Barone, and Len Darcell. Darcell, she said, was a "weird psycho" who had an explosive temper and who sexually harassed the women who worked there. He'd threatened to kill one of the other employees, Kramer complained, and punched her in the mouth one day.

Maybe Rob and Martha were destined for the bizarre. It showed up first in their selection of a house to purchase. It seemed cozy and ideal with a fireplace and plenty of room. Located across the Willamette River from central Portland, and ironically not far from Woodstock Avenue, the street address was 7734. They'd no sooner settled in their new home when neighbors informed Rob and Martha of something they would have preferred not to know.

It seems that the house had been the scene of a gruesome murder-suicide in 1989. The resident went berserk and shot her two daughters to death in a bedroom, then took her own life with the same gun. Martha felt a little twinge when told that the woman had also been a nurse. But the next revelation stunned Martha. The suicide killer was Vickie Cutsworth, whom Martha had known in OHSU!

The house had acquired a nickname from neighborhood children. They called it "hellhouse." They'd cleverly used the old trick of reversing and turning upside down the street number, 7734, to form the word hell.

Martha had owned two cars. She'd traveled west in a fairly decent little Honda, then wrecked it. She bought a used Volvo, but it had always been unreliable. Finally, she acquired the car she would fondly nickname "Maggie," a green 1966 Volkswagen bug. Rob preferred to call it "Willie." She attached a bumper sticker announcing that MIDWIVES HOLD THE FUTURE.

*   *   *

A cograduate of OHSU and good friend of Martha Bryant, Debbie Duran-Snell also felt the joy of helping deliver babies as a midwife. They'd met at the university, two of six students in the nurse-midwife program, and Debbie had joined the Healthy Start team five months after Martha. One night in early October, Debbie had an experience she would never forget.

She'd finished delivering a new baby at Tuality Community Hospital, a six-story red brick building ten blocks from downtown Hillsboro, and had washed up and changed clothes in preparation for going home. Debbie checked her watch a couple of minutes before midnight, and stepped out through the first set of double glass doors of the hospital foyer. Babies always seem to come late at night, she mused. Before exiting through the second set of doors, she glanced through the glass panes, and came to a quick halt. A man stood just outside, near the keypad in which a code must be punched in to allow entrance. At first, she chided herself for a foolish fear, then had second thoughts. Something about his stance and his staring at her set off internal alarms. He seemed out of place, just leaning against the brick wall, certainly not giving the appearance of someone preparing to enter the hospital or just leaving. And he stood near a locked doorway restricted for use by hospital staff only, not for use by the general public. Even the parking lot required a key punch code to enter, but it was foolishly simple: 1-2-3-4.

She stopped in her tracks, suddenly afraid to exit. The stranger outside continued to stare at her with an odd absence of expression.

Not knowing why, Debbie made a mental note of his description. He appeared to be between five-ten and six feet tall, with short "cropped hair at the top," cleanshaven, maybe in his twenties. The hair especially struck her as distinctive. A little longer on the sides, it appeared to have highlighted streaks on the top. He wore dark pants and a sweatshirt.

Turning as if to reenter the hospital, she sneaked one more look at him. He spun away from the wall, and strode into the dark parking lot. She waited. When she'd given him enough time to leave the area, Debbie worked up her courage, pushed through both sets of doors, and hurried to her Toyota van. As she opened the driver's door, she heard the sound of a car idling, and realized it was the one parked just a few feet away, inside the restricted area. She snapped the locks closed on her own vehicle, and caught sight of the stranger again, standing in the shadows near the idling car, staring intently at her. Jamming the accelerator, Debbie raced out of the parking lot.

Feeling safe as she sped along Cornell Road, planning to turn left on Cornelius Pass Road, her stomach lurched again when she realized a car had rapidly closed from behind and appeared to be following her. It pulled up alongside the van, dropped back, and the driver began flashing the lights off and on. She could make out the shape of the American-made car and the darkish lower portion with a light-colored top, but couldn't see the driver. In the lonely shadows of midnight, no other cars were in sight.

Feeling the first stages of panic, Debbie increased her speed, rounding curves at a dangerous pace, and saw the street coming up where she planned to turn. Trying to decide what to do, she finally spotted another car at the dark intersection also waiting to make a turn. Relieved to have someone else around, she jammed the brakes and came to a halt right next to the waiting vehicle. The follower slowed, hesitated, then made a tire-squealing right turn on Cornelius Pass Road and disappeared into the distant darkness.

Exhaling a huge sigh of relief, Debbie hurried on home where she woke up her husband to describe her frightening experience. They agreed to call the police and report it.

Michelle LaChance had worked for one month with Martha Bryant as a student-midwife and truly respected her colleague. Martha acted as mentor, directing Michelle in actual births. There were some personal traits about Martha that Michelle liked, too, and she recalled them: "She had great clothes. She dressed very colorfully. She liked tie-dye . . . she wore a lot of rayon and cotton and scarfs and colorful stuff. We all liked her clothes." And the way Martha spoke. "She had a low voice, and it was kind of loud. It—I guess that's how I'd describe it. It was very low and loud. It carried."

On the morning of October 8, the night following Debbie Duran-Snell's harrowing flight, Michelle admitted a young woman in labor to Tuality Hospital. She telephoned Martha to let her know the patient appeared to be nearly ready to have her baby "caught." Martha said she was going to be helping out at the Beaverton Healthy Start clinic that day, but would be wearing her pager. When Michelle needed her, Martha would hurry right over, since Beaverton was only twenty minutes away. The uncomfortable young patient was Christina Jerome-Johnson, who had worked in a Forest Grove nursing home with a couple of men named Barone and Darcell.

At seven, Michelle called. When she connected with Martha, she said the client was ready to start pushing. Martha said she'd be there as soon as possible, and arrived within the hour. The patient's labor, though, lasted for hours, and the delivery was finally completed at 1:30 A.M.

Michelle recalled it: "I think we stayed in the room for forty-five minutes to an hour, just doing repair and examining the baby and hanging out with the family. Then we came into the nurses' station to talk. She was giving me feedback and encouragement. And we probably stayed and talked for twenty minutes by the nurses' station."

Her voice choking, Michelle continued: "And then she went and changed her clothes, came back out, and told me that she had just remembered that she hadn't filled out her time card. She and her husband, Rob, were going away for the weekend, and she was very excited." Martha told Michelle that she felt it necessary to fill out the time card before going home because she wanted to assure the money would be on her next paycheck. She'd stop at the Healthy Start headquarters, four blocks away, then drive on home. "She reassured me that no one else would probably start labor soon, and that we'd done our work for the day. And she was very, very happy. I stayed for another forty-five minutes to finish charting and then I left as well." It was close to 3:30 in the morning of October 9.

Because she lived not far from Rob and Martha, Michelle followed the same route Martha drove along Cornell Road toward Portland. "I was very tired. I had a window open to try to stay awake, and I was looking out the left side of the car. And I saw three or four police cars, and I saw a lot of broken glass. I thought to myself, you know, something had happened. But I kinda wanted to make it home."

So Michelle LaChance didn't stop. And she didn't see the little green Volkswagen Bug, shot full of holes, sitting astride the sidewalk, empty. She paid little attention to the first officers who'd arrived on the scene, summoned by local residents wakened by loud outbursts of gunfire.

Chapter 8

0311 hours, October 9, 1992
911 Emergency Operator

"This is 911. Do you need police, fire, or medical help?"
"Yes, police, please."
"Yes."
"I just heard six shots in front of my house . . . It woke me up."
"What's your address?" The caller gave the street number on North East Ray Circle, Hillsboro.
"What's your cross street?"
"Uumm—Cornell, right at the corner of Cornell and Ray."
"Did you see or hear anybody out there?"
"I haven't even looked out yet. My husband's going to look—We aren't turning any lights on though." The voice sounded nervous, but gave her name, her husband's name, and their phone number.
"What kind of shots did they sound like?"
The voice turned away from the phone, asking someone else in the room, "Uumm—what kind of shots did they sound like?" The emergency operator asked if perhaps the noise was like a shotgun. But the answer came back far more specific than expected. "They sounded like semiautomatic gunfire and there are a couple of cars stopped over on Cornell, he said (apparently referring to her husband who had taken a look outside). He can't see the cars, just taillights."
"Okay, we'll check the area out. Thank you."

The first caller reported specific information. No more than a few seconds had passed when the 911 console lit up again. Some of the people trying to report what they'd heard or seen stammered nervously and had few details to offer while others spoke calmly, delivering precise observations. The number of gunshots reported by the sleepy residents varied from three to twenty. No one had written down a license number or an exact make of car driven by the phantom.

Gloria Thomas, age twenty-four, lived within eighty yards of the site where Martha Bryant's VW came to rest. She snapped awake at 3:15 A.M., according to her clock, startled by "three very loud gunshots" close to her home. Disoriented, Gloria leaped out of bed and heard muffled sounds outside which she later described to an investigator as "two male voices." At the front upstairs window overlooking North East Ray Circle, Gloria squinted into the darkness, but saw nothing. Yawning, she started to crawl back between the covers when she heard the muted voices again. Since they now seemed to come from a different direction, Gloria opened the opposite bedroom window and saw movement under the street light on Cornell Road.

The activity took place at the mouth of a 200-yard north-south driveway or alley between her back fence and a large open field. A long row of giant overhanging oak trees on the east side of the driveway obscured most of its length, but the view at the Cornell sidewalk was blocked only by the height of the six-foot wooden fence. As her eyes adjusted, Gloria could make out a man standing next to a car and could hear the engine rumbling in a throaty idle. The vehicle, Gloria said, was parked in the long driveway at its entrance, and stood between her and the man. Because of the fence, her field of vision was limited to only the top six or eight inches of the car while it remained in place with the engine still running. The voices she heard spoke in short, abrupt bursts of conversation, but Gloria couldn't make out what they were saying. She believed the man whose facial features she could barely distinguish was one of the speakers, but she never even caught a glimpse of the other person.

Within moments, according to Gloria, the man climbed into the bigger car and it backed out unhurriedly into the

westbound lanes of Cornell Road, facing east. The car
drove away at a normal rate of speed, giving her an unobstructed rear view of the vehicle. She described it as "a
very shiny, silver or white, mid to late sixties, two-door
sedan. The front and back seemed rounded, and it had a
chromed straight rear bumper, with rectangular horizontal
taillights, not broken. The engine had a deep sound, lots
of power. Looked like a '68 or '69 Chevy Nova, but not
a Nova."

Greg Thomas, Gloria's husband, said he'd been ill and
in a deep sleep when the noise started. But he still vaguely
thought he heard three shots, which prompted him to crawl
out of bed. Groggy, he listened as Gloria asked him if she
should call the police. "Did you see anything?" he mumbled to her. She replied that she'd seen a car and a man
down there in the alley. They decided not to call 911.

Neither Gloria nor Greg saw the bullet-ridden Volkswagen until a few minutes later when the flashing lights from
emergency vehicles reflected patterns on their bedroom
walls. At that time she looked out again to see what had
happened, and realized that someone else must have reported the incident. They would be interviewed later that
morning.

Officer Kerry Aleshire of the Hillsboro PD responded to
an emergency 911 dispatch at 0316 hours related to gunshots heard in the vicinity of Cornell Road and Ray Circle
Drive. When he arrived, Aleshire spotted a green Volkswagen Beetle parked at an angle, across the sidewalk on the
north side of Cornell, just past a deep driveway. No occupants could be seen in the car.

On closer investigation, he found the ignition key
switched on, but the engine not running. The right-turn
blinker had been activated, and still eerily flashed a useless
signal. The little green Beetle had been pierced by numerous bullets, some of which had broken out the front passenger window and shattered all of the glass on the passenger
side plus the driver's window. Aleshire searched the dark
shadows around the silent car and aimed his powerful
flashlight beam in the area of the oak trees, but saw no one.

0325 hours, October 9, 1992
911 Emergency Operator

"This is 911. Do you need police, fire, or medical help?"

"Yes, I'm here on Northwest 231st Avenue in Hillsboro . . ."

"Uh-huh."

"Right near the Toshiba, um, building, turns off from Cornell."

"Uh-huh."

"There's a man laying in the road, bleeding. I just passed him and there was a strange car taking off from the scene."

"Can you describe the car for me?"

"The car looks like a—umm—El Camino. It's a '70 or '71, somewhere in that era. It has oscillating headlights like a police car, but it wasn't a police car."

"So the headlights were moving?"

"They were, they were not oscillating—excuse me, they were flashing alternately."

"Okay."

"Like police headlights and then there is a man laying in the road, bleeding, not moving. I don't know—"

"Where is he bleeding from?"

"He looked like he was bleeding from the head and possibly the face and chest. I'm not sure."

"Okay, so he's on the corner of Northwest 231st?"

"He's in a little ways, umm, south of Cornell Road, on 231st. It's where the corners are."

"Okay, near the Toshiba building?"

"Right."

The caller said he didn't stop at the scene. He'd hurried past the figure on the road to telephone 911. He paused for a moment, then confessed that the presence of another car driving away had made him reluctant to stop due to the potential danger. The operator thanked the caller and said someone would be sent out right away.

Two other reports came in almost simultaneously, of a man lying on 231st Street, about a quarter mile off Cornell Road, near some railroad tracks. No one had stopped to try to examine the extent of the injuries or to apply first aid.

Officer Aleshire was still in the process of inspecting the
Volkswagen scene, and no one thought of connecting the
two emergencies. HPD Officer Vernon "Andy" Schroder
responded to the second incident, racing to the scene with
lights and siren to determine if the "person down" on 231st
Street needed an ambulance. Within moments, he radioed
in. "I have the subject. Advise fire (department) I'm south
of Campus Court. It (the downed person appears to be in
the middle of the roadway. He's not moving."

With the fire department EMT team notified, Andy
Schroder moved in to check the prone figure and could see
a fresh pool of blood to the left side. His eyebrows shot
up when he noticed something else. His boss, Sergeant Tom
Robinson, radioed, "Give me a status on the victim."

Schroder answered, his voice registering surprise. "The
victim is not ambulatory, and she's a *female* victim in the
roadway. I don't know what the circumstances are."

The dispatcher cut in to advise the officers that the earlier shots had been heard a quarter mile away. Now, the
connection had been established.

Sergeant Robinson, cognizant of the danger that the
shooter might be concealed out there somewhere in the
predawn darkness, or could possibly make a U-turn, return
to the scene, and take a pot shot at the officer, warned
Schroder. "Watch your back, just in case he comes back
up there behind you."

Schroder acknowledged but returned to the downed victim anyway. She was sprawled in the center of the dark
road, with her blue slacks and underpants pulled down to
her ankles. Schroder noted, "Her arms were at her sides,
bowed slightly as if her hands were resting on her hips.
The hands were turned up slightly and the position of the
arms and hands did not seem comfortable or natural." The
woman wore an orange blouse and a triangular button imprinted with the words, NO ON 9 (the ballot issue regarding
homosexual rights). One of her black Birkenstock shoes lay
on the pavement next to her left foot. No identification
could be found on her person or nearby.

Within seconds the EMT team arrived, and found the
woman still alive, but barely. One of them noted, "Upon
quick examination, the patient had labored breathing with

the right eye protruding and open, fixed, dilated pupil and left eye closed. . . . She was unconscious, unresponsive, in agonal respiration, with a pulse and what appeared to be a laceration to the left side of her forehead."

Working rapidly with the help of his partner, the technician cut open the orange blouse Martha Bryant wore along with a bloodied white sports bra, being cautious not to damage evidentiary bullet holes in the cloth. They could see the gunshot wound that left a bloody hole close to her chest where the slug had torn its way out, so concentrated on that trauma. They tried to insert a tube in her trachea to facilitate breathing, but found Martha's teeth tightly clenched and the "oral pharynx" full of blood. So they "logrolled" her onto her right side, which helped relax the clenched muscles, but still had trouble inserting the tube. The changed position also exposed the bullet entrance wound.

Sergeant Robinson arrived while the EMTs rapidly and efficiently tried to stabilize any vital signs. They told him that they'd requested a LifeFlight helicopter to transport her to OHSU where top-rate intensive care might help her survive.

Robinson asked the fire department lieutenant in charge if there was any chance the victim might be able to speak, or make a dying declaration. The lieutenant said the prognosis didn't look good. Hoping for the best, Robinson ordered Officer Schroder to be ready to accompany the victim to OHSU, with a tape recorder.

After the helicopter arrived with the giant blades battering the air into noisy gusts, and settled onto the roadway, the technicians belted Martha onto a longboard with a "stiffneck" collar, and placed her inside, still working feverishly to save her life. The huge propeller sent autumn leaves blowing again as it lifted off over the still dark crime scene at 4:02 A.M. Bright moonlight reflected from the whirlybird's polished red surface as it ascended and headed toward Portland.

While two HPD officers secured the area, Sergeant Robinson drove the short distance over to the Volkswagen where Aleshire and Officer Randy Lapp had sealed off the area with yellow tape. Robinson leaned into the glass-strewn car, withdrew the registration certificate, and saw that it had been made out to Martha B. Bryant. A travel bag and a purse lay undisturbed on the passenger seat. The shooter evidently hadn't been trying to rob her. Robinson had everything inside the car photographed before checking the purse's contents, where he found a driver's license for Bryant. He recognized the photograph as being the victim over on 231st Street, who now lay fighting for her life in the hospital at OHSU, where she'd won her degree two years earlier.

Aleshire, with the help of Officer Jim Kelly had already diverted the light traffic on Cornell and searched the street for evidence of the shooting. They'd turned up several 9 mm bullet casings, and had identified the exact sites of the gunfire by the pattern of broken window shards on the pavement. Under Robinson's direction, they chalked key spots, photographed everything, then collected the casings.

The officers also noted spots of blood on the Volkswagen's passenger seat and on the driver's backrest. Robinson sent three newly arrived officers to search the vacant field east of the Volkswagen, more than 100 acres. They found nothing.

Detective Derald Riggleman, HPD, paid a call to the home of Gloria and Greg Thomas to take their full statements. First, she described what she'd seen, then Greg gave his brief account. Gloria thought about it for a few minutes, then added some details and some subtle changes. She'd heard male voices before, but now she thought it was only one deep male voice, and he'd been yelling. She also now recalled going to the front door to see if the popping noise came from a neighbor's car that often sounded like firecrackers.

Riggleman showed her photographs of various 1968-model American cars and asked her if any of them resembled the car she'd observed leaving the scene. Gloria thought an Oldsmobile 442 and a Chevrolet Chevelle seemed very similar. The Chevy, she thought, might be the one, because she'd once owned a mid-sixties Chevelle.

Asked if she could recall any more details about the suspect car, Gloria said it was silver or white, very clean and shiny. A "muscle" car. Regarding the man, she thought he was about six feet tall, medium build, midtwenties. But the feature that stood out the most was his hair. Brown and wavy, trimmed shorter on the sides, it appeared to have lighter highlights on the top which "stood up a little." Riggleman thanked the cooperative couple, left, and passed the information on to Tom Robinson. He in turn, relayed it to Lieutenant Lila Ashenbrenner who would act as PIO, public information officer, to feed information to the voracious news media.

As the first pink rays of dawn broke to warm the chilly October morning, at 6:45 A.M., Vern Schroder called from OHSU. In a subdued voice he informed Robinson that the victim had expired without ever regaining consciousness. Schroder had been told about two gunshot wounds the woman had suffered; the one that had ripped through her upper body but hadn't caused lethal damage, and another one which had caused her death. Someone had put a small caliber gun to the victim's right temple and delivered the coup de grâce, an execution-type slug to the brain. The bullet was still in there.

This case, Sergeant Robinson decided, would require a top priority approach. He began making arrangements for a full multiagency homicide investigation team to be formed for the purpose of solving an "aggravated murder."

In most cities, the district attorney delegates crime scene visits to deputies, but Washington County district attorney Scott Upham wanted first-hand knowledge of this one. He arrived to join Tom Robinson in scrutinizing every detail. If they could ever bring anyone to trial, Upham wanted first-hand knowledge of the evidence to be used against the savage killer who had executed Martha Bryant.

Sergeant Tom Robinson had seen a long parade of murder victims during his twenty-two years as a Hillsboro cop, but few to match the cold brutality with which Martha Bryant had been snuffed out. He wanted to catch all of the killers perpetrating the ten or fifteen homicides committed each year in his town, but especially this ghoul.

From his northern England ancestors, Robinson had in-

herited sun-sensitive fair skin, set off by blue eyes and
sandy brown hair neatly parted and trimmed. He'd learned
honest Midwestern values in his hometown of Parkman,
Ohio, where he grew up in the healthy environment of the
family farm. Following his graduation from nearby Mid-
dlefield, Ohio, High School, he spent another year in his
home state attending college in Hiram before moving to
Oregon. By 1971, he'd earned his B.S. degree in business
administration at Forest Grove's Pacific University. On
campus, Robinson had worked part time as a lab assistant
and in town as a car salesman, which led to his "accidental"
career in law enforcement. A fellow salesman belonged to
the reserve police squad and bragged to Tom about it. Robinson figured if his buddy could do it, so could he, and
besides, he could use the extra cash. He applied, and became a reserve officer the same year he finished college.
Soon afterwards, a gruff voice asked him on the telephone,
"Wanna' job? I gotta know by tonight."

Robinson pondered the idea for two seconds, and replied, "Yes." He became a full-time HPD officer the next
day. At that time, with a population of about 9,000, the
town had two police officers, a night patrolman, and a supervisor. (It would grow to a total staff of 80 by 1996.)

A solidly built 5'9" tall, soft spoken most of the time,
but able to growl when necessary, Robinson fit perfectly
into the law enforcement circle. He accepted a promotion
to sergeant in 1990. In the interim, he met the beautiful
woman whose framed photo occupies a prominent spot on
his desk, and married her. They have one son. He's a
reader in his spare time, but prefers to avoid "cop or lawyer" books.

Robinson's team of detectives doesn't admit it to him,
but they love and respect the guy. Barbed humor and zing-
ers are exchanged daily, and Tom responds in kind with
his quick, tilted grin. He speaks with pride about his fellow
officers, and especially about the "clean" department,
meaning free of the insidious corruption or political influence that infects some police organizations in a few large
urban areas. Robinson also cites the teamwork between
HPD and the Washington County sheriff's department as
a super example of efficient law enforcement.

Nothing in Martha Bryant's purse had given any hint that she was married. Because her driver's license showed a Portland address, Robinson called that city's PD. They dispatched an officer to the address and woke Martha's husband, Rob.

Five hours after the first reports of gunshots, Tom Robinson, along with a police chaplain, and two detectives, interviewed Rob in a waiting room near the intensive care ward where'd she been pronounced dead. Desolated, Rob listened to efforts by the chaplain to comfort him, and struggled to maintain his composure while trying to answer the detectives' questions.

One of the first steps in the murder of a married woman is to examine the whereabouts of the husband, since a large proportion of such murders are committed by the spouse.

Rob said he'd been working the previous day in Tigard. After quitting time, about 5:00 P.M., he'd driven over to Germantown Road to continue some extra chores he'd been doing for a friend. He'd arrived home at about seven that evening, and found Martha absent. That wasn't unusual, he explained, because of her on-call status with Healthy Start. She rarely bothered to leave messages for him when duty called. He'd gone to bed, anticipating a weekend trip with her when she finally arrived home.

No, Rob, said, he could think of no reasons anyone would want to harm Martha, much less kill her. And they certainly had no marital problems. While Rob had no witnesses to prove his whereabouts, Tom Robinson mentally ruled him out as a suspect, and his gut feelings usually proved reliably accurate.

Dr. Karen Gunson, a nine-year veteran with the Oregon Medical Examiner's office, had performed more than 2,500 postmortem examinations, which were required when suspicious circumstances surrounded any death in the state. On the same morning of Martha Bryant's death, Dr. Gunson began the autopsy at nine twenty-five. After she'd cleaned the tiny hole in the victim's right temple, the doctor found that, "the gunshot wound was characterized by having charred or blackened edges and very fine skin tearing around the edges. And there was no gunpowder residue on the skin." The slug had entered through the temple into the brain, taken a circuitous and destructive path through the lobes, and wound up in the soft tissue behind a cheekbone. "We found that there was gunpowder blown into the soft tissue beneath the scalp, between the scalp and the skull." In other words, the barrel of the weapon had been in contact with the skin when the killer pulled the trigger. The pathologist carefully lifted the bullet and gave it to Detective Larry Harris for future examination.

The lethal shot to Bryant's head had been made by a .22 caliber weapon, while a 9 mm slug had torn through Bryant's upper body. Her assailant had roughed her up before killing her, as indicated by other injuries Dr. Gunson identified. "There was bruising or contusions, with laceration or skin split, and some abrasions present on the back of her right hand, and bruising around her right elbow. In addition . . . she had bruises on the inner surface of her left upper arm and around her left elbow. A torn fingernail. Also, bruising and abrasions present in her right upper chest, along the outside surface of her right thigh, on the front of her left thigh, and on the shin regions on both legs." The inside of Martha's mouth had sustained several injuries as well. And, Dr. Gunson noted, the victim had an abrasion or scraping away of the surface in her vagina.

Detectives Harris and Officer Schroder observed the entire autopsy procedure, took notes and photos, and reported back to Sergeant Robinson. All three masked the anger boiling inside them.

Martha Browning Bryant would never again "catch" a newborn baby.

Chapter 9

Using the age-old investigative technique of door-to-door canvassing, officers assigned to the Bryant murder case pounded the pavement through every block of the residential tract west of the abduction site. They turned up a half dozen residents who had been wakened by a varying number of shots, but few had seen anything. The best vantage point for the entire incident would have been from four stories of office building windows directly across the street. Each office, on the south side of Cornell, had an unobstructed view of the spot. Tom Robinson hoped there'd been at least a few employees burning the midnight oil, or security guards on duty, or possibly a late-shift cleanup crew who'd looked out the windows. But his hopes were dashed by the first inquiry of building owners and occupants. Not a soul had been inside. The night cleaning crew had completed their work before midnight. Nevertheless, the large plate glass windows did help in one sense.

The occupant of a corner home at Ray Court and Cornell had heard "eight or more gunshots" he told Officer Andy Lapp. They sounded like "a semiautomatic pistol being fired as fast as you can pull the trigger." The observant resident looked outside and could see across Cornell, reflected in the office building windows, a clear image of two sets of taillights. One of the sets, he said, had three or more lights over the bumper on each side. The other set, obviously the Volkswagen, were single lights and much smaller. The man instructed his wife to call 911, hurriedly pulled on some trousers, and rushed outside to his backyard where he peered over the wooden fence in the direction the cars had been parked. All he could see, by that time, was the VW Bug with broken windows and the lonely flashing of a

turn signal. The second car had already vanished into the
night. Officer Lapp noted every detail of the witness's report. Any little piece of the puzzle could eventually help.

By driving the 200 yards under the overhanging oak trees
lining the east side of the long driveway in which the killer
had parked to abduct Martha from her VW, Tom Robinson
met the owner of the secluded house. She had heard absolutely nothing during the night. Stunned to see all the police
activity when she rose in the early morning, she did her
best to cooperate. She would later write a note to the HPD
stating how courteous and professional the officers had
been, especially Sergeant Robinson. "This wonderful
Sergeant . . . he is the best of the best," she wrote. Not
forgetting the other investigators, she noted that all HPD
personnel had been very nice, but said Robinson was "the
cream of the crop." Tom Robinson smiled and took it in
stride, but an astute observer could see faint tinges of blush
in his fair-skinned face.

A search of the Volkswagen interior by criminalist Chris
Johnson of the Oregon State Police Crime Lab revealed
precious little to help unravel the deepening mystery. The
best hope, Tom Robinson figured, was Bryant's personal
directory he'd retrieved from the car, which listed eighty-
four people she knew well enough to keep their addresses
and phone numbers. Perhaps at least one of them could
shed some light on who might have reason to kill Martha.
A few of the entries, though, were in cryptic initials, which
would require even more laborious tracing to identify. Always frugal, Martha had been using a 1991 calender to jot
down appointments for the current year. Each of the entries would have to be probed. Nothing came easy.

Among the contents of the travel bag Robinson had
found in the VW passenger seat, he discovered a thick
packet of papers outlining case histories of three maternity
patients plus a list of women to whom she'd attended during the week of October 5. It contained fifty names.

Other personal possessions of Martha's included her L.L.
Bean Swiss Army knife, a clock, some books and pamphlets
related to natal care, and four one-dollar bills.

Inside her purse, the contents of an envelope quickened

Robinson's pulse; a round-trip airline ticket to Boston. Did the flight have anything to do with her death? Had someone with whom she had planned to travel backed out? Perhaps a secret entanglement that had gone sour? Nah! Too simple. Robinson soon found the tickets were for a perfectly innocent nurse-midwife convention Martha Bryant planned to attend with a female colleague.

In the gray morning hours, a group of Special Interest Explorer Scouts, the organization to which sheriff's detective Michael O'Connell had once belonged, arrived to help search the rolling vacant land adjacent to the shooting site. Supervised by a detective, the boys fanned out and walked for hours, but discovered nothing related to the abduction or murder.

During the next few days, all of the lists of people, patients, witnesses, and appointments were subjected to laborious, time-consuming visits, hours of driving, and endless telephone calls. Very little of value turned up. Murders are often motivated by large insurance policies, and Robinson explored that possibility. Yes, Martha did have a $15,000 policy through her employment with Healthy Start, with her husband Rob listed as the beneficiary. Robinson knew that legions of victims had died for far less, but realized that insurance, in this case, was a dead-end street.

The news media jumped on the case as soon as Lieutenant Ashenbrenner fed them the first tidbits of information. A full-color five-and-one-half-by-eight-inch photograph of the green Volkswagen, still astride the sidewalk, appeared in the Saturday edition of Portland's major newspaper, the *Oregonian*, along with a twenty-column-inch article and an inset photo of Martha Bryant. The story told of the murder, witness reports, and described the suspect vehicle sought by the police. DA Scott Upham was quoted as saying, "The key to this case is the car."

In the Sunday edition, the same paper reported that more than sixty tips had been received from the public regarding the case. The article also commented that the shooter's car apparently struck Bryant's Volkswagen in an effort to run her off the road before the attack.

The *Hillsboro Argus* reported the police had revealed

Bryant was sexually assaulted, and quoted Sergeant Robinson as saying, "That does appear to be the probable motivation for the abduction." Some 200 tips had come in, the article said, and included photographs of a 1968 Oldsmobile 442 and a '68 Chevrolet Chevelle as representative of the "muscle car" as the objects of a police search. Authorities had not released details of the sexual assault or the caliber of weapons used, the report noted.

Tom Robinson and Lila Ashenbrenner had deliberately withheld the information about Bryant's pants and underwear being pulled down around her ankles, and that two calibers of guns, .22 and 9 mm, had been used. Only the killer or someone close to him would know that.

Every lead had to be checked out thoroughly, even the one called in by a security guard at a company located a few blocks from the shooting scene. In quiet, hesitant voice, the caller said, "I saw a guy walk through the fields that night with a flashlight. He wore dark clothing and acted real strange. Then, about twenty-five minutes later, I heard screams, heard a woman screaming.

"And then something really bothered me, and I wanted to talk to you about it. Now I've got another security guard here who just started a few nights ago. He works two places. There's a little restaurant that's been closed down for quite a while, and he sets in there at night. I asked him to go with me and check out where the incident occurred because there were police cars all over the place.

"He told me he saw a vehicle [that night] smashed up with the windows all broken out." The caller laughed nervously, then continued. "Now this guy doesn't even have a car, 'cause I've been driving him all over the place. So, don't you think it's kind of strange that he could go see a vehicle somewhere when he doesn't even have no way to go?"

Pausing, the caller said he challenged the other guard and got a strange answer. "He said he'd heard about the smashed-up car on the radio. Now I've been doing security work for a long time, and I know that police are not going to give out information that quickly."

Asked specifically what the suspected man had heard,

the caller said, "He heard that there was a rape-murder and there was a blue Honda Accord involved somehow. That bothered me. I got home and I couldn't sleep."

To an officer's query for more details about hearing a woman scream, he replied, "It was a godawful scream . . . I couldn't . . . you know, I didn't have a flashlight. All I do is patrol in the parking lot with my car." He paused for nearly a minute, and stammered, "Maybe I have an overactive imagination, I guess."

Finally, the caller described the man he said he'd seen walking in the field. "He was a tall, white male and has short, short hair and he, you know, walked right by my car."

Tom Robinson dutifully logged the call in his growing stack of reports on the case. He'd have to send a detective out to interview the security guard in more detail, but Tom didn't have a great deal of confidence that it would lead anywhere. He was right.

Maybe, Robinson hoped, he'd have better luck with the .22 caliber slug surgically removed from Martha Bryant's head and the 9 mm shell casings picked up from the street where the gunshots had been heard. They'd been sent to the Oregon State Police Crime Lab in the capital city, Salem. If the criminalists there could identify the type of weapons used, it would at least give the detectives something specific to hunt for. Meanwhile, the team could continue searching for the suspect vehicle in hopes that Gloria Thomas could make a positive identification.

George Rogers Park, about fifteen miles south of Portland, adjoins the narrow waterway connecting the Willamette River to Lake Oswego. In the late afternoon of Saturday, October 25, as sun filtered through cathedral-like evergreens forming long shadows on the grassy parkland, over 100 friends and associates of Martha Browning Bryant gathered to mourn her passing and celebrate her life. Many of the young women in the crowd carried infants Bryant had helped coax into the world. A colleague of Bryant's said, "There is incredible rage and terror at the randomness of it all. She spent her life making people whole. Someone has taken that away, taken away the courage she gave to other people." Trying to hold back tears, the speaker added, "Right now, I just miss her."

The assembly linked arms to sing favorite songs, and listened as songwriter Holly Near sang one of her own compositions. Another mourner said, "We loved her . . . The community has lost a gentle soul."

The tips called grew to 400, then 600, but the usable leads remained slim.

In their usual spirit of interdepartment cooperation, the Washington County Sheriff's Department assigned Detective Michael O'Connell to join the homicide investigation team on October 26. He and Tom Robinson had known each other for years, and Robinson welcomed his help. That same afternoon, O'Connell rolled up his sleeves to help officers dismantle the impounded Volkswagen for the purpose of finding any hidden bullets or fragments. They dug out four pieces and sent them to the OSP crime lab.

O'Connell hadn't yet given up his intensive personal search for a pair of Reebok ERS running shoes, size eight and one-half, but still hadn't spotted any. The Bryant case gave him new challenges even though the shoes remained in the back of his mind. He followed up on an early bit of information. Robinson had learned that Martha had ended a relationship, while in OHSU, with a singer-actor. A tip about the jilted suitor suggested that he'd been a drug user and the parting was an unfriendly one. O'Connell traced the man and found that he had no criminal record and that the drugs he used were prescribed by a doctor. One more dead end.

It's an axiom among homicide investigators that if a solid lead isn't developed within forty-eight to seventy-two hours after a murder, chances to solve the crime drop off sharply. One month after Martha Bryant died, not a single suspect had been identified.

Joining Detective Jeff Martin on the early afternoon of November 11, Michael O'Connell drove to Gloria Thomas's home, picked her up, and continued toward Portland.

She'd agreed to look at vehicles in used car lots to see if any one of them was identical to the suspect car she'd seen on the night of the murder.

Known as automobile row, 82nd Street in Portland is lined with auto sales lots featuring hundreds, perhaps thousands of cars waiting for the right buyer. At the first stop, Thomas thought a '72 LeMans looked "similar." The second place had a '74 Ford Torino and a Chevy Nova, same year, which Gloria examined. No, she said, the Torino was nothing like it, but the Chevy bore some resemblance. From agency to agency, they stopped, looked, watched hustling salesmen's crestfallen faces, and moved on. Gloria focused on an Oldsmobile, a '75 Nova, another older Nova, and a '69 Chevy Chevelle. That last one, she said, looked the most like the suspect car, but the different colors didn't seem right. They gave up the search at 3:40 P.M. and headed back to Hillsboro.

A small reward had been offered by community groups shortly after the murder for information leading to the capture of Martha's killer. By mid-November, public-spirited organizations and businesses increased the reward to $21,000. More telephoned tips poured in. Tom Robinson answered one, and heard a male voice identify himself as a representative of an insurance company. The voice curtly demanded the most recent information about the investigation into the murder of Martha Bryant. In his explanation, he claimed he needed to know if Bryant had been shot to death or had died in the crash of Volkswagen, which would make his company liable. He must obtain this information, he said, to determine whether or not to pay off on the policy.

Robinson patiently explained that the caller should follow regular procedures; to write a letter on the insurance company's letterhead. The request should list specifically what is needed and why. In an angry voice, the caller protested the need for a letter, and refused when Robinson asked to speak to a supervisor, then hung up. Robinson's daily log on the incident noted his doubts about the veracity of the caller, wondering if it was someone trying to gain confidential information. Possibly, it was the killer attempting to learn if the police were getting close.

*   *   *

As October wound down, and the Oregon weather turned threatening, Tom Robinson heard a glimmer of encouraging news from the Oregon State Police Crime Lab. Criminalist Chris Johnson had identified the bullet casings as 9 mm Winchester Luger shells. Now, detectives could seek records of purchases. A few days later, the lab also reported that a partial palm print lifted from the Volkswagen might have enough detail to compare to a suspect's prints. Now, all they had to do was find a suspect. The bad news from the lab was that all bloodstains collected from the VW belonged to the victim. The killer had left none of his blood that could tie him to the crime.

Standing in splendid domination of northwestern Oregon's horizon, Mount Hood beckons skiers year around to schuss down the ever-white glaciers. A dormant 11,239 foot volcano, the mountain's peak is the highest point in the state and the focal point of a verdant national forest spreading over one million acres. High up on Mount Hood's slope, just above the elevation where the thick fir, spruce and pine forests grow, stands historic Timberline Lodge, built by the Works Progress Administration (WPA) during the Great Depression of the thirties and dedicated by President Franklin Delano Roosevelt. A high-ceilinged, rough-timbered lobby warmed by a massive stone fireplace offers cozy comfort to visitors when snowstorms howl outside. The lodge has hosted several movie companies who found the setting perfect to film Jimmy Stewart's *Bend of the River* in 1952, Jack Nicholson in Stephen King's *The Shining*, 1980, and Marlee Matlin in *Hear No Evil*, 1993.

While investigators worked night and day to find a lead in the slaying of Martha Bryant, Cesar Barone and his companion, Ray Cardenas, drove seventy-five miles east of Hillsboro to Timberline Lodge for a day of skiing and possibly some other recreation. On that same Thursday, October 22, two young women who'd been enjoying the new powder covering twenty-six inches of hardpack snow took off their skis an hour before noon, and made their way into the big lobby for some refreshments.

Pam Evans and Ashley Price settled into comfortable

chairs, and noticed two men staring at them, A short, heavy-set girl with brown hair sat between the men, but they seemed to be paying little attention to her. One of the guys looked "kind of short" with dark hair and a full mustache. The other man, about five-eleven, stood up and walked over to their table. He wore a white turtleneck (one of Ted Bundy's favorite garments), dark blue ski pants, and a ski jacket in two shades of dark blue that looked too small for him. Introducing himself as Cesar, he spoke in a friendly manner, had appealing features, and "seemed like a nice guy," telling them he was from a tropical place with far different winters. After buying them a round of drinks, Cesar invited both women to ski with him and his buddy, Ray. Pam and Ashley accepted, finished their drinks, and followed the two men outside.

The foursome skied the fresh powder the remainder of the afternoon until long shadows and a chilly wind drove them back into the lodge. They stopped in the bar, noticing the girl who'd been with Cesar and Ray had left, and had another drink. In a dark corner of the big lounge area, the four passed around a marijuana joint, then returned to the bar. The girls downed more Bloody Marys while Cesar and Ray drank whiskey and 7-Up. Ray paid for all the drinks, while Cesar did most of the talking, telling them he worked in a nursing home and traveled a lot.

By 9:00 P.M. other guests had dwindled away, leaving the lounge nearly deserted, so the bartender announced he was closing up. The foursome went outside where only two cars occupied the big parking lot, Cesar's and Pam's blue Honda Prelude. Saying goodbye, Pam and Ashley tried to open the locked car doors. Chagrined, Pam realized she'd left the keys in the bar, now also locked up. While Cesar and Ray waited, the women found a snow-plow operator who managed to gain access to the bar for the embarrassed pair, where they recovered the keys.

Once again bidding the men goodbye, Pam mouthed a silent curse when she found the car's battery was apparently dead. Cesar came to the rescue with a jumper cable. They got the Honda started three times, but as soon as Ray would disconnect the big spring clips from under the hood, the engine died. Cesar got out of his car and he and

Ray stood next to the Honda offering advice. He suggested
they could all get a room in the lodge. No, the girls said,
they didn't think so. Cesar showed them a square-shaped
bottle of cheap rum he wanted to share with them, but they
politely declined. Because the temperature had dropped
rapidly, and the whole area was shrouded in darkness, the
two women finally did allow Cesar and Ray to climb into
the Honda's back seat. Within minutes, they were sorry.

Cesar's conversation, which had earlier been courteous
and pleasant, turned to "weird sexual remarks." Both
women shrank down in their seats, uncomfortable and ap-
prehensive. Pam hinted that she had a gun in the car and
Cesar's chatter tapered off to a tense silence.

Pam persuaded them to try the jumper cable again, and
once more her engine sputtered and died while Ray still
leaned into the engine compartment. Suspicions crept over
her and she asked Ray to move away. He frowned in anger,
muttered a few words, jumped into Cesar's car and
slammed the door. Cesar walked around to Pam's open
window and apologized for his companion's behavior. He
asked the women if they would meet him later down in a
Vancouver bar, across the Columbia River from Portland,
where he'd buy them some Mai Tais. No thanks, they said
in unison.

Cesar tried another approach. His clothes were damp
from skiing all day. Could he and Ray come to the women's
residence and at least change clothes so they wouldn't
freeze to death?

"No." But they both realized that they needed to curb
his persistence without making him angry. They hinted that
maybe they would stop in Vancouver for just one drink.
When he wanted their phone number, Ashley gave him one
she made up on the spur of the moment. With absolutely
no intention of keeping the rendezvous, they hoped they
could just get away from these two bozos.

With the engine running fine now that Ray no longer
had access to it, Pam rolled up her window, both girls
waved, and Pam drove down the slope toward Highway 26.
When she reached a convenience store, she stopped in the
parking lot to buy some beer. Cesar and Ray pulled in right

behind her. Ray appeared to be "too drunk" to get out, but Cesar followed the women into the store.

At the counter, Pam laid her identification on the counter to prove her age and glanced away for a moment. When she reached for her card, it had vanished. A search by both women, Cesar, and the clerk failed to locate it. The hell with it, Pam said. She just wanted to get out of there. She suspected Cesar had grabbed it, and felt glad that it didn't contain her correct address.

Once more on the highway, Pam could see Cesar's headlights close behind. A couple of times he recklessly passed her, doing nearly ninety miles per hour, then dropped back again.

Finally, when they reached the city freeway traffic of Portland, Pam managed to lose the car that had tailed her for fifty miles, happy at the prospect of never seeing those two faces again.

Never say never. It would take many months, but they would see the face of Cesar Barone again.

On the night before Christmas Eve, a seventy-three-year-old woman lay in her bed at a senior health care center in Forest Grove. Paralyzed from the waist down, and suffering from multiple sclerosis, she still anticipated the holidays, still treasured memories of children singing carols, family laughter during the exchange of presents, the aroma of cooking turkey, the color, lights, and joy from long ago. She drifted peacefully off to sleep with these things in her mind, and awakened in fear, adrenaline pounding through her. A man hovered over her in the dark room, breathing rapidly. He shoved his hand down the front of her nightgown and fondled her breast. Afraid to breathe, she heard him tell her not to worry, that he was checking her heartbeat. After a few moments, he crept silently out of the room.

In the shadows, she didn't get a good look at his face, but later said, "I will never forget his haircut."

Within moments, an employee of the center spotted a man climbing out a window, carrying a television set. He thought it better not to intercede, so he called the police. In his report, he said he was sure he could identify the man if he ever saw him again.

Chapter 10

Over a month had passed since Martha Bryant's death when Sergeant Tom Robinson received a phone call from an anonymous tipster who said he knew someone who could shed a lot of light on the case. The caller said that a guy named Frank Ellison hung out with a couple of young men at a party who'd made some admissions about Bryant's murder. Robinson listened, wondering if it could be the break they were looking for, then contacted Michael O'Connell and Detective Jeff Martin with a request for them to have a talk with Mr. Ellison.

They drove to the business address given by the anonymous caller, which happened to be not far from the crime scene, and asked to speak to Frank Ellison.

Not very happy at being fingered by the caller, Ellison scowled and gritted his teeth, seeming reluctant to divulge what he might know. That damned cousin of his, who had to be the guy who called, he said, shouldn't be shooting off his mouth. Ellison grumbled but agreed to answer questions.

"Look," he said, "I have a couple of friends, if you could call them that, who fit the description I read about in the newspapers. They're the right age of the guy that was near that lady's Volkswagen." Even more important, he told the investigators, one of the men owned a muscle car that could be the one the assailant drove away.

"What are your friends' names?"

"Tony Campbell and Doug Hunter. Tony owns the car. I don't know what kind it is but it's white and sort of a hotrod and real shiny, too. It's kind of strange, but I haven't seen the car for three or four weeks. Ever since that murder. Matter of fact, the last time I saw it was over at the

7-Eleven store on Cornell Road just a couple of days before that lady was killed. Tony was driving it on his way home."

"Where do they live?"

"That's one of the things that makes me suspicious. They live on the east side, in one of those older houses right near where the body was dumped. Both of 'em stay in the basement of Tony's parents' house." Ellison said Campbell and Hunter were both twenty-three years of age.

"How do you know these guys?"

"I was friends with Tony Campbell a long time ago." And Ellison had attended high school with Doug Hunter. Their friendship had lasted until about two years ago.

"And what is it they said that made you think they're involved in this case?"

Ellison stated that Doug Hunter had once mentioned his desire to see someone die. That was about the time their friendship ended. The thing that made Ellison seriously believe the two men might be suspects was Hunter's deep interest in Satanic worship. Once, Hunter had shown Ellison a Satanic bible, which gave him chills. He didn't want anything to do with that, or with the two guys anymore.

Hesitating as if reluctant to continue, Ellison sighed and said there was another thing. Doug, he divulged, had been accused of raping more than one woman.

Michael O'Connell had been waiting for that shoe to drop. He'd already recognized the name Doug Hunter, and remembered one of the rape allegations he'd personally investigated. The accusation had been made in January of 1991 by a young woman with a dubious reputation for telling the truth. The district attorney had dropped it due to a lack of evidence and the unreliability of the witness. Just four months ago, O'Connell had encountered the same young woman, who again claimed she'd been raped. His inquiry proved the allegation was unfounded, whereupon she admitted lying about the whole thing. O'Connell cited her for initiating a false police report. One more thing came rushing back in his memory. The young woman was Frank Ellison's wife!

Seemingly unaware that O'Connell knew about his wife's spotty past, Ellison said that he'd also heard stories that

Hunter once shot someone in Utah. Now on a roll, Ellison dug even more recollections from his memory to share about his ex-friend, Hunter. He said that Doug used to enjoy hanging out the passenger window of moving cars and yelling at other motorists or pedestrians. It had happened several times on Sunset Highway. One man he yelled at retaliated by pointing a gun at Hunter, and Doug challenged the guy to go ahead and shoot him. "Doug has no fear of anything," Ellison said. The daredevil even rode on the roof of cars sometimes.

When is the last time you saw Hunter?

"About a year ago at a KISS concert." Hunter, Ellison said, was high on methamphetamine at the time. Besides that, Ellison added, Doug is obsessed with guns and knives. "He stole my .30-30 Winchester." Asked for more details on the theft, Ellison modified the assertion. He'd loaned the rifle to Doug who later claimed he'd lost it.

As Ellison continued, he enlarged his mounting indictment of Hunter's morals and behavior. The guy was not only obsessed with guns and knives, but he was into violence and pornography.

Ellison described Hunter as tall, 160 pounds, and well built, with brown hair, which he characterized as having an "untamed" look.

The other guy, Tony Campbell, according to Ellison, was about the same size but had longer, darker hair, Tony was "a follower" who was easily persuaded by Hunter to go along with anything. If either of them was the shooter, Ellison insisted, it would be Hunter.

Despite the false rape reports previously made by Ellison's wife, O'Connell and Martin couldn't rule out the possibility that the two young men might be involved in the Bryant murder. They drove slowly by Tony Campbell's address to see if they could spot the "muscle car." An old Volkswagen parked at the curb could hardly be called that. Neither of the two young men was at home.

Detective Martin confronted the original informant, Ellison's cousin, later that afternoon and heard that Tony Campbell's car was a light-colored sedan. No, the tipster said, neither Campbell nor Hunter had made any direct confessions regarding the Bryant homicide.

Unable to find the two men despite more drive-bys, during which they never saw any vehicle remotely resembling the suspect car, O'Connell and Martin talked to Tony Campbell's father. In his written report of the conversation, O'Connell described the father as a hardworking, honest citizen. The detective also remembered him from an incident during the previous summer when the father had dug up some bones near his property and had called the police thinking he'd found a murder victim. The old bones turned out to be nothing but some animal remains.

No, the father said, Doug Hunter didn't live in the basement of their home, but Tony did. And Tony had never possessed any kind of a car that resembled the one police were searching for. "He drives a steel gray '85 Ford. I gave it to him." Sure, he said, Doug Hunter comes around and visits Tony with some of their pals. He couldn't recall any of the fellows' cars that might fit the one the officers had described.

Tony, the father said, worked steadily in the housing construction industry and still maintained a close friendship with Doug Hunter. Doug's driver's license had been suspended so he had to rely on Tony for transportation.

O'Connell left a business card and asked the man to have Tony call him. To O'Connell's surprise, the call came promptly the next morning. The detective made arrangements to meet Tony Campbell at a job site near the Sunset Highway.

At the meeting, Campbell stated that Doug Hunter once had a 1969 Pontiac, but he'd sold it. The vehicle was later towed to an impound lot and never recovered. Tony repeated what his father had said about Doug's having lost his driver's license. "He's on probation. He has kind of a problem controlling his temper, especially when he's doing drugs." Tony said that his pal was receiving counseling for these problems.

"What's he on probation for?"

"A shooting he was involved in over in Utah." So Frank Ellison had been right about that bit of information. The incident stemmed from problems with a neighbor of Hunter's grandmother. Doug used a small .22 caliber pistol to blast a warning shot into the air hoping to scare the man. The mention of a .22 renewed O'Connell's interest. Martha Bryant had been executed with a weapon of that size.

O'Connell asked Tony if he knew where Hunter was on the night Bryant was murdered. Sure, Tony said. He was at my house. They'd played guitars in the basement, after which Tony had driven Doug home, over in Hillsboro, at about eleven-thirty that night. Afterwards, Tony returned to his own house and went to bed.

The story provided no real alibi for either of the men, so O'Connell probed a little deeper. He listened as Tony explained that Doug's temper and drug problems had "mellowed out over the last year or so."

Just to see how Tony would react, O'Connell mentioned the $25,000 reward offered for Martha Bryant's killer. Licking his lips, Tony said he'd sure like to have that kind of money, and if he knew who'd done the murder, he wouldn't hesitate to turn the guy in. But he really didn't have any idea who had killed her. All he knew was what he'd heard on the news.

The Ford Tony's father had described was parked at the job site. O'Connell looked closely at the tail lights, and realized they were rectangular in shape, and horizontal, closely resembling the ones described by the witnesses who'd seen the suspect car.

Enough loose ends still existed regarding Doug Hunter to keep O'Connell exploring him as a possible murder suspect. He contacted Washington County probation officer Brad Sperb, who had been assigned to supervise Doug Hunter. Sperb verified the story about Hunter being on probation for an April 1991 shooting incident that took place in Utah. The case file had been transferred to Oregon. Hunter had also been sentenced to some jail time, but hadn't yet served his sentence due to overcrowded jail conditions. The neighbor's version of the incident differed in some aspects, mostly in the assertion that Hunter had fired directly at him instead of at the ground. The gun was described as a .22 caliber derringer. Nothing in the records indicated where the gun was now.

O'Connell telephoned the records division of the town's police department in Utah, and learned that the police file gave no description of the gun or its current location.

One more report O'Connell obtained regarding Doug Hunter was a psychological evaluation which had been filled out while he was still in school. His mother had requested the examination, which recorded that Hunter had developed a drug problem by the time he was sixteen, and had a long history of behavioral problems.

While a number of factors pointed in the direction of Doug Hunter as a suspect, and possibly Tony Campbell as an accomplice, Michael O'Connell had his doubts. He'd keep that branch of the investigation open, of course, but certainly not to the exclusion of other possibilities. At the same time, he'd continue the maddening search for a pair of elusive Reebok ERS shoes.

At the same time, Sergeant Tom Robinson got wind of another possible suspect in the Bryant case. He learned of a kidnap, rape, and attempted murder of a woman dragged away from a bus stop in Clackamas County, to the east. The victim's ATM card had been stolen by her abductor, who forced her to give him the personal identification number. He used the card to make withdrawals from her bank account, and had been videotaped in the act by a hidden camera at the automatic teller machine.

At Robinson's request, an Oregon State Police officer delivered a copy of the report and still pictures made from the video. The same images had been broadcast by television news reporters in Portland, giving widespread coverage of the crime to the public throughout western Oregon. One television watcher took a special interest in the photos.

The viewer picked up the phone and dialed Tom Robinson's number, as he had many times in the past in his role as one of the sergeant's most reliable informants. In the shadowy world of his daily life, and among the furtive figures who populated it, the tipster often observed and heard snippets of information he could use as bargaining chips in case he found himself in trouble.

"I know who that guy is in the ATM video pictures," the informant told Robinson. He gave the suspect's name, claiming that he'd known the guy for some time, and was positive of his identification.

Robinson ran the name through an on-line computer search, which regurgitated a description of a white male, DOB 03-25-70. In a phone conversation with an OSP lieutenant, Robinson learned that several other callers had named the same individual as resembling the broadcast photos.

The public tips worked, leading to the suspect's arrest the next day. He faced charges of kidnapping, rape, and attempted murder. OSP officers interviewed him at length, got a full confession, and shared the information they gleaned with Tom Robinson. The possibility that the same person had killed Martha Bryant evaporated like December morning fog on a sunny day. He'd been nowhere near the crime scene, and his car didn't bear any resemblance to the Bryant suspect car.

Well, there were over two and a half million people in Oregon. That eliminated one of them.

Two days before Thanksgiving, when the Bryant team had little to be thankful for, Chris Johnson, OSP crime lab, called again. He informed Robinson that the .22 caliber bullets were fired from a gun with ten lands and grooves with a right-hand twist. Only six manufacturers of .22 caliber handguns produced weapons with those characteristics, Johnson said, and none of them were very popular or numerous. Actually, he said, all of them fell into the class of "Saturday night specials." He listed the gunmakers-distributors: Herbert Schmidt, Rohm, R.G. Industries, Liberty Arms, EIG Co., and EMGE Company.

Tom Robinson promptly contacted a large retail agency selling handguns in Arkansas, and arranged to acquire photographs and diagrams of the six types of .22 caliber guns.

Typical of December in Oregon, the rains came to Washington County, but they didn't dampen the spirit of the approaching holiday season. Radio stations began playing the old traditional tunes and Christmas shoppers dashed to the brightly decorated malls.

*   *   *

Cesar Barone's ex-wife, Kathi, wondered if he would want to spend Christmas with his son. Barone had visited the boy regularly, generally once a week. Sometimes, Kathi thought, he seemed kind of spaced-out. She never smelled alcohol on him, but wondered if he'd been taking drugs.

In late December, some minor irritant erupted into a major argument during one of his visits. Kathi, when later recalling it, couldn't say what it was about but knew that Cesar's temper had exploded. He became hostile and brought up the issue of his monthly disability check that she received in lieu of child support. According to Kathy, he yelled, "Furthermore, I'm canceling the power of attorney and I have witnesses to this so you'd better not cash any checks."

When she received the next one in the mail, she wrote on the envelope, "Return to Sender," and popped it back in the mailbox. She never received another check. Merry Christmas.

The winter sun rose later and set earlier, making the long endless hours of chasing false leads all through December seem even longer. Tom Robinson, Michael O'Connell and the whole Bryant team listened to tips, reexamined the scant evidence available, and performed the plodding, routine work involved in the process of elimination. Every lead seemed to wash away like the first melting snowflakes.

The thirteenth day of December turned out to be an unlucky day for Andy Tremaine, the owner of the cabinet-making shop where Cesar Barone had often worked and was currently employed. En route to a job site where Cesar waited with the company van, Andy drove around a blind corner and slammed into the rear of a flatbed truck. Uninjured, he called for a tow truck and contacted Cesar to bring the van. When Cesar arrived, Tremaine unloaded some work material and personal possessions from his smashed car into the van, including his fishing poles and a long-barreled Western-style .22 caliber revolver. He rode with the tow truck driver while Cesar drove the van away.

Shortly afterwards, Cesar handed over the fishing poles, but not the gun. An oversight, Andy presumed. So a few days later, he asked Cesar for the revolver. "Well, I gave it back to you," Cesar said.

"No, you didn't," Andy said. "I'd remember if you gave me my gun back."

"Yeah, I did. I gave it back to you," Cesar insisted.

The Nazi propaganda minister during World War II, Joseph Goebbels, espoused the theory that if you told a lie often enough, people would begin to believe it. Andy Tremaine scratched his head, and started to wonder. Could Cesar have handed the revolver back? Maybe so, and it had just slipped his mind. He would give Cesar the benefit of the doubt, and search for the weapon in the usual hiding places.

Having almost convinced Tremaine, at least temporarily, Barone turned to other matters. He'd sold his car, and needed another one. At a Chevrolet agency, he found a white Hyundai, arranged financing, and drove it out of the lot on December 16.

The Christmas holiday provided some slight diversion for the Bryant homicide team, but the fact that a killer still ran around out there on the loose never completely left their thoughts. A few days after Christmas, events would take a dramatic turn.

Chapter 11

Two days remained in 1992 when Cesar Barone and Leonard Darcell escaped the chilly evening by sitting in a Cornelius steak house bar-restaurant on Baseline Road. They craved some female companionship. Cesar spotted a woman he'd met before, and approached her. After chatting for a few moments, he introduced her to his buddy, Len, saying that Darcell was just up from San Francisco. The threesome conversed several more minutes, and she finally excused herself to leave. No other opportunities presented themselves in the bar, so Cesar and Len left shortly afterwards.

A couple of blocks away, riding along Baseline in the Hyundai, they spotted the same woman walking with a teenage boy, her fifteen-year-old son. They pulled alongside and asked if the woman and boy would like a ride. She politely declined. Persistent, Barone and Darcell suggested she accompany them to a party in Portland where they could have a lot of fun.

"No," she said, her voice taking on a determined touch of harshness. The disappointed duo rolled up the car window and sped away in the direction of Portland.

Sixteen-year-old Heather Crane rushed out of her ex-boyfriend's house in Portland, and sprinted to the bus stop. If she hurried, she could catch her ride at 11:32 P.M. and arrive home before the black skies opened up again to douse her with freezing rain. She missed the bus by five minutes.

Worried about hanging around the corner until midnight, she walked the short distance to Sixth and S.W. Yamhill, Pioneer Square, in the heart of downtown where some of her crowd hung out around brightly lit shops and restaurants. She'd be safe there until another bus came.

The cold weather, though, had kept most people indoors. Heather sat on a bench about fifteen minutes before she saw a man she recognized. He wore a beret, and she knew him only by his street name, "Germ."

Germ recognized Heather easily; it was hard to miss her wild mane of hair dyed a garish orange-red and the excess of makeup. He asked if she wanted a ride. "No," Heather said, she'd wait for a bus.

"C'mon," Darcell urged. "I don't want you to catch a cold out here." She had to agree that the chilly air made for a miserable wait. After some coy resistance, she accepted his offer and walked almost three blocks with Germ to a parked car. Heather nearly backed out when she saw another man sitting inside the white four-door Hyundai, clad in gloves, dark pants, and a black leather jacket. Noticing Heather's slight hesitation, Germ spoke soothingly, reassuring her it would be okay. As they climbed in, Heather in the front passenger seat and Germ in the rear, he said, "This is my buddy, Cesar." Heather nodded and introduced herself while Cesar gave her an appraising look.

She asked, "Where do you guys know each other from?" Germ snickered and said they'd done some business together. Heather wanted to know what kind of business, eliciting another chortle from Germ who told her that she would see. Ignoring the nonanswer, she tried to make conversation by asking where they'd acquired the car.

"In California," Cesar answered as he started the engine and pulled away from the curb.

Because he headed in the direction directly opposite of Heather's home, she opened her mouth to protest. Germ interrupted, asking if she wanted to go to one of their friends' houses. "No," she snapped.

Germ sat in the backseat swigging beer and offered a drink to the now concerned young woman. Again, she refused. "I need to go over the Ross Island Bridge to get to my house," she pleaded. Relief swept over her as Cesar made a U-turn and headed toward the bridge. From the back, Germ announced he needed to urinate, and asked Cesar to pull over on a dark street because he was in a hurry. On 2nd Street, Cesar twisted the wheel and entered a parking lot surrounded by bushes. Both men climbed out of the car. Neither of them made any serious attempt to hide as they relieved themselves. At least Germ turned his back toward Heather, but Cesar, she thought, seemed to enjoy standing just a foot away and facing the car to be sure she could see him.

When they'd finished, as Heather recalled it, Cesar plopped back into the driver's seat, next to the girl while Germ stayed outside several paces from the car. She'd taken off some tight shoes purchased the same day and placed them on her lap along with her purse. Without warning, Cesar grabbed both shoes and the purse and slammed them to the floor, growling that she wouldn't need them. Her eyes like saucers and her throat constricted, Heather could do nothing but stare at him. From nowhere, he produced a silver-colored pistol that looked to her like an Old West gunslinger's weapon. He poked the barrel against her neck and ordered her to perform oral sex on him. If she didn't, he snarled, he'd blow her head off. He repeated the demand several times.

Heather would later say, "It was like, 'why are you doing this to me? There's no way. I'm not going to do it. I don't understand why you're doing this to me. Please don't.'" Later, she would recall that in refusing, she told Cesar he'd have to kill her because she wasn't going to do what he demanded.

Germ opened the back door, climbed in and said, "Don't do this to her, man," then repeated it. According to Heather, he argued for several minutes, babbling something about Heather being "cool" and that she wasn't the "skinhead" girl. It would be okay, he said, to do this to the skinhead. Heather had no idea who that girl might be.

At one point, Germ leaned forward and jammed his forefinger between the cocked hammer and the chamber to prevent the gun from being fired.

More tense moments dragged by, what seemed like hours to Heather. She wouldn't allow herself to tremble or cry, fearing that it might provoke both men. At last, Cesar let his wrist go slack, put the gun down, started the engine, and skidded out of the parking lot on slippery pavement.

Snow crystals flurried against the windshield and the wipers slammed back and forth as he headed for the Ross Island Bridge. Then he began to laugh. In spite of Cesar's chuckling, she thought he seemed "frustrated" at Germ.

He slid to a stop in a fast food restaurant parking lot she pointed out, across the street from her mother's house. Heather gratefully leaped out of the Hyundai and watched as it sped away, the red taillights reflecting in the wet, mirrored asphalt.

Through the remainder of that night, Heather sat up for hours, thanking her lucky stars to still be alive. Yet she didn't call the police to report the attempted rape.

In the same neighborhood where they'd dropped Heather off, Cesar Barone and Leonard "Germ" Darcell paid a visit to one of Darcell's Portland friends, who was known as "Doc." Now past midnight, they pounded on Doc's front door to wake him up. The sleepy resident recognized Darcell and invited both men inside. He sensed a tension between Darcell and Barone from their conversation. Over beers, Doc heard Barone take snipes at Darcell's character, hinting that the younger man hadn't lived up to certain expectations. "You don't deserve to wear the beret," Barone barked at Darcell, "but you'll get your chance later." Perhaps Cesar was harkening back to his days as a Ranger when wearing the beret signified status and strength.

Somewhat surprised, Doc waited for Darcell to snap back at his friend. This couldn't be the cocky, confident, self-assured Germ that Doc knew. Why was he just sitting there taking this abuse? Oh well, it wasn't Doc's problem. They finished the beers and Doc wasn't unhappy to see the pair depart a few minutes after one o'clock, Wednesday morning, December 30.

Chantee "Elise" Woodman was no stranger to people who liked to hang out in the Old Town section of Portland where counterculture nightclubs could be found. She'd learned how to survive on the streets of several cities in California and Oregon. At twenty-three, slender, with black hair and brown eyes, Chantee walked with a limp and sported small tattoos on various parts of her body. One blue imprint on her right arm contained the words, MY WAR. In some places, people knew her as Dantee Oshita, the name given to her at birth. In reference to her light olive complexion, she was often called a mulatto. But inhabitants of the street don't ask too many questions, and tend to accept others for their behavior and personalities, not for their breeding or backgrounds. They liked Chantee's upbeat energy and positive outlook.

She'd been searching for a better place to live in recent months, and found one in the last week of 1992. Chantee moved into a Northwest Portland house where she made a deal with the owner, an antique dealer, to keep the entire house cleaned spick and span in exchange for room and board. She liked to spend nights at spots like the Howling Frog Cafe, the X-Ray Cafe, and the Satyricon, where, as in the famed fictional bar of the *Cheers* television series, everyone knew her name. Often referred to as a "groupie," Chantee made no secret of her affinity for bands that played loud rock music, and the band members. She would usually ride a bus between her new residence and the Old Town section north of Burnside Street where tourists and locals visited Chinatown, upscale restaurants (including the one where Martha Bryant had celebrated her wedding) and partied at a variety of nightclubs appealing to all tastes. Sometimes, when she was broke, Chantee would walk the three-mile distance.

At about the same time Heather Crane accepted a ride with Germ and Cesar, Chantee Woodman entered a cafe in Old Town. Cold wind whipped sheets of rain and tiny snowflakes along the wet streets, making the warm interior a welcome haven from the weather. It was a gathering place for a variety of people with eclectic interests, where they could play checkers, chess, or just sit over coffee and talk.

A thirty-one-year-old fencing instructor who taught at a local college spotted Chantee and wondered why she didn't have a raincoat or even warm clothing, just jeans and a lightweight black sweater over her flannel shirt. He asked her if he could give her a ride anywhere. No, she said, but courteously explained why. A friend of hers worked at the nearby Satyricon Club as a musician. He had a sore throat, and Chantee was bringing him some hot tea. She just needed to kill a little time until he could take a break. To prove it, she held up a red plaid thermos bottle. Anyone who knew Chantee would have recognized it because she always carried the colorful thermos with her.

"Well, okay," the fencing instructor said, and offered to drive her the few blocks to the Satyricon. Chantee accepted. When they reached the club, he didn't especially want to go in, so he waited in the car while she hurried inside to deliver the tea. Her sick friend, though, couldn't be found. Back out in the fencer's car, Chantee listened as he suggested they return to the cafe where'd he met her, but she wanted to stay at the Satyricon a little longer. They discussed it and couldn't come to an agreement. He handed her a few dollars so she could buy some food or drinks, and said he'd be at the cafe they'd left if she got bored and changed her mind. Maybe, he suggested, they could see each other some time in the future. That seemed agreeable to Chantee, so they exchanged phone numbers. She stepped back out, waved, and went into the nightclub. The fencing instructor departed into the wet night.

Another man chatted with Chantee a little later, after she'd had a few glasses of wine. She complained that she'd missed her bus and needed a ride home. But he was going in the other direction.

Chantee stood near a bus stop in Old Town. A white four-door Hyundai rolled to a stop, and the passenger window slid down. The two men inside had watched an African-American man approach her. As they came to a stop, he wandered away.

Len Darcell had seen Chantee in the neighborhood on previous occasions, but didn't know her name. "Hi," he greeted. She greeted him in return and smiled. "Are you all right?" Darcell inquired.

"I'm okay." Her eyes sparkled and her speech slurred slightly, hinting of too much wine.

"You know that guy?" Darcell tilted his head toward the man who'd scuttled away. Chantee shook her head no. Encouraged, Darcell said, "It's kinda dangerous and wet around here. Do you want a ride?"

Chantee would have a long wait for another bus, and the Satyricon had closed. With few alternatives available, she accepted the offer. Inside the car, in the passenger seat, she spoke to the men in a friendly manner and gave directions to her residence, three miles away.

While Cesar Barone drove, Darcell gave a beer to Chantee. He kept slouching down in the backseat, pulling a beret down over his forehead, worried that a cop might see them drinking and pull them over. He was on parole already and didn't need to spend any more time in jail. The partially consumed case of Milwaukee's Best beer they'd bought earlier in the evening also worried him, because the cops would certainly assume they were under the influence in a motor vehicle and nail them with a DUI.

Darcell asked Chantee if she wanted them to drop her off right away or if she would like to stay for a while, maybe go to a party at his buddy's house. According to Darcell's recollection of the night and the conversation, "Chantee said she'd go with us." They headed towards Hillsboro and quaffed a dozen more beers during the ride.

While they drove the slick streets through the edge of Beaverton, Aloha, Reedville, and into Hillsboro, Barone didn't say much. Finally, as they passed a video games store, he volunteered, "Hey, I used to play video games there when I was a kid." Then he clammed up again. The trio passed through Hillsboro, entered Cornelius, and came to a stop at the two-story house where Barone lived on the lower floor and Darcell sometimes stayed.

Inside the house, according to Darcell, he and Chantee walked toward the kitchen and Barone toward his bedroom. They caught sight of him removing a gun from his pocket.

Darcell and Chantee shared some leftover food, he recalled, but he didn't want her to eat very much of it because he thought it was moldy. Cesar came in from the bedroom, still carrying the gun. He sat down at the kitchen table, and shoved the long-barreled .22 caliber weapon over toward Darcell, who shoved it right back. They repeated the exchange. Tired of the goofy game, in which Darcell thought Cesar mumbled something about "backing his play," Darcell took Chantee into a windowless bedroom. His sleeping bag was on the floor. They talked, he said, and listened to music on the radio. Just wanting to crash and to protect Chantee by keeping her away from Cesar, he sat with her. He hadn't planned to have sex, he claimed, but it just happened, on the sleeping bag.

As Darcell recalled it, Cesar walked in the bedroom while they were still locked together in passion, and began complaining that it wasn't fair. "It's my money, my beer, my place, and you make off with the girl," Darcell quoted Cesar. It was rude for Len and Chantee to have sex and exclude him, Cesar grumbled.

They completed the act, Darcell said, then Chantee asked to be taken home. Now 5:00 A.M., Darcell felt sleepy and tired but offered to take her back to Portland. He had no car, though, so they'd have to wait for the early morning bus. His thoughts, he recalled, were confused and foggy and all he could think was, "Wow, what a screwed-up night," just like a lot of nights in his past. He really didn't want to make the long ride to Portland, so he offered her a couple of bucks for bus fare, but, in his recollection, she protested going by herself. It would be easier to drive, so he asked Cesar if he could have the car keys. Barone replied, according to Darcell, with a refusal and commented that the request was "very rude."

At that point, Chantee got dressed, grabbed her Thermos, and acted as if she had decided to make her departure. Darcell recalled that Barone began fondling the pistol in a threatening way and asked her to be "nice" to him.

"I argued with him," Darcell would later report. "I told him he was out of line. I'd never said that before to Cesar, but I stood up to him. We were getting ready to fight. I was at the point where my brain short-circuited, where I don't think very well. But I reminded myself that he had a gun in his hand. I thought about kicking him in the nuts or somethin'. I told him that she wasn't going to have sex with him. But Chantee puts her hand on my arm, tells me to be cool, everything's all right. She said 'this has happened to me before.' "

Darcell recalled that Cesar was gloating as he led Chantee from the kitchen into his bedroom. There was no door between the rooms, just a blanket nailed over the door frame, so Darcell could hear them in the bedroom. "I heard Cesar tell her to get undressed, and [sounds] like popping, like he's undressing her." What he heard, Darcell imagined, were sounds of rough sex. He thought Chantee said, "Fine, just break it. No need to destroy it, it's the only one I've got." He had no idea what she meant, but figured that Cesar was ripping the buttons off her flannel shirt.

When they'd finished, and came out of the bedroom, Cesar said to Darcell, "Everything's cool now. I'll take her home." But, according to Darcell, he insisted on going with them, still feeling protective of the girl.

As they stepped outside, Darcell said, Cesar grabbed Chantee by the hair, jammed a gun in her back, and ordered her to close her eyes. He'd guide her to the car.

In the Hyundai once more, with Cesar at the wheel, Chantee in the passenger seat, and Darcell in the back, they drove out of the muddy Cornelius yard. Instead of turning right, in the direction of Portland, Cesar Barone made a left turn, west, toward the mountains separating Cornelius from the stormy Pacific Ocean.

Chapter 12

Sunset Highway, U.S. 26, from Portland to the Pacific beaches, for the first sixteen miles is a straight shot of freeway intersecting Washington County urban developments and farmland. Then it narrows to two lanes and meanders across rolling agricultural tracts before winding through the thick evergreens of Clatsop and Tillamook state forests. Most of the one hundred miles is interrupted only by scattered small communities. Though scenic and pastoral, the highway has a reputation for being one of the most dangerous stretches of road in Oregon, largely due to impatient speeders making lethal attempts to pass slower vehicles. For the most part, though, it is a peaceful, refreshing drive from the city to several spectacular coastal resorts.

Dark, threatening clouds still hovered over the highway and all of Tualatin Valley after sunrise on Wednesday morning, December 30. Francis Steffey, a sanding truck operator for the State of Oregon steered through a gradual curve on a long, lonely stretch of Sunset Highway, scattering sand on the slippery pavement. At 8:40 A. M., something lying on the south shoulder of the road caught his eye, not far from a traffic guardrail, so he pulled over to check it out. The sight sent his pulse rate spiraling and twisted his face into sadness. A young woman lay sprawled on the ground in frozen silence, her face battered and bloody, her dark hair matted. She wore a blue plaid flannel shirt, black pants and sweater, and black tennis shoes, inadequate protection from the chilly weather. But she was far beyond ever again feeling the cold, or anything else for that matter.

Because the body was discovered just inside the northwest border of Washington County, Sheriff's Detective Scott Ryon drew the duty of investigating the homicide.

Mindful of the slick pavement, he headed west on Sunset Highway, passed the junction peeling off to Vernonia, and halted among a cluster of other emergency vehicles parked between mileposts 44 and 45.

Examining the body, Ryon shook his head in disgust and pity. The killer had poked the barrel of a gun under her chin and pulled the trigger, execution style. From the facial bruises and blood, Ryon knew the last moments of her life had been a nightmare.

A search of her clothing produced very little. She had no purse with her, and no identification papers. Nothing. Only a tiny slip of paper found in her pocket. Someone had scrawled a telephone number on it.

Ryon, along with deputies, searched the area around the body for any possible evidence. They found nothing helpful, but felt sick at the discovery they did make. Tiny pieces of her flesh blown off by the blast of the gun had impaled themselves on boughs of fir trees. Before the body was hoisted into a coroner's van, a criminalist put bags over the victim's hands to preserve them for fingerprinting.

That same morning, Ryon traced the telephone number found in Woodman's pocket to a fencing instructor she'd met the previous night in Portland. The startled man expressed his astonishment, then told Ryon all he knew. Her name was Chantee, she had a sick musician friend to whom she wanted to deliver some tea in a red plaid thermos bottle, and she'd given the instructor her telephone number, which he readily passed on to the detective. Before the day ended, Ryon talked to Woodman's landlord, the antique dealer, and learned her full name as well as her residential address. Ryon verified the name by comparing her fingerprints to records on file. Chantee Woodman was no longer an anonymous Jane Doe. Investigators could begin tracing her associates and activities in hope of tracking down a brutal executioner.

At the autopsy the next morning, performed by the busy pathologist, Dr. Karen Gunson, Ryon took notes and observed. Gunson examined the bullet entry wound under the victim's chin, and informed the detective that it was a close-contact injury, seared by powder burns. Even more disturbing, she identified a cluster of "puncture wounds" in the soft flesh around the bullet hole. They'd probably been inflicted by someone repeatedly jamming the pistol barrel's tip and gun sight under her chin, and doing it with extreme force.

Chantee's face had also been subjected to a series of blows leaving "blunt force trauma" injuries. It could not be determined what hit her; maybe a fist or beer bottle, or possibly the butt of the gun. Bruises marred her lips and the skin around her mouth. The left cheek had been struck with a heavy blow and her scalp had been pounded with some object.

Dr. Gunson removed the bullet, which had been distorted to a flattened piece of metal. Ryon arranged to send it to Chris Johnson at the OSP crime lab. Johnson would also conduct DNA tests of the swabs taken from the body, which had already revealed vaginal and anal sexual penetration. Of course, DNA tests would have value only if a suspect could be found to which the results could be compared.

One at a time, Detective Ryon tracked down Chantee Woodman's circle of friends, the musicians she liked, the men she dated, and female pals, but none of them could shed any light on her tragic death. He arranged for patrol officers to observe any suspicious stops by motorists at the body discovery site. At each of the clubs in Old Town, Ryon circulated, asking strangers about her. Much of the repetitious, routine work of detectives produces meager results. This case was no different.

The landlord of the house into which Chantee had recently moved came under intense scrutiny. A young woman who gets full room and board for cleaning the place might be providing her benefactor with other favors, or there could be furtive arrangements better kept from the eyes of a law officer. Not this time. The dismayed fellow had nothing but the purest motives and absolutely no connection to her death.

A press release went out of the sheriff's office requesting public assistance. A few tips filtered in, but revealed nothing new. The media dutifully covered the homicide, but had little information to report. The sheriff had agreed with

Detective Ryon to keep confidential all details about the gunshot wound being under the chin, the beating injuries, and the sexual assault. If any suspect spoke of these matters, he'd be revealing involvement in the crime or at least an association with someone involved.

Ryon had hit the same dead-end wall as Sergeant Tom Robinson and Detective Michael O'Connell in the cases of Martha Bryant and Margaret Schmidt. But none of them had given up.

Before the first week of 1993 had expired, cabinet shop owner Andy Tremaine and his wife happened to drive past the Cornelius house where Cesar Barone lived. They spotted Cesar outside, loading boxes into a van. Andy had never found his Western-style .22 revolver, and it irritated him. Cesar, he told himself, had lied about returning it. With a quick twist of the wheel, Andy turned on 4th Street and pulled to a stop in the big muddy yard.

With no preliminaries, Andy snapped, "Cesar, I want my gun back." Barone gave him a blank stare. Andy explained that he'd given Cesar the benefit of the doubt before, but now believed he had never returned the gun. Perhaps, he suggested, while packing those boxes, Cesar had found it and would give it back now.

Barone's eyes turned hateful, and the hair on the back on Andy's neck bristled. They exchanged harsher words. Barone, though, held his position that he'd returned the weapon. Andy Tremaine, frustrated and furious, left without his long-barreled, silver-colored Western-style revolver.

The relationship between Barone and his girlfriend Sheila Hawkins had been on a sporadic basis lately, and he'd been seeing more of Denise Nichols, a thirty-seven-year-old waitress at a steak house restaurant and bar in Cornelius. She lived in a single-story complex of barrackslike apartments on North Adair Street in Cornelius, close to her friend, Betty Williams, another employee of the restaurant, and within a short walk of the old house where Cesar had been renting the ground floor. They'd met the previous October, and started dating a few weeks later, often using her chocolate brown 1969 Mercedes-Benz.

Cesar had sold one car, lost his Hyundai when it was repos-
sessed, drove unreliable old clunkers, or used "borrowed"
cars, so he liked using the Mercedes. Although Denise was
attracted to a number of things about Cesar, a lingering
suspicion and disapproval troubled her. His evasiveness
bothered her enough to do a little checking up on him.
When he told her he worked at Emanuel Hospital, she
telephoned the place and asked for him, only to learn
they'd never heard of a Cesar Barone. Repeatedly, he told
her that a Mafia hit man was after him, so he often carried
a semiautomatic pistol in a waist holster.

Her huge, fawn-colored dog liked Cesar, and what was
good enough for the big pooch was good enough for Denise. He stood nearly four feet high, and could intimidate
the most aggressive of men, so she always felt safe at home
or on walks with the big fellow on a leash.

Cesar could be a lot of fun, and then again he could be
a real jerk. Denise still fumed when she thought about Cesar's most recent birthday in December. In a burst of romantic generosity, he took her to the White House, a Portland
bed and breakfast establishment. The enchanting ambience
and his lavish attentions swept her away, until his temper
shattered the whole thing. They'd bickered about some triv-
ial matter. It escalated. He steamed and fussed and yelled,
then jumped into the car and left her stranded alone in
Portland to make her way home any way she could.

During their relationship, Denise became the victim of
theft, twice. The first time, someone broke into her apartment and stole her VCR, her television set, and several
smaller items. Astonished that her dog didn't frighten the
burglar away, she chewed him out for being such a pansy.
The second time, some cash and a ring disappeared. She
noticed the loss shortly after Cesar had left one night, and
realized then who'd ripped her off both times. No wonder
the dog had remained docile and allowed him to plunder
the apartment.

Rather than call the police immediately, Denise telephoned Cesar's number, planning to demand the return of
her property. His new housemate, Ron Price, answered the
phone. No, Cesar wasn't there. When Denise insisted on
talking to him, Price said he'd be glad to give Barone the

message. Cesar didn't call back, but Price did, with a hair-raising account of poor Cesar being in a bad auto accident and undergoing care in a hospital. That turned out to be another lie, so she made the report about her stolen possessions to the Cornelius PD.

A forgiving woman, though, can sometimes be too lenient. Maybe Cesar just needed the money and had too much pride to ask for it. Maybe he'd return the stolen items as soon as he achieved some financial stability. Denise didn't know that Cesar had already pawned her ring in Portland.

Barone rarely introduced Denise to any of his friends. She'd met only one, a short swarthy man with a mustache, named Ray Cardenas, who she thought was "handsome." Women, she realized, took up a disproportionate amount of Cesar's thoughts. Denise knew about Sheila Hawkins but had never met her.

And Denise hated the way Cesar would just show up at her apartment at odd hours of the day or night, never keeping any kind of a regular schedule. Late Wednesday evening, January 6, he asked her if they could get together that night after her shift ended. She stunned him by saying she couldn't because another man was coming over to her place that night.

Betty Lou Williams had wrestled with booze for much of her life, and often lost. At age fifty-one, she'd abused her body with poor diet, cigarettes, and liquor over a period of many years, to the point where her health had dangerously deteriorated. The early stages of emphysema racked her lungs. She wasn't obese, but chubbier than she should have been. Her liver had enlarged, and her coronary arteries were choked off with cholesterol. She'd had a complete hysterectomy years earlier. Despite her critical health problems, Betty wouldn't, or couldn't stop eating fatty foods, drinking, and smoking.

With the exception of some time in North Dakota, most of Williams's life had been spent in the green vales of Washington County and the lush forests of neighboring Tillamook County where she was born. She'd moved to Cornelius in 1990.

A sociable gadfly, Betty had a pleasant, amiable laugh that brightened her smooth, round face. Ringlets of dark hair outlined her high forehead, and oversized glasses gave her a sweet but mischievous look. She lived alone in the same apartment complex as her friend, Denise Nichols. With other companions, she liked going to dog races and betting a few bucks, but her extended family meant the most to Betty. Her four adult sons sometimes brought grandchildren to stay all night with her. She usually spent holidays with them and had joined a gathering for dinner and exchange of presents at Christmas.

Even though she didn't feel very good, Betty Williams worked steadily as a waitress with Denise at the steakhouse restaurant. The two women socialized off the job as well, and kept each other informed of local gossip and the comings and goings of various men. Of course, Denise told Betty about the guy she'd been dating named Cesar Barone and introduced her to him. Betty thought he was a likable guy and enjoyed getting together with him and Denise after work to have a few drinks. She'd seen Cesar in the restaurant on December 29, when he and his buddy, Len, had eaten and flirted with a woman accompanied by a teenage boy. *That Cesar,* she laughed, *he really liked women.*

One of Betty Williams's sons felt a gnawing unrest on Thursday, January 7, when his mother didn't answer the telephone. He called one of her neighbors, who knocked on Betty's door, but got no response. By two-thirty that afternoon, the son's unrest grew to alarm. He checked the restaurant, but Betty hadn't been there. Denise Nichols hadn't seen her that morning. The worried son contacted several other acquaintances of Betty's, but no one had seen or heard from her.

Now panicky, he rode his bicycle the few miles over to her apartment, hammered his fist against the front door, then used a hidden spare key to gain entry. Inside, he saw a bra lying on the floor. She wouldn't leave it like that. He called out, checked the bedroom, then walked into the bathroom. An unthinkable nightmare any offspring automatically shuts out of the mind became a stunning, horrific reality.

The dead body of Betty Williams, bent over the rim of her bathtub in a V shape, back toward the ceiling, one leg entangled in the shower curtain, the other dangling over the tub's edge, and her face submerged in a few inches of water, lay cold and motionless. Black tights and gray sweatpants clung to her left ankle, the right legs of the garments dangling limply to the floor, turned inside out as if they'd been hastily and forcefully peeled from her leg. Her upper body was still clad in a red sweater with no bra underneath.

Horrified, the son instinctively pulled the drain plug to let the water swirl out, then ran outside in confusion, spilling his cigarettes, dropping his gloves. Finally he dashed over to Denise Nichols's apartment to call for emergency medical help. EMT personnel arrived, but the lifeless body of Betty Williams was long since beyond any chance of revival. Technicians had no way of knowing whether she'd died of natural causes or as a result of foul play. They summoned the police.

Sergeant Mark Christy, Cornelius PD, arrived at the apartment complex to see if foul play could have been involved. Having been in law enforcement for fifteen years, he knew his way around a crime scene.

A native Oregonian from Bend, Christy had spent his youth in the bucolic high country around Burns, a small crossroads town where Highways 79 and 395 peel off from the east-west U.S. Federal Route 20. He worked on ranches while attending high school, but also found time to become a member of the student-police program and wound up as a cadet captain. During two years at Southwestern Oregon Community College in picturesque Coos Bay, majoring in law enforcement, he also served on the county sheriff's reserves. Following his 1977 graduation, Christy landed a job as a patrolman in Washington, but soon returned to his hometown, Burns, to join their police department. They promoted him to sergeant in 1981. In the following years, Christy moved his wife and two daughters to Coos Bay, again serving with the county sheriff, then back to Burns, where he added to his family by participating in a foster-home program.

In February 1989, the Cornelius PD made him an offer he couldn't refuse, and he uprooted his family one last time.

Slim, wiry, and light complexioned, with a blond mustache and a cleft in his clean-shaven chin, Christy had a disarmingly easygoing manner, but no one took the job of investigator more seriously than the veteran sergeant. He hated the bad guys, especially perpetrators of sex crimes.

To Mark Christy, the circumstances of Williams's death looked more than suspicious. The distorted position of her body in the tub seemed peculiar, as did the tights and sweatpants pulled from one leg only. And why would a bra be lying on the otherwise immaculate living room floor while the braless woman still wore a sweater? Her son told Christy that he knew Betty was in poor health, but he couldn't believe it had caused her death in this bizarre position. Anyway, he said, his mom always showered in the morning so it was ludicrous to believe that she'd died while trying to bathe during the night. Furthermore, he said, the dead bolt, which his mother always locked when she was inside the apartment, was unlocked. And a shelf, ordinarily propped against the back door, lay unused on the floor. Her purse, which normally would have contained some money, was completely devoid of any cash.

One of the officers spotted a gun under a desk, and pointed it out to Sergeant Christy. Clearly, there was nothing unusual about a single woman keeping a gun around for self-protection. But Christy made note of it anyway and photographed the silver-colored Western-style, long-barreled .22 caliber revolver, encased in a camouflage holster.

The top of the desk also caught the sergeant's attention. A rectangular impression approximately two inches by seven inches had been left in the light layer of dust, by something recently removed. He couldn't figure out what it was, but entered the observation in the report.

Outside, officers discovered several pennies scattered around an area covered with freshly broken glass.

The case could be a homicide, or it could be death by heart attack. No stab wounds. No bullet holes. Nevertheless, Sergeant Christy felt it suspicious enough to have the body autopsied.

Once more, the skills of Dr. Karen Gunson provided necessary information. The cause of death, she said, could be easily determined. Betty Lou Williams had unquestionably died of a heart attack. Sure, she had some slight injuries to the top of her head, and a small one-inch laceration of the vagina, but these had not been fatal, or even serious wounds. The woman's health and severe arteriosclerosis, Gunson said, made her a perfect candidate for a heart attack. Moreover, Williams's blood alcohol level soared to .33, more than three times the amount of legal intoxication. She had died at least eight to twelve hours before her son had discovered her body.

In the same hours Dr. Gunson performed the autopsy, Cesar Barone sat on a couch in Denise Nichols's home, picking up the phone every fifteen minutes to telephone the public information officer at the Cornelius PD. Claiming to be a concerned friend of Betty Williams, he anxiously wanted to know if they'd found a cause of death yet. Recognizing that his repeated calls might arouse suspicion, he asked Denise to call. She reluctantly complied, and heard the announcement that Williams's death had been declared the result of a heart attack. Instantly jubilant, he left in a great mood.

An FBI agent named John Douglas had pioneered a specialty in crime-scene analysis to develop "psychological profiles" of killers. His remarkable success had made him famous in law enforcement circles. It was said that he could simply examine photographs of the circumstances in which the victim was murdered, and draw incredibly accurate conclusions about the killer. In one case, he looked at a stack of snapshots and without asking a single question of the investigators, he began rattling off his observations.

Douglas told the astonished observers that when the victim ended up in water, such as in a bathtub or shower, the killer was probably not making an attempt to destroy the evidence, he was more likely rearranging the body, the clothing, and other items present to change the appearance so it would be consistent with his personal preconception of what it should look like. Using water, Douglas said, was a method to portray something kinky or bizarre.

*　　　*　　　*

Perhaps Sergeant Christy could have used the professional advice of John Douglas, but at this point in the death of Betty Williams, investigators couldn't even prove it had been a homicide, much less profile the killer. Christy's gut feeling told him that she'd been murdered, so he left the crime scene tape up for a full twenty-four hours and continued to probe for more information. He interviewed her coworkers at the restaurant and learned names of her friends, including a man named Cesar Barone and a woman he often dated, Denise Nichols. Christy also found another one of the dead woman's girlfriends who had driven by Betty's apartment at three in the morning and noticed the light still burning. The woman had thought little of it and didn't bother to stop. She mentioned that Betty would ordinarily have about twenty-five dollars worth of tip money, earned at the restaurant, after a night's work. Christy's eyebrows shot up, because no money had been found anywhere in the apartment.

The friend came up with something else. Betty kept a coin separator on her desk, usually full of change. And when it overflowed, the pennies would be dropped into a glass jar kept in the living room. One piece of the puzzle had fallen into place; Christy knew what had made the odd-shaped indentation on the desk. The investigator later verified with Betty's son the existence of a jar for pennies and a coin separator. He added that Betty's rent was due on January 5, and her habit was to save one-half of the payment from one paycheck and one-half from the next check, then pay the rent in cash. To Christy, that gave even more weight to the absence of money in the apartment. Someone had been in that apartment, caused Betty's death, and taken all of her money. Unfortunately, the theory had no foundational evidence to support it.

Betty's son, heartbroken and horrified over the cruel way his mother had died, painfully gathered her clothing, furniture, and personal treasures she'd collected over her half century of life. The grieving son stored them away, including the .22 revolver he assumed belonged to her.

Officially, Betty Williams had died of a heart attack. To Mark Christy, she'd been murdered, and he planned to keep his eyes open for any leads.

* * *

Andy Tremaine still fumed about the pistol that he regarded as stolen by Cesar Barone. That's why he couldn't believe it when Barone came marching into the cabinet shop on Friday morning, January 8, acting as if nothing had ever happened. He hadn't worked there for some time, so his arrival didn't make sense to Tremaine.

"Andy," Barone said, an excited edge to his voice, "did you see all that commotion up the street on North Adair?" Tremaine gave him an apathetic stare. Barone ignored it, and continued. "Did you see all the police cars, and all the firemen?"

Wishing that Barone would just go away, or return the pistol if he wanted to repair the friendship, Tremaine answered, "No, Cesar, I didn't. I'm busy."

Almost jumping with nervous energy, Barone said, "Oh, man, you should have seen it. You should have seen it, you know. They thought it was a homicide at first, but then they found out it was a heart attack."

Tremaine looked up in disgust, considered asking for his pistol again, and then decided to hell with it. He felt relieved when Cesar Barone left, still chattering about the event on Adair Street.

Chapter 13

Cesar was glad he'd moved. After he unpacked his boxes, threw a mattress with some wadded blankets on a bed frame, and settled into a caramel-colored, single-story two-bedroom house in eastern Hillsboro, with his buddy Ron Price, he was glad. He'd left the ground floor of the old house in Cornelius where too many things had happened and people knew too much. It would be better, he figured, to put a little distance between himself and curious folks who might create problems by snooping around. Since Betty Lou Williams died, it seemed even better that he'd removed himself from the close proximity to her apartment where nosy people might ask too many questions. The rent he had been paying in Cornelius had been a problem, too, because he hadn't earned a regular paycheck for some time now. In Ron's place, he'd only have to pay a couple hundred dollars each month, and they could share other expenses. To most people, Ron Price might not have been the ideal roommate. Cornelius police knew him well. Short of stature, about five-two, tattooed, usually filthy dirty and unshaven, with stringy brown collar-length hair, Ron did not make the social register of Cornelius. He consumed booze like most people drink water. Usually, his income was from untraceable sources, but at least he worked when he could find a job, most often in gas stations, recently as a laborer in the cabinetmaking shop where Cesar had often been employed.

Despite a few obvious shortcomings, Cesar liked Ron, and chose to occupy a house with him. By pooling their resources, they could make a go of it. Things were looking up for Cesar.

*   *   *

Sergeant Tom Robinson had reexamined the entries in a dozen bulging binders, all related to the murder of midwife Martha Bryant. He gritted his teeth in frustration. The shooter who drove the "muscle car" was still free to dish out more torture and death if he so chose. There had to be a link somewhere to identify the fugitive and slam barred doors in his face. Maybe it would help to make another appeal to the general public with increased emphasis on the reward which had grown to $25,000. A national television program, *America's Most Wanted,* hosted by John Walsh, who'd lost a small son to some monster, had generated some remarkable success, and law enforcement agencies across the nation had welcomed the help.

Robinson knew that the police chief and the sheriff had already refused to air the case with one of the most popular talk show hosts, Oprah Winfrey. That program, officials agreed, focused more on the social implications of crime and the effect on victims, rather than emphasizing the urgency of capturing the suspect.

When *America's Most Wanted* returned their calls, though, they felt no such reluctance. Robinson, Lila Ashenbrenner, Michael O'Connell, and the entire task force had no qualms about participating, readily agreeing to present the facts to John Walsh and company. By mid-January, a deal had been struck, and the show's producers planned a trip to Hillsboro within a month to begin filming.

Still juggling his relationships with women, Cesar Barone continued to see his ex-wife Kathi and their child, at least once each week. Usually, they wound up at the home where Kathi lived with her mother, Joyce Scarbrough. They often dined there and later congregated around the warmth of the cheery fireplace with family members, including Kathi's grandmother who also shared the home.

On January 21, Kathi gave her little son a party to celebrate his second birthday. Cesar dropped by for a couple of hours and Kathi thought he acted peculiar. "The thing I remember most vividly is that he appeared to be quite drugged at the time. He . . . spent a lot of time leaning against the wall, and seemed to be having trouble staying awake. When he got there, he [acted] very energetic and excited, and then he just kind of crashed." Asked if it concerned her, she replied, "It did, yeah. I didn't particularly want my son seeing that kind of thing." She discussed the matter with her mother who commented that she'd also noticed the same kind of stupor, several other times.

Kathi had to admit, though, that while she'd frequently seen Cesar drink alcohol, especially beer, she'd never seen him ingest drugs.

Joyce Scarbrough had developed a certain affection for Cesar, even though her daughter had divorced him, and despite some of his eccentric habits. She'd never believed his preposterous yarn about descending from noble Italian ancestry or of having been in Italy. She found too many discrepancies in his various stories, but chose to disregard them. To her, "C" simply liked to exaggerate as most people do at one time or another. Nothing but harmless self-aggrandizement, she rationalized.

Perhaps a bit naive, Joyce carelessly punched in her personal identification number at her bank's automatic teller machine, allowing Cesar to watch, never suspecting that he might memorize the valuable code. She carried the First Interstate Bank ATM card in her purse, and kept a spare which had her son's name imprinted on it, at home. Three times, she even handed her card to Kathi and Cesar, together, and asked them to withdraw some cash for her. On one occasion, Kathi said, "Mom, you'll have to give me the PIN number again."

Nonchalantly, Cesar remarked, "Oh, I have it."

Joyce didn't keep the storage place of her spare card secret, either. With innocent trust, she tossed it into a desk drawer in full view of Cesar.

Joyce and Kathi shared not only a mother-daughter relationship, and lived together at Joyce's Hillsboro home on N.W. 338th Street, they also regarded each other as best friends. Since Joyce worked regularly as a nurse on the night shift at Emanuel Hospital, and Kathi worked days as a paralegal, they shared the duties of caring for Joyce's ninety-one-year-old mother. All three generations of women appeared to be in reasonably good health.

That's why the shock nearly flattened Kathi on Thursday, February 4, at about 2:00 P. M., when her brother found their mother dead on the carpeted floor of the family recreation room. Her still body lay partially beneath the pool table, with no signs of trauma nor disheveled clothing.

A cursory medical opinion suggested that she'd probably suffered a heart attack, but no autopsy was performed since the death appeared to be natural. They buried her in the small community of Beavercreek, south of Portland, in the morning shadow of majestic Mount Hood.

It went unnoticed for a nearly a week that someone had been using Joyce's ATM card. Substantial withdrawals had been made from her checking/savings accounts, $300 to $500 dollars each time. Made at ATMs Joyce had never been known to use, the transactions had started five days before she died.

Sheila Hawkins often wondered how Cesar ever had any money, in view of his frequent unemployment. He dropped by her house on Saturday, February 6, and she expected him to be broke as usual. She couldn't believe it when he pulled a wad of crisp, fairly new twenty-dollar bills from his pocket. Grinning, he told her to count the cash. She tallied forty-five of the bills, exactly $900.

"Where'd you get all the money?" she asked. Cesar gave her a vague, involved story in which he'd collected an unpaid drug debt for some anonymous person, and been rewarded for his brave assistance. The grateful fellow had paid him $1,200, he said.

In a magnanimous mood with his new wealth, Cesar bought Sheila a pair of seventy-five-dollar boots, a dress that cost $105, and slipped her two twenties to give to her daughter. The couple also went shopping at the Beaverton mall where they examined the flimsy, sensual garments on racks and tables inside a shop specializing in sexy clothing for women. In a libidinous burst of generosity, Cesar bought her a revealing camisole, some panties, and a lacy see-through bra.

On Sunday, three days after Joyce Scarbrough's death, Cesar Barone initiated a chat with Kathi's brother. Barone announced that he'd seen Joyce on that Thursday morning, in her house just hours before the body was found. He'd arrived, he said, at about nine or nine-thirty, and had a conversation with Joyce in which she told him how weary she was. According to Barone, Joyce had said she'd had a very busy night, wanted to make some breakfast for her elderly mother, and then go to bed. Even though Joyce had appeared tired, Cesar said, she'd certainly been okay when he left.

The still bereaved son wondered where all this was leading, and why Barone was even there during the family's grieving period. As if reading Tim's thoughts, Cesar said he'd dropped by to borrow a wrench to remove his car's oil filter. This made the son even more curious because he remembered seeing Barone take the wrench two days earlier. He frowned, shook off the prickly feeling Cesar's comments had brought on, and watched Barone walk down the driveway, past the giant birch tree, and speed away in his car.

When Joyce Scarbrough's son began the difficult task of examining his mother's financial affairs, he stopped, looked again, and had to double check the figures. Something was wrong. Money had been withdrawn from her accounts not only before her death, but *continuing four days afterward*. Nearly $3,000 had been taken, virtually draining the balance. Certain that no one in the family would have done such a cruel thing, he immediately suspected Cesar.

Rather than telephone a report to the police, the angry man marched directly into the sheriff's office on February 11 to personally deliver what he'd discovered. He told Detective Roger Mussler about the depleted bank account and about Barone's access to the card and the PIN number. That, in itself, did not provide enough evidence to make an arrest, so Mussler thanked him and said they'd launch an investigation.

Mussler, six feet tall, light complexioned, and beefy enough to motivate most bad guys to avoid physical confrontations, had been chasing felons for fifteen years. He'd spent the most recent five years with the WCSD "Person Crimes" unit, investigating assaults, rape, robbery, and homicide.

The first step taken by Mussler involved VICAP, the national data base controlled by the FBI, in which criminal information records are kept for the use of police agencies across the country. Mussler learned of Cesar Barone's juvenile crimes, that his birth name was Adolph Rode, and of his adult criminal history which sent him to Florida State Prison at Starke.

While Roger Mussler assembled this information and prepared to investigate Mr. Barone in greater detail, a woman Cesar knew received an unexpected visit.

It had been more than five weeks since Cesar moved from the two-story house in Cornelius, where fifty-eight-year-old Matilda Gardner had expressed a wish to take over the downstairs space vacated by Barone. But she hadn't yet made the relocation. On Saturday morning, February 13, Barone knocked on the front door. When Matilda answered, he smiled and asked to use her telephone explaining that his car had broken down nearby. She generously invited him in and allowed him to make his call on her cordless phone while standing in the stairwell.

As soon as he'd spoken a few muffled words into the mouthpiece, Cesar hung up, handed the phone back to Matilda, and expressed an urge to use the bathroom. Matilda hesitated momentarily, blushed, and led him upstairs. She waited for him to finish, and watched as he stepped out and approached her, apparently to offer his thanks. He leaned close to her face and commented about the moisture in her eyes. She told him that it was caused by an allergy. With apparent compassion, he leaned closer yet and used his thumb to brush away a tear. Sensing something morbid, she fought the urge to rush into her bedroom and slam the door behind her. She waited too long to take counsel of her own fears.

Barone's gentle demeanor abruptly vanished. He lunged forward, jammed a knife against her throat, and demanded that she sit down. Trembling now, holding back the flow of tears, Matilda sat and felt a surge of terror course through her body. Barone unzipped his jeans, dropped them to his ankles along with his underwear, and thrust his pelvis toward her face. He demanded that she perform oral sex on him.

Her voice barely audible, Matilda said no. Using coarse street language, Barone repeated his demand. She again refused. But realizing that her rejection of him could very well cost her life, she spoke again. This time, Matilda pretended to capitulate, and choked out a hoarse whisper, "You know me. You don't need that knife." Barone guided Matilda onto the floor where she disrobed from the waist down. While she forced herself not to scream or throw up, he mounted her. But the rape Matilda had steeled herself to suffer through did not happen. Barone failed to get an erection. Seizing the opportunity, Matilda warned Cesar that a friend of hers was due to show up at any minute. She hinted to Cesar that he could return a little later. He glanced around trying to make up his mind, rose, pulled his jeans up, gave her a last look of abject disgust, and trotted downstairs to make his escape. Matilda let the dam burst, and cried uncontrollably. At last, she composed herself enough to telephone a friend who relayed the call to the Cornelius PD.

That same Saturday morning, Sheila Hawkins, suffering from painful menstrual cramps, decided she needed some Advil, and hoped Cesar would be willing to bring some by for her. She knew he'd recently moved in with Ron Price, so she called the number there. It irritated her when she was able to connect only with an answering machine, but she left a message for Cesar anyway.

Barone returned the call at about one-thirty that afternoon, agreed to bring her the pain reliever, and arrived at her apartment an hour later. She wondered aloud where he'd been that morning, and he tossed off an answer about "crabbing" over in Tillamook with some dude he'd met in a bar. Couldn't even recall the guy's name.

Barone's words were slurred, his eyes glassy, and Sheila knew why. She asked him what he'd been smoking. Cesar acknowledged that he was "wired" and admitted he'd been "doing crank," which came as no surprise to Sheila. She'd seen Cesar under the influence of amphetamine on previous occasions, and easily recognized the effects, which made her wonder how he'd managed to drive the old brown Toyota she'd seen him using lately. When he left, Sheila hoped he wouldn't get in any trouble due to the drugs.

That wasn't the kind of trouble Cesar worried about at that moment. A much greater concern gripped him; to avoid being any place where the police could find him. Knowing very well that Matilda Gardner could certainly finger him, Cesar made himself scarce. When the police traced him to Ron Price's place in Hillsboro, they could never find him at home.

Barone may have felt some sense of satisfaction at the success of his evasive tactics, but his lust had not been sated.

On a Wednesday night, eleven days after Matilda Gardner had barely escaped being raped, Sarah Ross, age eighty-three, rose from her easy chair to answer a loud knocking at the front door of her modest little 1940s-style home on S.E. Oak Street in Hillsboro. She opened it a narrow crack because she lived alone and didn't want to take too many risks at 8:30 P.M., well after dark. A young man, about five-eleven she thought, 150 to 170 pounds, with brown hair combed back, stood on the tiny front porch, three steps up from the ground, with a worried expression on his face. In what Sarah perceived as a touch of Southern accent to his excited voice, he said there'd been an automobile accident down the street and he needed to use her phone to call 911.

Now Sarah couldn't refuse emergency help to someone in distress, even if it meant ignoring the potential risk to herself. So she opened the door and invited the man in to use her telephone.

He brushed past her, quickly spun around, and grabbed her from behind. With one arm locked around her neck, he groped her right breast with the other hand then tried to unbutton and tear off the blue, green and white flannel shirt she wore.

Sarah was not a woman to be trifled with. Instinctively, she kicked one foot backward and whacked him solidly on the shin with the heel of her sturdy shoe. And she hadn't thrown all caution to the wind when she allowed the over-sexed beast into her home. Sarah wore a device suspended from a necklace, a personal alarm to summon police or medical help. She grabbed it and pushed the button, not only alerting an operator, but setting off an earsplitting siren inside the house.

The startled intruder, smarting from the pain in his shin, and astonished at this woman's swift reactions, released his grip on her. Fury colored his face. His need for sexual gratification had apparently wilted, but he needed to salvage his assault somehow, so he grabbed her purse from the floor and made a wild dash for the exit. He nearly stumbled as he leaped off the porch and raced away into the darkness.

Emergency medical help and an officer from the HPD arrived within a couple of minutes. The medics checked her out while the feisty Sarah insisted she was okay. She just wanted the police to arrest the vile person who had tried to have his way with her. Her description of him sounded like the same man who'd assaulted Matilda Gardner.

The same evening Sarah Ross whacked a clumsy potential rapist in the shin, February 24, Cesar called his ex-wife, Kathi, for what seemed to her a very odd reason. He said that he'd talked to the Hillsboro police and a deputy sheriff, and been informed that they did not consider him a suspect in the theft of her mother's money.

Doubting the veracity of his statement, Kathi waited until the next morning to telephone Detective Mussler and report the weird call. The detective arranged to interview her within the hour. Barone's ex-wife, Mussler figured, would be the most likely person to know of his habits and possible whereabouts.

She cooperated readily with the detective, and would have helped Mussler find him if she could, but truly had no idea where he'd been hanging out during the last couple of weeks. Answering Mussler's questions, she described how she'd met Barone through a personal newspaper ad, subsequently married him after his release from prison and move to the Northwest and that they'd separated about a year ago. She stated that she didn't know what crimes had sent him to Florida State Prison, though. Cesar, she said, was completely estranged from his Florida family. He'd served in the Army and his employment record afterwards was sporadic. Kathi rolled her eyes while telling the detective that Cesar had several different girlfriends.

When Mussler brought up the theft of money from Joyce Scarbrough's bank accounts, Kathi admitted that she suspected Cesar, since he was the only one outside the family with access to the card and PIN number. Kathi produced detailed account statements which recorded all of the transactions. Mussler noted that each ATM withdrawal had been conducted at machines where no cameras had been installed to record the user's image. Fortunately, the family had not permanently lost the money. Kathi produced a letter from Scarbrough's bank. They'd taken a remarkably generous and responsible action by crediting the account with the amount lost due to unauthorized use of the bank card.

Trying to recall any previous financial shenanigans by Cesar, Kathi said he had passed a bad check the month before, on a bank account they'd closed the previous year. She'd heard from Cesar only a couple of times since her mother's death, and wondered what other trouble he might be in, but Mussler thought it better not to tell her about the alleged sexual assaults.

While Roger Mussler hunted for Cesar Barone in connection with the attacks on Matilda and Sarah, his colleagues from three departments continued to seek clues in several troubling homicide cases. None of them appeared to have any connection to the others. In the murders of Margaret Schmidt, Elizabeth Wasson, Martha Bryant, and Chantee Woodman, scant clues existed and no likely suspects had been identified. Over in Cornelius, Sergeant Mark Christy remained convinced that he had yet another unsolved murder; the odd death of Betty Williams.

Sergeant Tom Robinson, HPD, kept hoping that the "muscle car" driven by Bryant's killer would turn up. WCSD detective Michael O'Connell continued his search for an unusual pair of Reebok shoes. And Sheriff's Detective Scott Ryon remained confident that he'd eventually find the .22 caliber weapon used to savagely end the life of Chantee Woodman.

In the interim, though, they had other cases to research, reports to make, court testimony to give, and the infinite list of time-consuming duties to perform that fill the daily lives of cops everywhere. Fictional detectives can devote all their time and energy to that one important case. In the real world, bureaucracy exists, and less exciting routine cases drain resources.

And then some creep starts molesting older women, and needs to be taken off the street.

PART THREE

Misplaced Trust

Chapter 14

Sergeant Mark Christy, accompanied by officer David White, had the pleasure of arresting Cesar Barone on Saturday, February 27. They found him sitting in a tavern located on Pacific Avenue, the main east-west thoroughfare through Forest Grove. Barone gave them no resistance, only a sick smile.

When Barone asked what he was being hauled in for, Christy informed him that he was wanted on suspicion of rape, attempted sodomy, burglary, and menacing the victim. Each charge related to Cesar's alleged assault of Matilda Gardner in the Cornelius house where he'd lived until recently. If Barone breathed a sigh of relief, no one noticed. Christy dutifully informed Barone of his constitutional privilege to remain silent, the Miranda rights, which Cesar waived with a brief comment and shrug of his shoulders. Christy could ask anything he wanted, unless Cesar interrupted the interrogation by demanding the aid of a lawyer.

First, Christy wanted to know about the alleged attempt to rape Matilda Gardner. Barone vehemently denied it, and hinted that Gardner had flirted with him in a sexually suggestive way. He stopped as if in deep thought, then asked to make a phone call. If he called a lawyer, the session would come to a screeching halt, and the possibility of a confession would collapse. Mark Christy had nothing against legal representation for a suspect, but like most investigators trying to get at the truth, he knew that an attorney would advise Barone to promptly shut his mouth.

Barone didn't call for legal help, though. Instead, he contacted his housemate, Ron Price, and directed him to hurry over to the jail as soon as possible to retrieve Cesar's personal possessions such as his wallet, jewelry, and keys, which he didn't want to leave in the officers' custody. Ron would have to use those keys to carry out Cesar's next request, to pick up the Toyota he'd been forced to leave parked near the tavern.

When he completed issuing instructions to Hank, Barone telephoned Sheila Hawkins. He wanted to explain, he said, about the phony charges the police had trumped up to frame him. Adamantly insisting that Matilda Gardner had lied, Barone said that she must be trying to protect her own reputation, because she was the one who had started it. She'd tried to kiss him but he'd resisted her unwelcome advances, and when he was on his way out she'd made it plain she wanted him to come back later so they could have sex together. He certainly wanted no part of it, he said in the voice of a virtuous choir boy. Why in the world would he want to fool around with a woman nearly twenty years older? It was ridiculous, Cesar said.

Trying to assess the credibility of his plea, Sheila asked Cesar why he'd found it necessary to go to the house where Matilda lived.

Well, Cesar explained, he just wanted to tell the landlord about the headboard of his bed he'd left there, and to request the property owner to leave it outside by the shed so Cesar could pick it up later.

Sheila thought that sounded completely phony for two reasons. In the first place, Cesar had already told her he'd cleared everything he owned out of the house. In the second place, she knew the landlord didn't even live there. It would have been much easier for Cesar to telephone the request if, indeed, he really had any reason to speak to the property owner. She hinted to Cesar that she doubted his story.

If talking faster was persuasive, Cesar would have convinced her. The speed of his words accelerated like a deflating balloon in frenzied flight, telling her that he wasn't guilty and that the police had falsely arrested him based on a pack of lies and he was innocent and he'd be out of there pretty soon since they couldn't prove anything anyway because they had no evidence.

When Cesar finally ended his tirade, he left Sheila in serious doubt. She pondered her next move. Sheila had never met Barone's ex-wife, but decided to give Kathi a call to find out what she knew about Cesar's plight. The two women chatted, trying to be congenial but both feeling somewhat strained. Neither of them could cast much light on Barone's nocturnal roaming or secret desires.

And only one person knew of the crucial mistake Cesar had made. No one could guess the torment grinding in his guts while he desperately hoped the investigators wouldn't discover his hasty, clumsy error.

Having patiently waited while Cesar spewed his self-assessed purity into the telephone, Mark Christy resumed the questioning. Did Cesar own any guns?

According to the reply, Barone owned a small arsenal. He listed a .30–06 rifle, a .308 rifle, a .444 elephant gun, a 9 mm Browning semiautomatic pistol, and a .357 revolver. He mentioned nothing, however, about any .22 caliber weapons. And Cesar evidently assumed that since he had changed his name from Adolph Rode, the convicted felon from Florida, to Cesar Barone, a man with no criminal record, it wouldn't be noticed that his possession of guns was illegal.

How about knives? Do you own any knives, Mr. Barone? He did, but he preferred not to talk about them.

Next, Christy wanted to know if Barone had ever stolen anything from his girlfriend, Denise Nichols, specifically a gold ring. Of course not, Cesar said. Hell, nobody would stoop that low. He'd pawned a few things of Denise's, but with her permission.

Since Betty Lou Williams had lived in the same apartment complex as Denise, Mark Christy thought he might as well find out what Cesar knew about the strange death. "By the way," he asked, "where were you on Tuesday night, the fifth, into the early morning hours of Wednesday, the sixth, at the time Betty Williams was last seen alive?"

It didn't surprise Christy to hear Barone admit knowing her, which was common knowledge, but it caught the sergeant slightly off guard when Cesar blurted out that he was the last person to see Williams alive. He'd been at Betty's apartment, he admitted, and saw that she was "extremely drunk." Denise Nichols came over, Cesar said, and he didn't want his lady friend to see him at Betty's, so he tried to hide in the hallway. But he realized he was being foolish, so he came out of his hiding spot, said goodbye to Betty, and walked Denise over to her apartment. Later, when he headed home, he noticed that Williams's front door was standing open, so he stopped, went to the door, looked inside, and saw Betty alive and well sitting on the living room floor. She was fully dressed, Cesar said, but seemed much too drunk to even get up, so he reached inside, flipped the lock, and pulled the door closed. No, he didn't enter the apartment, and no, he didn't speak to her. He just left her sitting there in a happy stupor, safe and sound, and made sure her door was locked.

Christy asked what time all this had taken place, and Barone answered that he'd left Betty at about one o'clock in the morning. "Yeah," Barone mused, "I'm the last person to have seen Betty Williams alive."

Mark Christy had no trouble believing that Cesar Barone was, indeed, the last person to see Betty alive. And probably the first person to see her dead.

As the interview wound down, Michael O'Connell, at Christy's invitation, joined them in the interview room and took some photographs of the suspect. While Christy continued the interrogation, O'Connell had a "six-pak" prepared, an arrangement of two-inch by two-inch pictures portraying six different men, including Barone. It would be used for a "photo laydown" presented to victims and witnesses for the purpose of selecting the photo most resembling the perpetrator they'd seen.

Detective Derald Riggleman asked to use the six-pak first. He knew that Barone had been arrested on suspicion of sexually assaulting Matilda Gardner over in Cornelius, and suspected that the same perp had been the one who lied to Sarah Ross to gain entry into her home for the purpose of trying to rip off her clothing and grope her body. Riggleman drove the few blocks over to Sarah's little house, and spread the folder open on a coffee table. Even though she was eighty-two, Sarah didn't waver for an instant, pointing unequivocally to the photo of Cesar Barone as the man who'd assaulted her.

Now, Barone had two victims willing to testify against him.

* * *

Wanting to know more about Cesar Barone's background in Florida, Detective Roger Mussler called Lieutenant Tony Fantigrassi of the Broward County sheriff's office. Fantigrassi remembered the man quite well, only he knew him as Adolph "Jimmy" Rode. The lieutenant would never forget arresting Rode for attempted murder following the brutal beating and strangling of Mattie Marino, the youth's grandmother. Sounding disgusted, Fantigrassi told Mussler that Rode had been acquitted of those charges. He speculated that the grandmother hadn't revealed the whole story, possibly because there'd been some sexual assault involved and the poor old lady had been too embarrassed to discuss it. And she also might have been terrified at the possibility of Rode returning to seek even more violent revenge.

His voice sounding considerably more enthused, Fantigrassi said Rode had been convicted of parole violations related to an earlier charge of trying to break into a Corvette. He'd gone to the slammer on those charges.

While Mussler scribbled copious notes, Fantigrassi told of a 1981 case in which an eighty-one-year-old lady was beaten to death late at night in an unincorporated area of Fort Lauderdale. It occurred about ten miles from the site of Mattie Marino's beating. To Fantigrassi, the modus operandi appeared quite similar, and he suspected that Rode had been involved, but on the books, the case remained unsolved.

Roger Mussler made an official request for copies of Adolph Rode's file from Broward County. He was especially interested in a notation on the documents stating, DEFENDANT IS A SUSPECT IN A MURDER HERE IN BROWARD COUNTY. It referred to the death of Alice Stock, the woman Rode had menaced back in 1976. So Barone was a potential suspect in at least two Florida murders, the one described by Lieutenant Fantigrassi and the Alice Stock case.

It seemed increasingly probable to Roger Mussler that Mrs. Scarbrough had been murdered, and he began to wonder if Cesar Barone could possibly have killed her in order to cover up his theft of money from her account. There had been cases in which a murder victim had been smothered, with a pillow for example, and no marks of violence were left on the body. Since no autopsy had been performed on Mrs. Scarbrough, no one knew for certain exactly how she had died. Mussler had to know. He made some calls and filled out the appropriate paper work to seek the answer.

Under the leaden skies of Thursday, March 4, 1993, a crew of workmen began digging dirt away from the still fresh grave of Joyce Scarbrough at the Moehnke Cemetery in Beavercreek. With Detective Michael O'Connell in attendance, they lifted the casket out, slid it into a van, which headed north up to Portland. In the Multnomah County medical examiner's office, Dr. Edwin Wilson performed a belated autopsy on the body. O'Connell observed and later reported, "Dr. Wilson told me he was unable to locate a cause of death." The body had been embalmed and prepared for burial, so examination of the internal organs didn't reveal very much.

When O'Connell called Mussler to let him know what had happened, they both decided to press the pathologist for more information. In O'Connell's report, he noted, "Dr. Wilson later told Detective Mussler and I that he did not believe that Scarbrough died from a heart attack, that his ruling would be the cause of death was undetermined . . . [and] appeared to be suspicious in nature." O'Connell added, "I know, based on experience and training as well as discussions with Dr. Wilson, that it is possible to smother a person without leaving any physical signs."

As soon as he'd returned to Hillsboro, O'Connell and Mussler took a drive to Ron Price's workplace and gave him a ride to the sheriff's office. In an interview room, they asked Price what he knew about Cesar Barone. The scraggly man lit a cigarette with shaking hands and decided he'd best not try to hide anything. He told them of the arrangement for Barone to move into his house and that his buddy had telephoned him from the jail and asked Ron to drive his Toyota home from the tavern. Price paused, cleared his throat, lit a second cigarette, and tried to look anywhere but at the faces of his interrogators. They waited in silence, staring at him while Price scratched and fumbled, then at last he spoke again. Barone, Ron muttered, had told him to take some items out of the car, including Cesar's pistol, cellular phone, and a knife concealed in the door pocket.

"Did you do it?" O'Connell asked.

"Yeah," Price grunted. He'd taken the 9 mm pistol and the cell phone out of the car and put them in the house, but left a "Rambo"-style knife in the car pocket. To the officers' query about any other knives, Price described a razor-sharp nine-inch blade with a handle of wrapped electrical tape plus a bayonet owned by Cesar.

Mussler asked Price the source of Cesar's income. Crinkling the cellophane covering of his cigarette package and stammering, Price said Barone supposedly worked in a home for elderly people, but it was strange how he never seemed to have to go to work. But oddly enough, he still appeared to have plenty of money. Not long ago, Price said, he'd asked Cesar where he got all the money, to which Cesar replied that he had a bank card he could use to make withdrawals. Ron had chosen not to inquire further, and Barone had volunteered nothing more.

Cesar, Price said, had called again from jail a few days ago, and asked Ron if it was okay for Cesar's lawyer to depend on Ron to testify. Price would be expected to say that Cesar was with him all day during the time Matilda Gardner had been assaulted.

"What did you tell him?" O'Connell asked.

"Well, I hesitated," Price answered, "but I said 'Yeah.' I knew it was a lie though, and I didn't want to do it."

Cesar had a bunch of stuff stored in their garage, Price said, but most of his things were in his bedroom, in the southwest corner of the house.

After they taxied Ron Price back, O'Connell made a call to the bank Joyce Scarbrough had used. He heard from a manager that the spare ATM card had never been recovered.

Working overtime that same Thursday evening, Mussler and Michael O'Connell visited Sheila Hawkins at her apartment. She responded courteously to their questions, describing the relationship with Cesar from the time she met him in June of 1991 when they both worked at the nursing center at Forest Grove. She'd lived with him for several months in the house where Matilda Gardner resided upstairs.

To their questions about the last time she'd talked to Cesar, she described the phone call he'd made to her when he was arrested and how he'd tried so hard to convince her of his innocence. Sheila also told of the message she'd left for him on that Saturday morning, February 13, when he later claimed he'd been "crabbing," and that when he showed up at her place, he was high on "crank."

Regarding Cesar's finances, Sheila readily admitted the recent spending spree at the Beaverton mall.

Back at headquarters, Roger Mussler spent the next couple of hours writing an affidavit for a search warrant to be conducted at the home of Ron Price and Cesar Barone. In the document, he asked for authorization to seize a specific bank ATM card, the knives Ron Price had described, a telephone answering machine on which Sheila Hawkins had left a message, and several guns Cesar Barone professed to own, including a 9 mm Browning semiautomatic pistol.

It was nearly midnight before the two weary detectives rubbed stubbly dark chins, tugged at neckties that had long since been loosened, donned coats over rumpled white shirts, and headed home for the night.

Chapter 15

The sun had been up less than two hours on Friday when
Roger Mussler, Michael O'Connell, and Mark Christy
drove past a turquoise mailbox and a white picket fence
into the driveway of the caramel-colored house in east
Hillsboro. Ron Price tried to force a smile of greeting, but
it was an agonizing effort and not very successful.

They showed him the search warrant signed by a judge,
and entered the house. Clearly, the two tenants hadn't
earned a place on the honor roll of good housekeepers.
Dirty clothes littered the floor, beds appeared to have never
been made up, and food-encrusted dishes filled a soiled
kitchen sink. All three detectives dug in their pockets for
some gloves.

Price, still stammering and hesitant, said he didn't want
Barone's junk in his house anymore. He handed over a
black sheathed filet knife which fit Matilda Gardner's description of the blade Cesar had held to her throat. Asked
about any guns Cesar might have, Price led them to the
Browning 9 mm semiautomatic pistol he'd previously removed from the Toyota at Barone's request. The weapon
was loaded with a clip containing eight bullets. Mark
Christy placed it in a box, along with a Velcro holster.
Price produced two more clips containing eight and thirteen
rounds of ammunition, which the officers also confiscated.
The arsenal of rifles Barone had described could not be
located; he'd either lied about them or they were stored
elsewhere.

In Barone's bedroom, equally messy, the two detectives
located a PhoneMate telephone answering machine. They
also collected his certificate of discharge from the Army
and two bills of sale for vehicles. Other documents they

picked up in the living room included Cesar's petition for name change and his Florida birth certificate listing his name as Adolph Rode.

The warrant also allowed Mussler and O'Connell to search the brown four-door Toyota Barone had been driving, which Price had dutifully driven from the tavern and parked in the driveway. From the car's interior, they seized the black "Rambo"-style knife and a sheath-encased bayonet. In the unattached garage, they found a partial box of .30-06 rifle ammunition.

The detectives had hoped to find Joyce Scarbrough's ATM card, but had no luck.

Accompanied by Sergeant Mark Christy, the officers drove to Cornelius where they showed the filet knife to Matilda Gardner. She affirmed that it was the one Cesar had used to threaten her.

With the eyewitnesses and the evidence the officers had seized, they had enough to nail Barone with the crimes against Matilda Gardner and Sarah Ross. District Attorney Scott Upham agreed and set in motion the procedures for Barone to be indicted.

Even though the search warrant had been served, the investigators hadn't heard the last of Ron Price. Two days after the search of Price's house, Roger Mussler returned to the address to check out a fire department report of arson. The house had indeed been partially burned, but only in a couple of rooms. Mussler called O'Connell to tell him that Ron Price was strongly suspected of torching the place. Not so mysteriously, Price's dogs and several weapons had been removed prior to the fire.

The cabinet shop owner, Andy Tremaine, who'd given Cesar a job several times, had recently been employing Ron Price. Detective Mussler had a few questions for Tremaine. At the shop in Forest Grove, Mussler missed Andy but ran into Mrs. Tremaine. She said she didn't care much for Ron Price or his buddy, Cesar Barone. She told Mussler that Price had divulged to her the subject of a telephone call he'd received from Cesar after the search warrant. Price had been running scared ever since. According to Price's comment to Mrs. Tremaine, Barone had said, "Thanks a lot for giving them my gun. Now I'm going to prison. You better watch your back."

Probing Ron Price's movements and associates, Mussler located a pal of Ron's who was willing to talk. The informant said he'd been out with Price on the same night the house burned, and Price had admitted setting the fire. When the drinking pal had asked Price why he wanted to torch his own house, Ron had mumbled something that sounded like "nobody would ever understand why."

One week after the search, Roger Mussler slapped cuffs on Ron Price's wrists and arrested him on suspicion of first-degree arson.

The 9 mm Browning semiautomatic pistol Mark Christy had taken from Price's house interested Michael O'Connell. Mussler had corroborated Cesar's ownership of the gun by comparing the serial number to a gun registration certificate found in Barone's wallet. Legally, the ex-con from Florida shouldn't even be in possession of a firearm, much less be able to register it. But he'd successfully covered his felonious tracks by changing his name.

O'Connell hadn't forgotten a report from criminalist Chris Johnson, OSP crime lab, who said the cartridges found at the scene where Martha Bryant's Volkswagen had been shot up were from a 9 mm pistol. Johnson had narrowed down the make of a gun to seventeen possible brand names. One of them was the Ruger brand, the same as the gun belonging to Barone. O'Connell arranged to have the weapon hand-carried by property evidence officer Geri Held to the OSP crime lab in Portland.

Another hunch took root in Michael O'Connell's mind. For months he'd been in quest of a pair of Reebok shoes, and had seen only one pair being worn by a young kindergarten teacher. Astonished at how extremely rare the shoes had turned out to be, he didn't know if there was much chance his hunch would pay off, but he had to give it a try. He telephoned Barone's ex-wife, Kathi, who agreed to another interview on March 8. O'Connell slipped a photograph into his pocket. It pictured a pair of Reeboks, the photo he'd personally taken at a shoe supplier's warehouse.

After talking with Kathi for a few minutes, O'Connell pulled the photograph out, handed it to her, and dreading the answer, asked if she'd ever seen any shoes like the ones pictured. She examined the snapshot for a few seconds while O'Connell held his breath.

"Sure," she said. "Cesar owns a pair exactly like that."

The detective had to control a rush of elation. She could be mistaken; it was only a photograph. "Do you know where he obtained them?" O'Connell's voice cracked, but only he could notice it.

"I think he bought them up in Tacoma. I really don't remember whether it was someplace in the Tacoma mall or at the Fort Lewis PX. I'm pretty sure it was one or the other, though."

"What size does your husband, excuse me, your ex-husband wear?"

Kathi suppressed a little laugh at the investigator's slip. "Eight and a half," she said. Another solid hit.

"Do you know if he still has them?" O'Connell realized they'd been separated for more than a year, but he hoped she might know since they had continued to see each other regularly.

"He probably does. He's a real pack rat and never throws anything away." She said she might have a picture of him wearing the shoes. The detective had an urge to slam a fist into his palm and yell "YES!"

She disappeared into another room for a few moments and returned with two photographs. The first one showed Cesar, dressed in jeans and a blue velour long-sleeve shirt, standing in front of a Christmas tree, his outstretched hands holding the paws of a big, black dog stretched upright on its hind legs. Barone wore white sports shoes. Kathi said, "I took this one at Christmas time in 1990."

She handed O'Connell the second photo, depicting Cesar seated on a dark couch, grinning as a toddler takes a step away from him. Again, Cesar is wearing white sports shoes. "That's our son when he was ten months old, in October of '91."

Maybe the shoes were the wrong ones, and maybe the whole thing was a big coincidence, but Michael O'Connell didn't think so. He instantly started forming plans to search Ron Price's charred house again. If Barone was a pack rat, as Kathi said, the shoes might still be there. Of course, it was much more likely that he'd disposed of them if they had, indeed, been worn during the commission of a crime.

In the county jail, Ron Price was separated from Cesar Barone so he faced no danger from his furious ex-roommate. Price would eventually plead guilty to first-degree arson for torching the house he shared with Barone. His attorney, Michael Sahagian, arguing that Price was forced by Barone to burn the house, asked the court for lenience. The judge agreed and ordered Price released after less than one month behind bars. Barone had more important things on his mind, though.

It's a necessity in prison or jail, to establish a place in the pecking order as early as possible. Sometimes, survival depends on status and associations. Barone picked out several fellow inmates whom he though worth impressing.

One of the individuals Barone targeted as a new friend was Troy Masters. Well muscled, "buffed" in prison parlance, with dark hair curling down to his beefy shoulders, he had what might be characterized as rock-star good looks. Outside of jail, Masters acted as a magnet to certain women whose appetite for male companionship tended toward dangerous liaisons. He radiated a powerful energy among men as well. Being in jail was nothing new to Masters. He'd been convicted of burglary and robbery in 1979, first-degree robbery in 1985, and was currently jailed for first-degree theft and delivery of a controlled substance. He knew his way around the prison yards, jail tanks, and among all kinds of convicts.

When he first entered Washington County Jail and landed in C-tank on the second floor, which housed anywhere from sixteen to twenty-four inmates, Masters took a measuring look around to see what it would take to bully the motley collection of men. Accustomed to being a ruler, in the same vein as schoolyard bullies, he demanded to see all of the men's "papers." Each jailed inmate had been given a document containing a brief outline of the reason for his incarceration. In most cases, prisoners prefer to keep that information to themselves. Some crimes are not acceptable in the peculiar moral judgments of men behind bars. It didn't matter to Masters what they wanted, though. His need to know was greater than their need for privacy. He moved with careless ease among the three cells bunking four men each, the two single-man cells, and the "day room" where he "persuaded" each of the inmates to show him their respective documents.

That power appealed to Barone. This was a fellow worth knowing and having on his side. From that first day forward, Barone made it a point to be near Troy Masters as much as possible, and to engage him in conversation whenever he could penetrate the wall of silence Masters usually maintained. He hurried to occupy the space next to Masters during workout or exercise sessions and while they ate their meals. When guards opened the cell doors to let men in C-tank mingle in the "day room," an area equipped with tables, chairs, a wall-mounted television, and a pay phone, Cesar sidled up to Masters as often as he could. Gradually, Cesar began to reveal little secrets about himself and then bigger ones in hopes of impressing this tower of strength.

Barone couldn't spend all of his time with Troy, so he selected the next best man, and worked on ingratiating himself with Dave Sparks, another tattooed con whose presence Cesar found interesting. Figuring that revealing a little about himself would motivate Sparks to do likewise, Barone entertained his new pal with details of his sexual desires and female conquests.

Two more men were chosen by Cesar to hear what he regarded as highly personal and powerful stories. There certainly was no danger in confiding in these men, Barone figured. After all, everyone knows about the inviolable code of conduct among inmates. They all shared in common a dislike for cops and stoolies. To inform on a fellow prisoner was unforgivable and deserving of a broken leg, a shank in the ribs, or worse. So Cesar Barone thought.

There was no doubt in Michael O'Connell's mind that Cesar Barone could be convicted of the assaults on Matilda

Gardner and Sarah Ross. Now the detective had hopes of solving at least a couple of murders, too. The first cracks in the stone wall he'd been battering himself against, along with Tom Robinson, Mark Christy, and a whole team of investigators, had now widened. A couple more breaks just might start an avalanche to bury Cesar Barone.

The phone rang in the sheriff's department office of detective Jeff Martin. An FBI agent told him that a woman named Karen Masters might have some information on a homicide in Washington County. It wasn't a federal case, the agent said, so it should be handled by local law enforcement officers. He gave Martin the woman's phone number. Nothing to be excited about. Routine crank calls came in regularly, but each of them had to be given serious follow-up. Martin punched in the numbers on his telephone keypad and heard a soft voice say hello.

Within a few minutes, Jeff Martin could hardly contain himself while trying to reach Michael O'Connell. The woman's husband, Troy Masters, wanted to talk to a detective about some unsolved murders that a fellow inmate, Cesar Barone, had confessed to committing.

Lunch could wait. At 11:35 A.M., Friday, April 9, 1993, the stone wall broke. O'Connell and Detective Jeff Martin brought Troy Masters from C-tank through some passageways and into a sheriff's office interview room.

Hesitantly at first, Masters said he'd heard an inmate upstairs talking about killing a lady. But it really upset Masters how the guy seemed to enjoy talking about it, and it made Masters sick that the victim was an older lady. Troy said he had a mother, and a grandmother, and he'd be damned furious if anyone molested them. It just wasn't right to pick on elderly women.

Chapter 16

Troy Masters exhibited not the slightest sign of embarrassment or reluctance to tell what he knew about Cesar Barone. There was no unwritten code against informing against a guy who would rape and kill grandmothers. They ranked down there with the sewer rats who abused or killed little kids. All bets were off in those cases. If Cesar thought he was impressing Masters, he'd been way off target. Masters had nothing but loathing for Barone.

O'Connell and Martin let him talk, prompting him with occasional questions. They opened the folder containing the photo laydown and asked Masters to examine it. He pointed to the snapshot occupying the number two position, the picture of Cesar Barone, as the guy who was doing all the bragging about hurting helpless women. The guy must have a screw loose, Masters suggested, and added that he thought Barone might be breaking down emotionally.

When did these conversations take place? O'Connell asked. Masters said most of Cesar's talk had occurred within the last couple of days.

Okay, just what did he tell you about elderly women?

Stroking his chin as if he needed to organize his thoughts, Masters finally said that Barone had spoken of murdering an old lady who lived on a street called "Brentwood, or something like that." And Barone had said he was worried that if the police found out he was the killer, he'd probably get the death penalty. "It wasn't very far from where Barone lived," Masters added.

O'Connell knew exactly the homicide to which Barone must have been referring. He later conferred with Detective Riggleman and Sergeant Robinson, and reached a consensus that it was the murder of Elizabeth Wasson back in September 1992. The poor little woman who'd been a missionary and who trusted everyone. There had been no obvious motive to the killing. She'd lived on Brookwood Avenue, not Brentwood, but that had to be the one Barone had confessed to Masters.

Other than that case, the sleuths asked Masters, had Cesar Barone mentioned any names, of victims?

"Yes," Masters said. "He sure did." He talked a lot about older women, but one of the women he said he killed wasn't that old. He said he "done" that lady, Martha Bryant.

Sometimes, after months of hard work, tracing false leads, driving hundreds of miles, chasing red herrings, endlessly reexamining minuscule bits of evidence, and spending long hours of overtime, the answer comes out with such a flat thud, and so matter-of-factly, it's hard to realize that the solution has finally been revealed. There it was. That simple. Martha Bryant had been murdered six months ago, and every single trail had gone cold. Now, the killer sat up there in C-tank, babbling about it to other inmates. *If Troy Masters could be believed.*

It wouldn't be the first time a prisoner had made up lies to get revenge for some dispute with another inmate. The Bryant murder had captured the imagination of the news media which splashed it across headlines and gave it wide television coverage. If Masters wanted to get Barone in some serious trouble, that's the type of case that would grab a lot of attention. The detectives would have to hear a lot more before they could accept the credence of this sudden revelation. They asked Masters to elaborate.

"Well," Masters said, "He was talking about one evening about how he had—it was late, after midnight, and he was out looking for—I can't remember the term—looking for something to do. And he came across, seen this lady in a Volkswagen, right?, and it was at a traffic light. And the car started driving off, and he hung his gun out the window, bam! bam! bam! shot at the lady's car, shot it all up, poppin' caps, shot her off the road, you know, pulls over right next to her, opens the car up.

"The lady is bleeding out the chest. I guess one of the rounds hit her, went through her, came out the front of her, was bleeding all over. He yanked her out of the car, threw her in [his] backseat. Jesus! And he said he had her pants down and was reaching back, messing with her, touching her and stuff.

"And he said he knew right off, because he could hear by the chest, the sucking chest sound, whoosh, you know—he went into elaborate detail about that, that he couldn't—this is what he said, that he couldn't fuck her. So he drove down further, drove up by some railroad tracks, he said, went down by the airport, Hillsboro airport, pulled her out of the car.

"The lady is still alive, and because she can't get his rocks off, he takes the gun and shoots her in the head and kills her, you know, kills her."

Recalling that witness Gloria Thomas, in her nearby bedroom, had thought she heard two male voices, O'Connell asked if Barone had been by himself on that night.

No, Masters said. There was some guy with him who helped drag that lady out of the Volkswagen. But the informant didn't know the accomplice's name.

So far, Masters's account of the Bryant murder was right on track, but most of it was public information, covered in great depth by the news media. Masters had mentioned only one thing that had been held back from press releases. It had been kept confidential that Martha's pants and underwear had been bunched around her ankles. But Masters hadn't been that specific, saying only that Barone had pulled her pants down in the backseat of his car.

Did he say what kind of a gun he used? The detectives waited, wondering if Masters would know that Bryant's Volkswagen had been punctured repeatedly with a 9 mm weapon, while the coup de grâce to her temple had been executed with a .22 caliber gun.

"Sure," Masters answered. "Barone said he shot the car up with a 9 mm. He bragged about owning a 9 mm Browning semiautomatic."

"Did he say what type of a gun he used to kill her?"

"He told me it was a twenty-two, a Saturday night special. He said the reason why he used that was because . . . a larger caliber, like, blows a hole in them, and a twenty-two will go in and scramble around in your head. Instead of making an exit wound, it will scramble your brains real good."

Both O'Connell and Martin had developed the thick skin necessary for emotional survival among homicide investigators, but this recitation by Masters of what Barone had said reached a new level of skin-crawling cold-bloodedness. Martin asked if Barone had said exactly where the .22 bullet entered the victim's head. Masters said that according to Barone, he'd shot her in the right temple.

No one but the killer or an accomplice could possibly know those details.

Martha Bryant's killer had trapped himself with his own braggadoccio, his own need for acceptance among men he thought were his peers. Big mistake. Troy Masters saw Barone not as a peer, but as a snake at the bottom of the inmate's social scale.

The informant sighed and rubbed his temples as if he'd grown weary. O'Connell and Martin had heard and recorded what they needed, which would provide a foundation from which to build a case of felony murder against Cesar Barone. And best of all, they already had the suspect in custody. It had taken over a half year, but they'd finally breached the dead-end wall. A formidable task still faced them of gathering evidence to corroborate the word of a convicted felon, which most juries would regard with sidelong glances and well-deserved suspicion. So the investigators must find sound supporting evidence. They released Troy Masters back to the jail, reported to WCSO captain Richard Underwood what they'd heard, and then regrouped to formulate a plan of attack to send Cesar Barone to death row.

Captain Underwood listened, maintained the calm dignity befitting his position while controlling his excitement, then telephoned Lieutenant Lila Ashenbrenner at the HPD. They agreed to assemble a joint task force of experienced investigators on Monday morning to probe every detail of the new information.

*   *   *

Michael O'Connell, still at work on Sunday, received a surprise telephone call from Karen Masters, Troy's wife. She said that Troy had heard more from Barone since Friday afternoon, and wanted to talk to O'Connell again. He arranged the meeting for Monday morning.

Over in the second story of the brick building on Second Street and Washington, Tom Robinson got the official notification from Lieutenant Ashenbrenner of the break in the case. In law enforcement circles, very little insider information comes as a surprise, especially something as big as this. Ashenbrenner told Robinson of the developments and that he would be a member of the task force, along with Detective Michael O'Connell, Sergeant Cleo Howell, Sergeant Rick Gordon, Sergeant Mark Christy from Cornelius PD, Detective Scott Ryon, Detective Roger Mussler, and Senior Deputy Larry McKinney. Ashenbrenner smiled and suggested to Robinson that he hurry over to the sheriff's office, where a second interview of Troy Masters was already in progress.

This time joined by Larry McKinney, O'Connell had arranged for Masters to be brought down from the jail again, and seated in the interview room. They turned on the recorder, and let him talk.

Masters said that Cesar Barone had continued his "confidential" revelations over the weekend, during which he'd talked more about killing Martha Bryant, and had revealed some other stuff, too. And another inmate, Dave Sparks, had also heard much of Barone's disclosures.

Picking up where he'd left off on Friday, Masters said that Barone had taken the badly wounded Martha Bryant from the Volkswagen, put her in the backseat of his car, and driven about a half-mile away on a dark street. One of the bullets Barone fired at the VW, according to what Cesar had told Masters, struck her in the back, pierced her body, and came out below her armpit. He pointed on his own body to the wounded areas, just as Barone had demonstrated to him. Masters repeated the previous account about the noise she made as she tried to breathe. The killer had described how her punctured lung resulted in a "sucking" sound. Barone had imitated the sound to Masters, who did his best to re-create it for the detectives.

According to Masters, when Barone reached the dark isolated curve in the deserted road, he braked to a halt and demanded that the victim perform oral sex on him. She couldn't and Barone said that "pissed him off." He killed her out of anger stemming from her failure to sexually accommodate him and because she'd bled profusely in the backseat of his car. He also worried that she probably could have survived the chest wound, and would have been able to identify him. Putting his right index finger to his temple, Masters demonstrated the trajectory of the final shot to Bryant's head, as Barone had shown him.

Just to be certain they had an accurate account of what Barone had revealed to Masters, O'Connell asked what Bryant had been wearing. Masters thought she'd had on "britches or pants," pulled down to her shoetops along with her panties. That was the specific information never released to the press.

Where had he shoved her out of the car? Masters tried to recall the numerical name of the street. It was two-thirty something, but he wasn't positive. Cesar had left her in the middle of a road in an industrial area near some railroad tracks.

Did Barone say what kind of car he drove that night? Masters had the impression it was a blue '74 or '75 Monte Carlo, which caused the detectives to wonder, because that style of car wouldn't fit the witnesses' descriptions. Barone had laughed, Masters said, because the cops were looking for the wrong kind of a car.

What happened to the car? It was left in a restaurant parking lot with the keys in the ignition. Maybe Barone wanted someone to steal it to lead investigators on a wild-goose chase. And on the subject of cars, Masters said, Barone had used a borrowed car once, and a stolen car another time, when he committed murders. The detectives jotted down notes to supplement the tape recording being made of the whole story. They'd get to those other murders a little later, but first they wanted to pin down as many details as possible about the Bryant case.

According to Masters, Barone had told him of working

in a nursing home with a guy named "Len Darrell." Then the informant dropped another bomb, information he'd just learned from Barone over the weekend. "That guy named Darrell," he said, had been with Barone on the night Martha Bryant was killed! He drove the car they used, Masters said, and Barone called him a "punk rocker." "They kidnapped her from the Volkswagen and left fast because they thought someone might see them." A lot of the windows were broken out of the VW, he added, as an afterthought.

Right after Barone had started shooting at the Volkswagen, the car hit the median divider on the four-lane road, Masters said, and then drove off the road, hit a curb which flattened the tire, and came to a halt. The detectives noted two errors in that part of Masters's statement. There was no median divider where the shooting had taken place, and the VW had no flat tire. Those were not devastating inaccuracies, and Masters's remarkable validity with other details made them believe that he was repeating exactly what Barone had said. If there were errors, they were probably Barone's, perhaps deliberate ones.

Masters had heard Cesar make a telephone call from the jail to someone named Ray Cardenas about moving a car before the police could find it. Cardenas, as Masters described him, was a short Puerto Rican who lived in Hillsboro not far from the jail.

Going back to the .22 caliber used in the execution, Masters described how Cesar had laughed about it. A photograph had been released to the press depicting the six types of handguns investigators had narrowed down as similar to the weapon possibly used by Bryant's killer. Barone thought it was hilarious that the gun in the upper right-hand corner of the photo was exactly like the one he'd used.

One thing that had really bothered Masters, he said, was how Barone said it gave him a real "rush" to kill someone, and that he really liked "older women with big tits." Especially repulsive to Masters was Barone's behavior while describing the killings. Cesar had shown signs of becoming sexually aroused, breathing hard and rubbing his genitals.

A mention had been made at the beginning of the inter-

view by Masters of knowing about some "other stuff."
O'Connell asked him about it.

Taking a deep breath, Masters said that Barone had told
him about murdering a young woman named "Chantel" up
on Sunset Highway. The killer had described this victim as
a "mulatto bitch." According to the account Masters had
heard, Barone and "Darrell" both had sex with the woman
and had also forced her to perform oral sex on them. Barone had held a gun with a six-inch barrel, possibly a .45
caliber, to "Chantel's" heart when he demanded the oral
sex. Masters' jaw muscles flexed when he added that Barone had bragged about having forced anal sex with the
victim, too.

Masters didn't hold back on any of the shocking clinical
details. Afterwards, he said, the two men beat her up then
took her up in the woods on the highway, and tossed her
out of the car. They drove away, but Barone ordered his
buddy to turn the car around, and they went back to where
she was. Then Barone put the tip of the gun's barrel under
her chin, and shot her. Barone claimed to Masters that the
shot blew off the top of her head.

The guy who was with Barone, Masters said, the one
named "Darrell" got scared and took off for Seattle after
the New Year's holiday.

Being familiar with the murder of Chantee Woodman,
O'Connell and McKinney knew that the .22 caliber bullet
had never exited the victim's head. For purposes of the
investigation, it didn't matter. They now had a pair of solid
suspects in another unsolved murder, and they knew their
colleague Scott Ryon, a member of the new task force and
the lead investigator in the Woodman case, would be
elated. He, too, had endured the frustration of finding no
usable leads for over three months.

Masters, winding down from the mental stress of repeating the repulsive stories told by Barone, seemed
drained. But the detectives had a few more questions. Were
there any other victims?

"Yeah, I think there were some in Florida," Masters said,
but Barone hadn't given him any details about those. Just
that they were similar crimes, and that Barone was worried
that sooner or later the Florida cops were going to come

after him. And, Masters said, Barone hinted about some similar activities up in Seattle.

While O'Connell and McKinney listened to the portentous litany from Troy Masters, Tom Robinson sat nearby in Captain Underwood's office where he was briefed by Detectives Gordon and Howell. At noon, O'Connell and McKinney came out, gave Robinson a summary of what had taken place that morning, and invited him into the interview room. They rewound the tape recording and played it for Robinson and Masters. At its conclusion, Robinson asked the informant if he would draw a diagram showing his understanding of how Barone had forced Martha Bryant's VW off the road. On a piece of eight and one-half by eleven inch blueline paper, Masters drew a remarkably accurate layout of Cornell Road, and the movement of two cars. He scrawled explanatory notes on it, and handed his finished work to Robinson.

After sending Troy Masters back to his cell, Robinson huddled with the task force members, and they jointly identified the three most important segments of the informant's statement which contained facts never given to the press or public. They were: 1) The exact location of the entry and exit wounds to Martha Bryant's back and chest, 2) The fact that Bryant's pants and panties had been pulled down around her ankles, and 3) The precise location of the head wound and the fact that it was a contact wound.

Robinson and O'Connell took the elevator up to the fourth floor, made their way through a labyrinth of hallways, and entered the corner office of Chief Deputy District Attorney Robert W. Hermann. Dignified, slim at age forty-four, mustachioed, imperturbable, Hermann sat behind his desk with hands interlaced behind his head and listened to two enthusiastic detectives outline the events of the last few days. He nodded his understanding, asked a few questions, and gave them the DA stamp of approval on the case.

At 3:30, Robinson and O'Connell joined six other officers in the first full-fledged meeting of the homicide task force appointed to root out every bit of evidence possible against suspected killer Cesar Barone and his alleged accomplice, whom they knew was Leonard Darcell.

Chapter 17

The already long day still hadn't ended for Tom Robinson, Michael O'Connell, and Mark Christy. While people who worked conventional nine-to-five jobs traded job stresses for the vexation of homeward-bound commuter traffic, the detectives arrived in Cornelius at the apartment of Denise Nichols, Barone's intermittent girlfriend. They glanced a few yards across the parking lot at one of the dwelling units where Betty Williams had died suspiciously. Christy knocked on Nichols's door hoping that she might be able to provide some answers about Cesar's activities, cars, habits, associates, and friends.

The harried blonde looked every bit her thirty-seven years of age that evening. She'd been dreading the arrival of cops ever since Cesar's arrest in February.

Denise invited the pair in, and admitted she and Cesar'd had a sporadic relationship that started in October of the previous year. She'd met him at her place of employment, in the steakhouse restaurant/bar on Baseline Street. It was her impression that he lived alone in the two-story house diagonally across the street. No, she'd never heard of anyone named Darcell; she'd only met one of Cesar's friends, a short guy named Ray. She didn't know much about him except that Cesar said Ray was his best friend. That seemed odd to her, though, because the only time she'd ever spoken to the guy, he acted like he barely knew Cesar. Oh, she said, she'd nearly forgotten another pal of his. When she reported Cesar to the police for stealing things out of her apartment, she'd met that scraggly guy, Ron Price, at a court hearing.

Taking short, quick puffs of her cigarette, and darting her eyes about as if waiting for someone, Denise said she'd often been annoyed at Cesar because he showed up at odd hours of the day or night, with never any warning or prearranged dates.

Trying to recall the various cars he'd driven during their six-month relationship, Denise thought Cesar had a "medium brown big fastback" when they first met. He'd kept it a very short time after that. Robinson and O'Connell exchanged a quick glance, both thinking it could be the suspect vehicle they'd been on the lookout for. But Denise had no idea what Cesar had done with it. On the subject of cars, she suddenly shrugged off her reticence and turned up her volume level several decibels. She complained that Cesar had borrowed her chocolate brown 1969 Mercedes and swindled her out of it. Ron Price had since poured fuel on that fire by informing her that Cesar sold the Mercedes over in St. Helens. On that matter, she planned to sue him in small claims court. Neither detective allowed their inner smiles to show, presuming that small claims court was a tiny pebble in the gravel truck about to run over Cesar Barone.

Cesar frequently showed up in different vehicles, Denise remarked. He'd told her he borrowed some of them, rented others, but she wondered at times if he stole cars when he needed them, and dumped them afterwards. In late 1992, he drove a little white Hyundai, then a "long blue heap," and more recently a brown Toyota.

Where did he work? She wasn't really sure. He'd told her he had a job at Emanuel Hospital, but she'd called there and they'd never heard of him. She was quite sure though, that he had once been employed at a medical care center in Forest View.

Guns? Yeah, she saw him carry a semiautomatic holstered on his waist a few times. That worried her because Cesar had once told her that he was taking a leave from Emanuel Hospital to "kill people." She thought it was some kind of a bizarre joke.

The interview ended with Denise commenting that Cesar had informed her his mother died when he was young and that his father remarried. He made a point of saying how much he disliked his stepmother.

*   *   *

Back in his office the following morning, Robinson embarked on the task of poring through previously accumulated data to see if Cesar Barone's name had turned up and been overlooked during the course of the Bryant investigation.

After an hour of tedious paper flipping, he figured he might as well try the LEDS, Law Enforcement Data System, computerized files. He performed an off-line search, examining records of police activity during the short time period before and after Martha Bryant was killed. Robinson's gaze landed on an item that virtually leaped in blazing color from the pallid data. BINGO! Robinson couldn't believe his eyes. But there it was in beautiful bold print.

An officer of the Forest Grove PD had stopped Cesar Francisco Barone at 0229 hours, in the 2800 block of 19th Street, about thirty minutes before Martha Bryant was shot to death. The license number of the vehicle Barone drove was JLD670, a 1976 Chevrolet. Quickly jotting down the vehicle identification number, Robinson grabbed his copy of a motor vehicle manual and compared the number to those listed in the book. He found that the VIN corresponded to a Chevrolet Chevelle two-door, certainly a vehicle many would call a "muscle car." Robinson also recalled that Gloria Thomas, the witness who'd seen the car from her bedroom, had first guessed the suspect car was a Chevy Chevelle. A quick check with the Department of Motor Vehicles revealed the car was currently owned by a man over in Multnomah County. Robinson called Michael O'Connell with the welcome development.

O'Connell had just disconnected from a conversation with Chris Johnson, the OSP criminalist reporting that he'd completed a ballistic test of the 9 mm Browning pistol delivered to him after the search warrant at Ron Price's house. Good news. He'd compared the test-fired casings with those picked up near the Volkswagen and found identical markings. Cesar Barone's semiautomatic pistol had fired the bullets into the VW.

Now, Robinson's call cinched the noose even tighter. O'Connell telephoned the Forest Grove PD. An officer riffled through some records and found that Officer Todd Stevens had stopped Barone on October 9, last year. Ste-

vens was there, and picked up O'Connell's call. He said
he hadn't forgotten the incident because he'd also arrested
Barone over a year ago for DUI, and remembered him.
Barone's rap sheet indicated he'd been stopped two other
times, in July 1991 while driving a pick up truck, and in
June 1992 on a motorcycle. On that night last October,
Stevens said, Barone was alone and driving somewhat er-
ratically. Stevens pulled him over, observed that Cesar was
nicely dressed in slacks and a dress shirt, and did not slur
his words. Even though Barone admitted having a couple
of drinks, he easily passed the field sobriety test, so Stevens
released him at 0244 hours. Before Cesar drove away, towards
Cornelius, he promised the officer that he was on his way
home. Martha Bryant was shot to death nearly thirty minutes later on 231st Avenue near Cornell Road, a distance
that could easily be driven in ten or fifteen minutes.

The next step was to have a look at the long-sought
"muscle car." Senior Deputy Scott McKinney, who wore a
red beard and mustache, drove to Gresham, in Multnomah
County, with Detective Ryon to check out the automobile's
status. Within two hours, McKinney called in to report that
he and Ryon had located the vehicle which turned out to
be a light brown Chevy Malibu Classic with a white vinyl
landau half-top. They knew enough about cars to realize
that General Motors had used the term Chevelle and Malibu to designate similar body styles.

"Did you find the new owner?" O'Connell asked
McKinney.

"Sure did, and interviewed him, too. He told me he'd
purchased the car last November, on the eighteenth, from
a wholesaler in Portland. And guess what. Not long after
he bought the car, he found a spent bullet casing inside
while he was cleaning it up. Not sure about the caliber,
though. I showed him a 9 mm cartridge and he said it
looked just like the one he found, had the same brass color-
ing." So had the ones picked up at the crime scene. Unfortunately, the new owner of the car had disposed of the
casing he'd found.

When he first got the Chevy, the owner told McKinney,
the backseat looked stained, was covered with dog hair, and
had a terrible odor. He'd vacuumed it out and scrubbed the

seat. O'Connell recalled that Ron Price had some big dogs and figured they were probably the source of the hair.

McKinney hadn't finished his report. He added that he'd contacted the Portland wholesaler, who produced records of having purchased the car from Cesar Barone on November 11, 1992. The efficient McKinney had made arrangements, too, to impound the car and have it towed to Hillsboro. O'Connell congratulated McKinney on a fine piece of work, and called Robinson to set in motion plans for bringing OSP criminalists to town for the purpose of scrutinizing every inch of the muscle car. Robinson, in turn, told McKinney to get a consent agreement from the owner and inform him that he'd be provided with a rental replacement to compensate for the inconvenience. When the man consented, Robinson personally arranged to rent a Pontiac Sunbird and delivered it to the Chevy owner.

While each member of the task force carried out a flurry of activity, another jail inmate brooded night and day, wondering what to do. Dave Sparks had also listened to the repulsive recitals of Cesar Barone, and watched as the man exhibited his sexual excitement while reliving his reign of terror over helpless women. It was more than Sparks could take without reacting. On Wednesday, April 14, he called the sheriff's office.

A sergeant notified Michael O'Connell that Dave Sparks had said it was "imperative" that he talk to the detective immediately. The name rang a bell. Informant Troy Masters had mentioned Sparks as being one of the inmates sought out by Barone.

With the red-bearded McKinney also in attendance, O'Connell brought Sparks to the interview room and asked what was "imperative." Just as his predecessor had done, the wiry inmate acted relieved at being able to unload the burden Barone had placed on him. He found the guy repulsive and didn't want Barone to ever be on the street again where he could attack old ladies. Sparks said Barone had confessed he'd murdered Martha Bryant.

Many of the same details related by Masters were repeated by Sparks. Barone had demonstrated exactly how he pulled his car close to Bryant's, peppered it with 9 mm bullets, forced her off the road, and kidnapped her. He repeated the gruesome account of dragging her into his backseat, driving a short distance, and then crawling back there with the victim where he tried to rape her and force her to perform oral sex on him. Unsuccessful, he told of executing her because she was no longer fit to satisfy his sexual cravings. Then he'd dumped her, still alive, in the middle of the road, with her clothing pulled down so she would be humiliated by being exposed to passersby as she died. Just as Masters had, Sparks drew an accurate diagram of the crime scene, explaining that it was a duplicate of one Barone had demonstrated using pencils and combs to represent the cars. And Sparks re-created how Barone had acted out his delivery of the final gunshot to Bryant's right temple, with the weapon in contact with her skin.

With chilling accuracy, Sparks used his own body to point out the precise locations on Martha where the 9 mm bullet had punctured her back, and exited near her armpit. And the inmate mimicked the "sucking sound" Bryant had made when she tried to breathe with a bullet hole through her lung.

The second murder confession Sparks had heard from Barone involved a girl named "Chantel" whose body he'd dumped on the Sunset Highway. Once more, information never released to the press or public had been revealed by Barone to the informer, including the exact location of the mortal wound under the chin, and the fact that she'd been subjected to both vaginal and anal intercourse prior to her death. Sparks was also able to point out that the body had been discovered close to a guardrail on the shoulder of the road. And, he said, Barone admitted having an accomplice in that caper, a guy named Len Darcell (Sparks had the name right). Someone had helped him in the Bryant killing, too, the informant declared, but Barone hadn't named him.

A new development had virtually ruled out Leonard Darcell as an accomplice in the Bryant murder. The bearded one, Scott McKinney, had traced Darcell's activities and whereabouts during 1992 and made an interesting discovery. Leonard Darcell had been locked up in Multnomah County jail when Martha Bryant was killed. That wasn't the case with the murder of Chantee Woodman,

Adolph "Jimmy" Rode was a darling little boy,
but even at the age of five he already showed
signs of the violent nature that lurked
beneath his charming smile.

Jimmy Rode as a teenager in Florida.

Note the sports shoes Barone (Rode) is wearing in this Christmas photograph. They became important clues in the police investigation of Margaret Schmidt's murder.

After a stint in the same Florida prison as Ted Bundy, Adolph Rode changed his name, married an Oregon woman he met through a personal ad, and moved to the Pacific Northwest to begin a new life — and his own killing spree on Bundy's old hunting grounds.

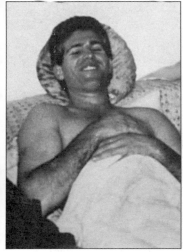

APPROX. ANGLES

1. 45°
2. 50-60°
3. 30-60°
8. 40-45°
9. 35-40°
10. Ricochet below to above

Scenario 1   Scenario 2

Martha Bryant's assailant pumped at least ten bullets
into her car and forced her off the road.

The police con-
ducted an intense
search for this car.
Although the car
had a new owner,
dried blood in the
backseat provided
investigators with
damning evidence.

These Reebok sports shoes, with their distinctive tread pattern, were a key piece of evidence linking Barone to the murder of Margaret Schmidt.

Leonard "Germ" Darcell, Barone's accomplice in the slaying of Chantee Woodman, guided investigators on a chilling tour of murder.

Detective Michael O'Connell, Sergeant Mark Christy,
and Captain Lila Ashenbrenner played key roles
in solving five previously unconnected homicides.

Sergeant Tom Robinson kicked off the
six-month investigation that led to
the arrest of Cesar Barone.

Deputy D.A. Roger Hanlon and Chief Deputy D.A. Bob
Hermann teamed up to prosecute Barone
in two murder trials.

Five murder victims:
(Clockwise from top left)
midwife Martha Bryant,
Margaret Schmidt,
Chantee Woodman,
Alice Stock, and
Betty Williams.

since Darcell had been released by that time. The reliable McKinney had verified with Darcell's probation officer that Leonard had been in the area until a few days after Woodman's body was discovered. If Cesar had told his confidants that Darcell had helped him abduct and kill Bryant, he'd been lying, which raised the uncomfortable specter of lies about other details. That added to the pressure on investigators to produce even more corroborating evidence to separate the facts from Barone's exaggerations or outright lies.

Expecting the account of two murders to end the interview, O'Connell listened carefully as Dave Sparks opened the door to a third homicide, and then a fourth killing. Barone had shared his experience of "doing" an elderly woman who lived not very far away from his own residence, along with his concern that he was going to be caught for it. The only detail he revealed about that one was that the crime scene tape had been up for a long time. O'Connell connected that fact to the murder of Elizabeth Wasson.

The next one was easy to identify. Barone had bragged of killing a helpless elderly woman who used a walker to get around. She had large breasts, Cesar boasted, and he made a big deal about how much that appealed to him. There was no doubt about this victim; it had to be Margaret Schmidt. O'Connell knew every detail of that murder. He'd been searching endlessly for the Reeboks which had left prints in spilled talcum powder. Now, if he could find those shoes among Barone's possessions, the frustrating hunt would finally pay off.

Dave Sparks mentioned that he knew about the house being torched, the one where Cesar had lived with Ron Price. Barone had laughed when he admitted to his cellmates that he'd insisted Price burn the place to destroy any evidence the police hadn't collected when they searched it.

Getting back to the subject of death, Sparks said Barone had talked at length about trying to force a woman to service him sexually when she suddenly keeled over with a heart attack and died. The informant thought it had taken place in Cornelius, but wasn't sure. O'Connell knew for sure, and made a note to relay the information to Sergeant Mark Christy as soon as possible. Christy would be gratified to know that his lingering suspicion that Betty Williams had been murdered could be confirmed.

Barone had told Sparks that he'd forced the victim to sit on the toilet to perform oral sex on him while he stood in front of her. It surprised him, Cesar had said, when she fell over in the bathtub and he figured she must have had a stroke or heart attack, so he left her there, face down in water. Hell, he'd literally scared her to death!

There might even have been a murder that task force members knew nothing about, since it had happened up in Washington. The informant told of Cesar's boast about killing other people, including a female hitchhiker at Fort Lewis. He'd taken her into the woods, he said, and held her there for two weeks before finally killing her.

Sparks emphatically identified Cesar Barone from the laydown of six photographs before he was escorted back to his cell.

While the interview took place in Hillsboro, Tom Robinson had joined OSP criminalists Chris Johnson and Susan Hormann to examine the Chevy Malibu Classic. Large stains on the backseat had been scrubbed, but not before they'd soaked deeply into the cushions. It didn't take long to make a presumptive test which concluded the stains had been made from human blood. Considerably more time would be required to put them through DNA testing in an attempt to determine whose blood it was, if possible.

That afternoon, O'Connell labored over the preparation of another affidavit for a warrant to search the partially burned house again. He couldn't really believe those Reeboks would be there, but he felt compelled to find out. Also, O'Connell wanted to hunt for any bloodstained clothing, .22 caliber pistols, ammunition, the red plaid thermos Chantee Woodman was known to carry plus anything else belonging to her, and a coin-sorting device. Meanwhile, Scott McKinney checked with an officer of the U.S. Army Criminal Investigation command, at Fort Lewis, Washington. The military official tentatively acknowledged that an unsolved murder had taken place there in 1989 and the circumstance seemed similar to those described by the informant. If Cesar Barone had tortured a female hitchhiker and killed her while he was in the Army, he would never be held accountable for it. The murder would remain unsolved.

Tom Robinson contacted the producers for *America's Most Wanted* and suggested they might want to postpone the scheduled broadcast because a possible suspect was in custody. They agreed, and set a new date of May 7 in case it was still needed or to update viewers on the recent events.

The rest of the evening Robinson helped O'Connell prepare the new search warrant.

While waiting for a judge to approve the new warrant, Robinson spent a good portion of Friday trying to find any available information on Ray Cardenas, Barone's Puerto Rican buddy. Two of the informants had mentioned that Cesar called Cardenas and asked him to take the brown Toyota away from Ron Price's house, and make sure the cops couldn't find it. They'd searched it once, and might do it again. Cardenas's house could be seen from the jail cell windows, the informants said, but that may have been more deception on Cesar's part because the investigators couldn't find anyone in the neighborhood who would acknowledge a resident named Ray Cardenas.

Robinson recalled that a personal directory had been found among Barone's possessions during the search. He rushed over to the property room, scanned the listings in the book, and found a telephone number for Ray Cardenas. The person who answered the phone said Ray was in Mexico, but he'd be back in a few days.

A judge signed the new search warrant on Friday afternoon. Each member of the task force agreed to meet early Saturday morning and tackle the dirty job of digging through the partially burned house once occupied by Cesar Barone.

Chapter 18

Seven of the eight task force members, plus an evidence property officer, assembled early Saturday morning to search the scorched house in Hillsboro. If the officers thought they were going to find it empty because of the damage, they were wrong. Ron Price still technically lived there and had occupied the rooms that survived fire damage until his arrest on March 17 for arson.

The team posed outside the house for a photograph taken by Chief DDA Bob Hermann, who also made an early appearance. He had a vested interest in the outcome, since he would handle the prosecution of Barone if enough evidence could be found to charge him with murder. Hermann's colleague, DDA Roger Hanlon, who also expected to be deeply involved, dropped by for a short time.

For the photo, Larry McKinney, grinning through his red beard, sat outdoors in a rocking chair. The others, all wearing casual clothing and holding paper cups of coffee, lined up to face the camera. Tom Robinson laughed. He was the only one who'd dressed in a dark coverall jumpsuit in preparation for the dirty job of pawing through charred rooms and filthy piles of scorched clothing and furniture. Scott Ryon drew the lucky duty of videotaping the project.

They waded in. The kitchen and laundry room had sustained the most fire damage, so there was little to be uncovered in either location, although Roger Mussler did pull a scorched plaid jacket out of the kitchen rubble and toss it into a collection box. McKinney rummaged through the detached garage and located a black leather jacket, apparently the one Cesar often wore. A cache of assorted women's undergarments, out of place in a bachelor house, caught Ryon's attention so he put the video camcorder down long enough to collect them. Confiscated knives and ammunition were placed in another container while a third box soon filled with a mishmash of clothing. The searchers found shoes in every room, some unmatched, some obviously for women, a few sports shoes, and some boots. One of the officers bagged a couple of military-style berets. They also turned up a small hodgepodge of drug paraphernalia, some yearbooks, a Ranger magazine, a pawn ticket for a rifle, silk bed sheets, and a few Mary Kay makeup items. Robinson located a letter from Leonard Darcell to Cesar Barone, establishing the first concrete link between the two men.

The team labored for seven grimy hours collecting 130 varied items of possible evidence. Roger Mussler listed each one on a Washington County Department of Public Safety Property-Evidence Report as the officers bagged and boxed them for easy future identification.

Tom Robinson had a knowing grin on his face when he carried a container outside and set it at the feet of Michael O'Connell. Inside the box, on top of a pile of assorted shoes, rested a pair of well-worn, white, size eight and one-half Reebok ERS running shoes!

After spending a fine spring day sweating, digging, sorting, and lifting, Robinson had planned to finally catch a little rest on Sunday. He shouldn't have answered the phone. It was O'Connell, who had just learned that Sheila Hawkins, Barone's long-time girlfriend, had a sister.

Okay, Robinson said. So what?

Just listen to this, O'Connell replied. That sister had a baby last fall at Tuality Hospital! Could there be a connection to Martha Bryant? Some kind of a revenge factor?

Robinson hurriedly pulled on some work clothes and drove over to meet O'Connell. Together, they went to the hospital and riffled through medical files, looking for anything related to Sheila Hawkins or her sister. It certainly seemed like a good lead, but they found nothing connecting either woman, or the birth, to Martha Bryant. The revenge motive went up in a puff of smoke.

Robinson gave one of his good-natured grins to his long-

time friend, O'Connell, and went home to catch even fewer
hours of rest.

   While the detectives dismissed any possible connection
between Sheila Hawkins's sister and Bryant's death, they
had been on the right track in wondering if there was something more to be heard from Sheila. Early that week,
Hawkins ended a long argument with herself and came to
a decision that there were some troubling thoughts she
should share with Tom Robinson. At her request, Robinson
and O'Connell drove to Sheila's work address where she
was employed as a certified nursing assistant.
   Speaking with soft hesitance, Sheila still wrestled with
the inner turmoil. Her feelings of loyalty to Barone, though
faded, pulled against her sense of moral responsibility to
do the right thing. She edged gradually into her statements
to the officers by treading over ground she'd previously
covered. Sheila said she'd met Cesar Barone nearly one
year ago, in June, when they both worked at a care center
in Forest Grove. Subsequently, they'd both been employees
of another facility for geriatric care in Aloha. She'd lived
with him on and off for a few months.
   The reason she'd called, Sheila finally said, was because
Ron Price had contacted her to state his opinion that Cesar
was probably involved in some of the crimes for which he'd
been arrested. Price had also described Cesar as "panicky"
because the police had confiscated his 9 mm pistol.
   Worse yet, Cesar had telephoned Sheila from the jail,
and said he needed to talk to Price as soon as possible. He
needed Ron to help him set up an alibi for February 13,
at the time Matilda Gardner was sexually assaulted.
   Sheila admitted that she still accepted calls from Cesar
because she felt sorry for him, regardless of her suspicion
that he'd abused her daughter while they lived together.
Maybe he'd been high on "crank" at the time, which Sheila
said he used during their relationship. Her facial expression
and tone of voice gave both detectives the impression that
her relationship with Barone had finally ended. Sheila confirmed it by admitting that she'd been seeing his old buddy,
Ray Cardenas. Ray and Cesar didn't talk to each other any
more, Sheila told them. They couldn't anyway, because Ray

had been in Mexico for a while. She thought he'd be back soon. Cesar, she said, had threatened to kill Cardenas if she went out with him.

Another old associate of Cesar's named Carlos, Sheila said, might know something about the criminal charges. Or perhaps his girlfriend, Norma, would know even more. Norma Thorpe and Carlos Romero had been laying low to avoid any involvement in Cesar's troubles.

The name Carlos Romero was familiar to both detectives. He'd been a local hell-raiser for some time, and had rightfully earned a berth in prison where he currently resided.

Robinson asked if Cesar had ever possessed any guns while he was with Sheila other than the 9 mm pistol. She replied that he did keep a .22 revolver wrapped inside a green glove hidden in the top of the closet. Did she know where Cesar obtained the gun? Hesitating and stammering, Sheila finally spit it out. Carlos Romero had given him the weapon last August. About a month before Romero went to prison, he'd left the .22 with Cesar for safekeeping. Norma had retrieved it in January, four weeks before Cesar was arrested.

Could you give us a description of Norma?

Sure, Sheila said, and gave the detectives a detailed word picture that included height, weight, hair tint, eye color, and types of clothing Norma wore, specifics that a man would probably have overlooked. Sheila paused, pursed her lips and focused her gaze directly into Robinson's eyes, signaling her intent to expose a secret, and then spoke. Cesar had confided in Norma that he'd been with that woman, Betty Williams, the night she died of a heart attack! He was in her apartment until past midnight, and saw her dead. Cesar admitted that he was "partying with Betty" prior to her death.

Having opened the floodgates, Sheila had even more to reveal abut her ex-lover. She believed he had sexually fondled an elderly woman at a care center in Forest View, and she recalled an incident where he put a washcloth in a lady's mouth. The poor old woman was a patient in the Alzheimer's ward. Sheila felt sure that Cesar had sexually abused that woman, too, but said it had never been reported because of the victim's mental disabilities.

At the end of the session, Sheila gave the officers Norma Thorpe's address. They thanked her for her cooperation, and drove away in the direction of Norma's Forest Grove apartment.

Robinson and O'Connell caught Norma at home, completely off guard and reluctant to speak with them, or to let them in. They managed to get a few answers from her through a narrow gap in the door she held part way open. Yes, Carlos Romero had requested that she pick up his revolver from Cesar last January, and she had done as he asked. She had left it at his mother's house.

A quick trip to the home of Carlos Romero's mother paid no dividends. She positively had never seen any gun that belonged to Carlos.

Back at his office, Robinson followed up on another item in his daily reminder list. He telephoned Karen Masters, the wife of informant Troy Masters. In Troy's statement to the detectives, he'd made a reference to some notes he'd been keeping on Cesar and that he'd given to Karen. Robinson wanted to know where the notes were. Karen admitted that Troy planned to write a book about Barone so he'd jotted down a lot of the information Cesar had passed on to him. Barone scared the hell out of her though, she said. In fear of retribution from him if he ever got out of jail, she'd destroyed all of Troy's notes.

Still thinking about the medical records he and O'Connell had dug through on Sunday regarding Sheila Hawkins's sister, Tom Robinson telephoned the woman at her home. He wanted to know what date she'd gone to Tuality Hospital to have her baby. She told Robinson she'd been in the hospital in the first week of December 1992, and had returned on three consecutive days to visit her infant child. Sheila and Cesar had accompanied her there each time.

There might still be more to learn from her sister, Robinson thought, so he and Cleo Howell dropped by the woman's house that afternoon. The sister divulged that Sheila had still been married when she started dating Cesar and had left her husband because of the romance with Barone.

Had the sister heard from Cesar since he was arrested? Yes, she groaned. He'd attempted to telephone her just last night, collect, a dozen times but she'd refused to accept the calls. She'd made intense efforts to get Sheila "straight" about Cesar, trying to convince her that Barone was not a good person, but her pleas had been ignored. Cesar had given Sheila several gifts, including a gold bracelet and a porcelain cat, all of which the sister felt sure he had stolen.

Because the woman seemed to know a lot about Cesar, Robinson asked if she had any idea who else he might try to call. She had an immediate answer. In her opinion, Barone would try to contact Carlos's girlfriend, Norma. Carlos, she said, had been Barone's cocaine supplier and had lived with Cesar for a short time over in Cornelius.

How do you know Carlos supplied the cocaine?

"Leonard Darcell told me," she said.

It was time for Robinson to pay a visit to Carlos Romero down in Salem, at the Oregon State Prison. The convict, age thirty-two, shuffled out to the visiting room dressed in prison blues. He acknowledged that he'd known Cesar Barone for about a year and a half. They'd been occasional drinking buddies and had some drug connections in common. Robinson already knew that Romero had been convicted of possessing and selling drugs which landed him in the graybar hotel. Did you ever give Cesar a gun? Sure, Carlos admitted. He'd given him a little .22 back in August. It was really Norma's gun, he said. Robinson would be able to confirm that very shortly, he figured, since Norma had coincidentally decided to visit on the same day, and sat out in the waiting room at that very moment.

Exceptionally cooperative, Romero told Robinson he would instruct Norma to turn the gun over to the police. He also promised that she'd be waiting for him with it in Forest Grove that same evening.

Had Romero instructed Norma to pick up the revolver from Barone? Yes, he had, he said. He'd wanted her to give the weapon to his mom to use for self-protection, but

Norma had never delivered it there. She'd kept it for herself.

At Robinson's request, Carlos described the gun. It was a small blued revolver, a Saturday night special with a set of white grips, and it fired .22 caliber short rounds. Robinson showed him the photographic layout of six guns that had been reproduced in several newspapers, the same photo Cesar had reportedly laughed about because the one in the upper right corner was exactly like the one he'd used to kill Martha Bryant. Romero pointed to the one in the upper right corner, and said it was a perfect copy of his revolver.

Do you know of any other guns Cesar owned or used? Yeah, man. He had that old 9 mm semiautomatic. He used to carry it with him most of the time.

Asked about other associates of Cesar's, Romero mentioned Ray Cardenas, and described him as a sharp dresser who sometimes wore boots.

A cloud seemed to pass over Romero as he fidgeted, paused, and wrinkled his forehead. He expressed hope that Robinson wouldn't divulge where he'd obtained all this information. He didn't want to be labeled as an informer. "A snitch jacket," he said, "is a very dangerous situation in prison."

On his return trip to Hillsboro, Robinson stopped to make a phone call. Concerned that Norma might race back to her place, change her mind about giving up the gun, and dispose of it, Robinson called O'Connell and arranged for him to be there waiting for Norma. The plan worked. O'Connell had the little .22 in his possession within the hour. It was an exact duplicate of the one in the photograph.

So far, with the concurrence of the sheriff and police chief, Robinson and O'Connell had not informed the news media that Cesar Barone was a suspect in the unsolved murders. As is often the case when a big story is brewing, a leak developed somewhere. On Friday, April 23, a Portland television reporter showed up saying she had obtained information from an anonymous source regarding a "secret investigation." She knew that Cesar Barone was in jail and that he was suspected of the Martha Bryant murder, plus some other crimes.

District Attorney Scott Upham explained to the reporter that splashing the details of the investigation all over the media might seriously compromise portions of it. Certain key people might vanish, and evidence could be destroyed. He urged her not to go public yet. The lid stayed on for four more days.

Chapter 19

Wayne Fallon looked forward to transferring out of the Washington County jail, down to the Mill Creek correctional facility five miles south of Salem. Housing only 229 minimum-custody inmates on a 2,000-acre working dairy farm, where they could take advantage of outdoor job-training opportunities, the facility would be a welcome change to Fallon. Wiry, twenty-two years old, and sick of the company in jail, Fallon hadn't been able to shake the knot festering his stomach during the last four weeks. Maybe it would ease up in another environment. But probably not.

When his girlfriend came to visit, and detected his discomfort, he told her of the tension and disgust he'd been feeling. She suggested it might be cathartic to talk to some official about it. Her advice usually turned out to be pretty good, and the idea grew more appealing to him every time he looked at the man who had caused it. Why had he had the misfortune of landing in C-tank at the same time as Cesar Barone?

From the first instant Fallon met Barone, sparks flew. And then when he heard from other inmates that Cesar was charged with rape, Fallon looked at Barone the way a lion watches a hyena. Regardless of his loathing, though, he would have done nothing except keep his distance if Barone had just kept his mouth shut.

By the last week of April, Wayne Fallon made his decision. He'd repeat to the cops every repulsive act Barone had described. This wasn't like squealing, it was more like stepping on a poisonous spider.

Accompanied by Sergeant Mark Christy, Michael O'Connell flipped on a tape recorder in the sheriff's interview room on April 28, a few minutes after nine in the morning. After noting the reason for the meeting and the names of the three men present, O'Connell asked for Fallon's address. The nervous inmate spoke with the speed of a running chain saw, and O'Connell had to interrupt. "Okay, talk a little slower because they have to type this out." Fallon did his best to slow down and speak clearly.

For the record, O'Connell verified Fallon's reason for wanting to meet with the investigators; he'd had knowledge about some murders. Fallon nodded and Christy reminded him that the tape recorder needed audible voices.

O'Connell also wanted it clear that whatever Fallon had to say couldn't be rehashed information he'd read in a newspaper or seen on television. He got the inmate's agreement that whatever information he would reveal was independent of anything he'd learned via the news media. If Fallon was going to talk about Cesar Barone, it probably would not have been from the news, O'Connell noted. There'd been only a brief local article speculating about some "new leads" in the case and a report that *America's Most Wanted* had filmed a re-creation of the crime. Barone's name had not been mentioned publicly.

As the detective had anticipated, Fallon said he'd been in jail with a group of men that included a guy named Cesar Barone. "I met him like, uh, March twenty-seventh. I went to jail and they put me in C Block, and that's where he was at." Again, the detective asked Fallon to slow down and speak clearly. "Okay. I ended up talking to him. I took a pillow out of the cell he was stayin' in, from this kid that was in there and Cesar came over and confronted me about it."

"Do you know the kid's name you took the pillow from?"

"No. I don't remember his name. But Cesar confronted me and I made a statement to him and told him not to talk to me like I was some kind of a punk, and he cringed down and wanted to shake my hand."

"That's how it got started?"

"Yeah. And then, the next day at breakfast time, I found out he's in there for rape." Fallon screwed up his face like a child who'd said a dirty word. "Then, anyhow, he came up to me and started talking. He was telling me he was in there for rape and that he was being investigated for multiple murders. As a serial killer."

"Did he talk about any specific homicide?"

"Uh, he started telling me about one where he was, him and a friend was over in southeast Portland partyin' and they left the place and picked up this girl out of a parking lot, took her out on Highway 26 and shot her after he molested her, I guess, in the backseat of the car while the other person was driving it."

"After who molested her?"

"Uhm, Cesar Barone."

"Did he say where on Highway 26?"

"No, he didn't. He just said he dumped her off up there. Somewhere up by Banks."

"Okay, and did he tell you that he killed her?"

"Yes."

"And how did he kill her?"

"He stuck a forty-four underneath her chin and shot straight up."

His information about the size of the weapon was inaccurate. Both O'Connell and Christy knew that the autopsy had revealed the murder weapon in the Woodman case was a .22 caliber firearm. But they were also well aware that a killer bragging about his feats might tend to exaggerate the size of the gun, perhaps wanting to make it sound more macho. "Did he demonstrate this to you?" O'Connell asked.

"Yeah."

"I know this won't show up on tape, but can you describe it to me and then we'll kind of narrate it? How did he demonstrate it to you?"

"He was just showing me how he put the gun underneath her chin and shot up in the air and it picked her up like, you know, off the ground."

Trying to create a visual image from the words, O'Connell said, "You just actually touched your finger to your chin to demonstrate?" Fallon agreed. "Okay, so he puts the gun under her chin. And did he describe the person who was with him?"

"No, no, he said—" Fallon struggled to remember, clapping an open palm to his forehead and deepening the crease between his eyebrows. "Well, he said—he told me the name, but I don't recall the name." Fallon added that he thought the guy might be someone he already knew.

"From where?"

"From MacLaren [correctional institution], I just remembered, well he mentioned the name to me, and I remembered it in the back of my mind, and it came back to me that I knew he was in MacLaren. I think that's where I knew him from."

"How would you describe him?"

"Oh, a couple of years younger than me, brownish-blond hair, kinda' scraggly and dresses rocker, punk rock." The description fit some of Leonard Darcell's features. Old arrest photos of Darcell showed him with long dark hair, but punkers often chopped their locks into bizarre styles and bleached all or part of it. Darcell was actually one year older than Fallon.

"So you and Barone had some conflict?"

"We kept getting in arguments, little arguments, and he came in the cell one day and says, you know, 'I could kill you like I do the rest of the people.'" According to Fallon, he'd paid little attention to the threat, whereupon Barone began trying to impress him by claiming to be under investigation for serial killing. Barone had smirked at Fallon, scoffing at the charges, asserting that there was no evidence against him. Fallon quoted Barone: "They ain't got the guns."

"Did Barone talk to you about any other murders?"

"Uhmm, yeah, he told me that he got into this old lady's house and had her in the bathroom and he was molesting her from behind and had her bent over and, uh, she had a heart attack—" Fallon began to mumble while Mark Christy tried to hear every word. This might be more confirmation he needed to verify that Betty Williams had been murdered. "—and so he filled the bathtub up and put her in it to make it look like she drowned." Fallon didn't know where it had happened.

"Did he say whether or not he knew her?"

"No."

Trying to word his question as tactfully as possible,

O'Connell asked, "Uh, did he—I don't want you to be embarrassed because we're on tape, I want you to try and re-create as best as possible the words he used. You used the term molest. Did he say molest?"

"No."

"What did he say?"

With a red face, Fallon described specific sex acts that ended when the victim had a heart attack.

Christy held his breath. On the next question could pivot the whole issue of consensual sex or rape, thus murder. O'Connell articulated every word. "Did he tell you she was doing this willingly or did he tell you he was forcing her to do it?"

"Forcing her." Christy exhaled. Fallon could recall no other details, such as the use of a weapon, the woman's description or name, the date of the incident, or even the name of the town where it had occurred.

"Did he tell you about any other murders?"

Not directly, Fallon said. But one day Barone was in his own cell talking to Troy Masters and Fallon had wandered in. "He's talking to him, in his cell and I walked in there and he was crouched down on the end of his bed describing how he shot this Volkswagen off the road with a 30-round clip of an Uzi twenty-two, and then, uh, shot her with a nine millimeter in the side, in the back left-hand side." Both detectives recognized Fallon's confusion about the weapons.

"Did he actually point out where she was hit?"

"Ya, ya." Pointing to his lower left rib cage, Fallon raised his voice. "He said he shot her right here in this area. And then, uh, he told her to get the fuck out of the car." Quoting Barone again: "You bitch, get in my car."

O'Connell hoped to clarify the weapons used. "Let's back up a little. What kind of gun did he use to wound her in the side?"

"A nine millimeter." Now Fallon was closer to the known facts.

After going over again what Barone had said to the victim, Fallon said, "And then she got in his [car] and he says he stuck a twenty-two pistol to her temple and shot her."

"Okay, when he demonstrated that, did he hold his hand

away or did he point with his hand touching her temple?"
Fallon formed his hand into the shape of a pistol, placed it
against his temple and spoke into the microphone to describe his actions.

To the officer's questions, Fallon reiterated that the conversation took place between Barone and Masters, with
Barone doing all the talking while Fallon listened. Another
inmate may have joined them for a while, he said.

"What else did Barone say?"

Again, Fallon hesitated, seeming reluctant. "He said he
likes big tits and when he, when he talked about women
with big tits he gets an erection and he starts touching himself on his private parts."

"Even in front of other inmates?"

"Yes."

"Did he masturbate in front of people?"

"Nah, but went in to take a shower. And I think he was
in there doing it."

"Was there anything else he did along those lines?"

Fallon's face flushed, not embarrassed, but angry. "He
said that if a woman can get him off he'd let her live after
he beat her, but if she couldn't get him off, that he'd kill
her."

Psychologists might say that Barone showed classic symptoms of hating women in general. One of the detectives
asked Fallon if Cesar had expressed such hate to him. He
hadn't, Fallon said, but he suspected that was the case. He
explained why. ". . . Cuz' his mother—cuz' he stated a few
times he hated his mom, he didn't like her and that if she
was alive, he'd kill her again."

"Okay, he would actually say 'again'?"

"Yeah."

"Would you describe him as normal, sexually, or
strange? Or how would you describe him?"

"As an individual if you don't know his—his dark parts,
you know, I describe him as an average Joe citizen."

"But after hearing all those conversations, how would
you describe him?"

"A pretty sick person." This from a twenty-two-year-old
inmate who'd been circulating among some violent, tough
company.

"What about his mood when he said those things? Did he appear remorseful and depressed?"

"No, he'd laugh. He was like totally calm and with no regret, you know, he wouldn't, his body wouldn't get tense or nothin'. He'd like really get into the story like it was some kind of a book he was reading."

"And at times, it's accurate to say at times he would become sexually excited?"

"Ya, yes."

"When he talked about killing the midwife, did he say he did it alone, or did he say someone was with him?"

"No, he didn't state—he just said 'I did.' " The implication was clear, Fallon said, that Barone had acted alone.

O'Connell shifted the subject to the Woodman murder, wanting to know Barone's version of how the "kid" with him had acted. Fallon said, "The kid, he just freaked out, from what Cesar was telling me. And then Cesar just pulled the gun over and looked at him and said, 'It could be you next.' "

The subject of the interview shifted to Barone's behavior while locked up in C-tank. Fallon said that Barone had a concealed "shank," or homemade knife.

"Where did that come from?"

"I think it came off his bunk," Fallon said. The officers knew how inmates sometimes could twist off a metal brace from the bunk, sharpen it by grinding it on the concrete floor or wall, forging it into a dangerous weapon. "He hid it up behind the TV and he told Troy Masters that he was gonna kill somebody with it. I think he meant me because we did have, uh, conflicts. One time he . . . had it wrapped up in a T-shirt and he put it down in the right-hand side of his pants. And he came walking towards me, but nothing ever happened."

"Did Masters ever tell you that Barone meant to harm you with the shank?"

"No. Troy just came up to me and told me that Cesar had a shank, but . . . that was after he walked toward me with it." Fallon speculated that Barone's action was meant to be a warning.

"Did he ever mention anything about Florida?"

"He said he did some time down there on attempted

murders. I think he said he got a pardon and he met Ted Bundy while he was down there and he thought that was really neat. He got out and joined the military for a few years. He said his uncle had gotten killed, so he went and killed a family of four over it."

"Was the family supposed to have killed his uncle?"

"Yeah."

"Did you believe everything he told you, or were there times when you thought he might be lying?"

"I didn't doubt anything he said."

"Why is that?"

"Because I just couldn't see how somebody could just come up with something like that, or even want to claim something like that." Most of the conversations, he said, were relatively short and took place "after snacks" at ten or ten-thirty at night.

Asked if Barone was trying to impress Fallon, the informant said no, it was more like intimidation.

The officers spent the next few minutes recapping parts of Fallon's statements. Fallon remembered one other thing he thought might be important. About the midwife, he recalled, "Barone said he'd met her before."

"Did he say where or how?"

"He just said he met her for a few minutes, like ten minutes." Fallon couldn't recall where it had taken place.

The interview ended with Fallon's acknowledgment that the officers had made no threats or promises, that his statements were voluntary and freely given.

Since the name Leonard Darcell had emerged, members of the task force had been on the lookout for him. They'd heard that he had left Oregon and headed up to Seattle. No one in Washington County had seen him for three months or more. He'd vanished from all of his known haunts, and investigators were beginning to wonder if his dead body would turn up in the forest along Sunset Highway.

The search for Darnell came to an abrupt halt in the latter half of April. The fugitive turned himself in to Clackamas County officials for violating his parole. He'd been convicted in 1992 on drug possession charges in Multnomah County, then later in Washington County for failure to appear in court after being cited for driving with a suspended license. During the first three months of 1993, he had failed to report to his parole officer. Clackamas authorities had locked Darcell up pending hearings to ship him to the state prison in Salem to serve out his sentence.

Detective Scott Ryon and Larry McKinney hurried over to the neighboring county jail and met Leonard Darcell in an interview room. Clad in orange coveralls and begging for a cigarette, Darcell trembled nervously. Ryon asked him about his activities in the last week of December. Darcell became evasive, mumbling nonsense. The two officers stood, turned toward the exit, and took a couple of steps when Darcell stopped them.

"Hold on a minute, guys," Darcell said, loud and clear. "I'm going to tell you something that will probably change the rest of my life."

Chapter 20

"I never thought Cesar would do anything like that," Len Darcell moaned to McKinney and Ryon, as he described the abject terror inflicted on Chantee Woodman on the last night of her life. Calling the victim Chantel instead of Chantee, Darcell told how he and Barone had picked her up in Portland and taken her to Cornelius. "She willingly had sex with me," Darnell claimed, which had made Barone angry, so he raped her. No, Darcell said, he hadn't actually witnessed the rape because Cesar took her in another room, but he'd heard the noises in there, and Barone had later confirmed it with his repugnant descriptions of what he'd done to the girl. Darcell told of his pleas to Barone to put "Chantel" out somewhere along the highway and leave her alive. But Cesar had shot her anyway. "Cesar was standing above her with the pistol and he was grinning." Barone had even taken the bullet casing out of the .22 revolver and handed it to Darcell as a souvenir. "Man, I didn't want that, so I threw it on top of the shed back at the place where we lived."

Woodman was not the first girl they picked up that night, Darcell volunteered. Just a short time before they met Woodman, a teenager with orange-red slicked-back hair also had accepted a ride in Cesar's car with them. Barone had tried to force her into a sexual act by threatening her with the revolver pointed at her head. Darcell gave the officers a detailed description of the weapon. The girl was really lucky because, according to Darcell, he had convinced Cesar to relent and drop her off at a fast food restaurant parking lot close to the girl's house.

After Barone shot "Chantel" and left her up there beside the highway, as Darcell reported it, Cesar had threatened his life. So he'd pretended to go along with Cesar's celebration of the crime, then hightailed it out of Oregon as soon as he could. He'd been hiding out up in Seattle, but he realized he'd finally be caught, so he came back and turned himself in.

Before they left, Ryon and McKinney convinced Darcell to accept a ride with them, scheduled in a few days, to point out what had happened and exactly where the sordid events had taken place.

In Cornelius, before the sun dropped over the western hills, Ryon and Sergeant Mark Christy greeted Matilda Gardner who had finally moved to the lower floor where Barone had lived. They asked her permission to look on the top of an attached shed. Of course it's okay, she said. Christy held the base of a ladder while Ryon climbed to the shed's roof. There, he carefully lifted a tarnished bullet casing and dropped it into an evidence bag.

With the second suspect now in custody, Michael O'Connell prepared another affidavit for a warrant to collect blood and hair samples from both men. In his summary of the facts, O'Connell pointed out that Leonard Darcell had been Barone's roommate in Cornelius, as verified by a rental agreement investigators had found. He described Darcell as having the appearance consistent with a person who leads a "punk rock" lifestyle, and that the suspect had a reputation of being a "gutter punk" and a probable skinhead gang member.

O'Connell, along with Tom Robinson, served the approved warrant on April 23, and collected blood and saliva, along with pubic hair and head hair samples.

That same afternoon, O'Connell learned that Ray Cardenas was back in town, and had returned to his job at a Hillsboro auction business. O'Connell hustled over, found Cardenas at work, and arranged to interview him. Sitting in the detective's car, Cardenas chatted amiably, recalling a New Year's weekend trip to Mount Hood and the Timberline Lodge with Cesar Barone where they'd met a couple of girls. He'd known Barone for quite a while, he said.

O'Connell asked, "Have you ever been with Cesar Barone when he hurt someone?"

"No," Cardenas answered emphatically. But he did wonder if Cesar had killed a woman. Explaining that statement, Cardenas said that one night in the previous October, he'd picked Cesar up after work, and they'd gone to a couple of bars in Beaverton. He recalled that one of the nightspots had country-western music. When the place closed, they started towards home, and about two-thirty in the morning a cop pulled them over. Cardenas was driving his black Mazda with no license plate, and figured he'd get a ticket for sure. But the officer just warned him, and let him go without a citation. Relieved, he took Cesar straight to his house, then made a beeline for home and went to bed.

A day or two later, he heard about the murder of Martha Bryant. Thinking back, he realized that it was the same night he and Cesar had been together. He wondered if Barone had done it.

The irony struck O'Connell. Apparently, Barone had been stopped twice that night by traffic officers. Once with Ray Cardenas, and once by himself in Forest Grove. But he'd still evidently chased down Martha Bryant's Volkswagen, shot it full of holes, then abducted and killed her.

One thing still troubled the detective. A couple of residents close to the VW scene had thought they heard two men speaking. Martha was known to have a very low, husky voice. So maybe there were two men present, or maybe her voice had been mistaken for a second man at the scene. Barone's buddy, Len Darcell, couldn't have been there, he was in jail at the time. Could Ray Cardenas be lying about leaving Barone and rushing home to his bed? Had he actually helped abduct Bryant?

"Would you come in to the sheriff's office and take a polygraph test?" O'Connell asked. It caught him by surprise when Cardenas readily agreed to do so.

Two days later, Ray Cardenas kept his appointment. O'Connell first asked him the same questions they'd discussed in the car, only this time with a tape recorder running. Then the detective turned Cardenas over to a polygraph examiner.

After an extensive session, in which Cardenas answered

questions designed to reveal whether he was withholding
any information or if he was present when Martha Bryant
died, the examiner said there was no indication that Cardenas had lied. He'd passed the test and was free to go, no
longer considered a serious suspect in the ongoing
investigation.

While one possible suspect was cleared, the evidence
against Barone continued to pile up. Criminalist Chris
Johnson had conducted tests on the .22 caliber revolver
Carlos Romero gave to Barone, which had been recovered
from Romero's girlfriend, Norma. Johnson reported that
he'd swabbed the inside of the barrel and found crusts of
blood in there. Apparently, it had been fired while in such
tight, close contact with a victim that blood had exploded
right back into the barrel. Johnson said he was sending the
tiny specimens he'd taken from the gun for DNA testing
and comparison with samples taken from Martha Bryant.

With the blessing of DA Scott Upham and Chief DDA
Bob Hermann, O'Connell and Robinson marched into the
jail at one-forty-five on the afternoon of Thursday, April
29, 1993, and announced to Cesar Barone that he was
charged with the aggravated murder of Martha Bryant.
Lieutenant Lila Ashenbrenner accompanied them. She
later commented, "I just wanted to see the look on his face
when it happened."

A few minutes later they attended a press conference to
let the news media reporters in on the events. Lieutenant
Ashenbrenner handed out the news release, which read:

"A Washington County grand jury handed down indict-
ments of four counts of aggravated murder against Cesar
Francesco Barone, aged 32, in the October 9, 1992, homicide of Martha Browning Bryant, age 42." The bulletin
named the task force members and summarized high points
of the investigation. It thanked Intel Corporation for providing a computer used to manage the data related to the
case, and made reference to other murders. "The task force
initially focused on the Bryant slaying but is also investigating the murder in April of 1991 of Margaret Schmidt, age
62, of Hillsboro and the September 1992 murder of Eliza-

beth Wasson, age 83, of Hillsboro. Both women were found slain in their bedrooms."

The public's help was solicited in regard to information about Barone's activities and vehicles. The press release also commented that "information about the identity of the second suspect believed to be involved in the Bryant slaying is still being sought. The maximum penalty for aggravated murder is the death penalty. The state will be seeking that punishment."

The task force, minus Tom Robinson, gathered in a conference room for a group photo, then spoke to reporters. "We had tons of leads," O'Connell said, "but they all led nowhere. It was very frustrating." He acknowledged that Sergeant Mark Cristy of the Cornelius PD had gathered enough evidence to arrest Cesar Barone on charges of sexual assault, after which new developments started pointing the team in the right direction. Referring to Barone, O'Connell commented, "We obtained information that clearly indicated we had to focus on this guy as a possible suspect."

Captain Dick Underwood, chief of the sheriff's detective division, credited O'Connell with contributing crucial footwork in the case. "He's the one who really did some serious digging and made the connections that put it together and got all the rest of us to jump on the bandwagon." O'Connell shook his head, and pointed to the detectives and officers making up the whole task force. "It truly was a team effort. Everybody had a little piece of the puzzle as it turned out."

While handing out the well-earned praise, neither Underwood nor HPD Police Chief Ron Louie gave the reporters many details regarding the evidence collected. Mention was made of the 9 mm pistol, but little else. Underwood explained, "We aren't just being secretive. If we give out anything prematurely, it could hurt us. People could disappear, witnesses can get scared, the public gets scared. We've just hit the tip of this thing and it's going to get bigger. It's a very involved case. The investigation may go on for months . . . It's a lot more involved that I can tell you about now."

He may not have realized exactly how profound his statement would turn out to be.

Lieutenant Ashenbrenner published another news release on the following day. "Task force investigators are renewing their request for information about the activities of Chantee Woodman whose body was found alongside Highway 26 on December 30, 1992. Authorities are seeking any witnesses who may have seen Woodman picked up near the Satyricon nightclub in N.W. Portland December 29." Following a description of Chantee, the bulletin added, "In connection with Woodman's murder investigators are seeking the identity and location of another woman detectives believe may have critical information about this case. The woman may have accepted a ride home from the Pioneer Square area late that same evening. She was driven in a white Hyundai to a parking lot near the Hawthorn bridge where a handgun was pointed at her head. About midnight she was dropped off at a fast food restaurant at S.E. 50th and Powell in Portland. The woman is described as approximately 16 years of age, with short bright red-orange hair worn slicked back in a punk style . . ." The document ended with a phone number to be called by anyone who might have helpful information.

Now, members of the task force could just hope that a sixteen-year-old "punk"-style girl would read a daily newspaper and recognize herself in the story. Not too likely.

You can't please some people. When the Chevrolet Chevelle, sought by investigators for months, finally turned up, it became necessary to impound the car to be searched for evidence. In an extremely courteous gesture, Tom Robinson didn't want to inconvenience the new owner, so he arranged to provide him with a rental car. Subsequently, with the financial help of the Hillsboro chamber of commerce, Robinson purchased the auto from the owner so it could be retained as evidence. It could have been confiscated outright, but that didn't fit Robinson's sense of fair play. The fairness went unappreciated. The man who sold it to the HPD didn't bother to return the rental car even after he'd been paid for the Chevrolet. Robinson repeatedly contacted the man, who kept promising to return it, and kept breaking those promises. Now the man and the car had vanished. As if Robinson didn't have enough to do tracking down killers, he had to spend unnecessary hours chasing the inconsiderate recipient of some very nice treatment, and trying to locate the missing rental car.

Finally, the Portland police rounded up the missing man and seized the filthy, battered car. The user had driven it nearly a thousand miles, then trashed it. Robinson personally cleaned it up before returning it to the agency. The rental company also demonstrated admirable generosity by not charging the HPD for damages. His patience exhausted, Robinson filed charges against the unappreciative man who'd abused the courtesy of a very considerate public servant.

Returning to the routine grind of digging for facts and evidence, Tom Robinson took a call from a neighbor of the late Joyce Scarbrough, Kathi's mother. The woman recalled that in the last two weeks of October 1992, she'd looked out her windows and seen Cesar Barone in a Chevrolet Chevelle. It was odd, she thought, that he parked about a block from the Scarbrough home. A short, "Hispanic-looking" man was with him. Both of them acted sneaky and strange, the tipster thought.

Robinson dutifully made a note of the report, expecting a flood of them now that the news had splashed the case all over front pages and television screens. Everyone would probably recall having some real or imagined past contact with Barone. Robinson could only hope that some of the tips would lead to hard evidence.

The arrest photo of Barone had been shown on evening television news, and it prompted an interesting call to Detective Jeff Martin on the last day of April. Debbie Duran-Snell, who had assisted Martha Bryant with "catching" babies, told Martin that she'd watched the Channel 2 news the previous night. She'd recognized that man, Cesar Barone, whom they'd shown as a suspect in Bryant's murder. Just three nights before Martha was killed, Duran-Snell told the officer, she had been terrified by a man she saw outside the hospital, standing in the parking lot and staring at her. He'd followed her as she drove her van along Cornell Road, and he had turned away in another direction only after she'd stopped next to another car. Detective Martin agreed to meet Duran-Snell to verify her identification of Barone.

He showed her the six-pak laydown of photos, and Debbie took only ten seconds to pick out picture number two. She shouted, "That's him," fingering Barone as the man who had menaced her that night. She told Martin that when she watched the program the previous night and spotted Barone, she'd stiffened in rage and terror. Her husband had immediately noticed the drastic change in her "body language."

The producers of *America's Most Wanted* still felt it would be worthwhile to air the show profiling the Bryant murder, but with some modifications. It should contain updates about the arrest of Cesar Barone and a request for public help in cementing the case against him. Tom Robinson and Michael O'Connell could write the new addendum to the script and Robinson would read it in front of television cameras. They put their heads together on Saturday, May 1, and knocked out the words Tom would deliver. They were:

"Local publicity generated by *America's Most Wanted* filming of the reenactment of the murder of Martha Bryant was a significant factor in renewing public interest in solving this puzzling murder.

"Important new information was received from the public after *America's Most Wanted* filmed this last February in Hillsboro.

"This new information gave detectives the vital piece of information needed to identify a suspect in the murder of nurse-midwife Martha Bryant. After the identity of the suspect was known, detectives were successful in finding the 1976 Chevrolet Chevelle believed driven by Barone during the kidnaping and murder of Martha Bryant. Detectives have also recovered both murder weapons, a 9 mm semiautomatic pistol and a .22 revolver.

"A Washington County grand jury indicted Cesar Francesco Barone on April twenty-ninth for the aggravated murder of nurse-midwife Martha Bryant.

"America's Most Wanted really works."

The show's anchor, John Walsh, would announce a "Call to Action," and say, "Detectives are currently focusing their investigation towards determining if Cesar Francesco Barone may be a suspect in other unsolved murders in the Northwest.

"Detectives have determined Cesar Francesco Barone moved to the Northwest from Florida in 1987. While in Florida he was known as Adolph James Rode. Barone is also believed to have used other names. Detectives are asking the public's help in determining Cesar Francesco Barone's, travels, activities, addresses, vehicles, employment, and associates since 1987."

Producers arranged for an Oregon freelance team to videotape Tom Robinson, seated outside on a chair in front of the Washington County courthouse, reading his script. The video photographers also were shepherded into the warehouse in which the Chevette was stored to tape some shots. Officers took extra precaution to be sure that no one made physical contact with the vehicle, which could give defense attorneys an excuse to exclude the car from being used as evidence. The new tape was sent overnight to the show's central studio in Washington, D.C., to be combined with the original footage shot previously. It would hit the airwaves on Friday night, May 7.

On Monday morning it was back to business with the daily task force meeting. The team set seventeen priorities, among which were:

—try to suppress a legal motion by the news media to unseal search warrant affidavits
—locate the "redhead" in Portland who accepted a ride with Darcell and Barone before Woodman was raped and killed.
—offer a reward for recovery of the .22 caliber weapon used in the Woodman killing

—interview any other jail inmates who might have had
contact with Barone.

The "redhead" turned up sooner than expected. Detective Scott Ryon listened on the phone as an excited man
who'd read the newspaper described a young woman he'd
seen get off a Portland bus. She "exactly" matched the
description of the girl police sought. Ryon asked where the
bus had deposited the young woman, scribbled the information down, and grinned as he dropped the note on Michael
O'Connell's desk.

With the help of the Portland PD, Ryon parked at the
corner bus stop the tipster had indicated, and began the
pavement-pounding, door-knocking labor of inquiring at
each house, in all directions. Sometimes it pays off, more
often it doesn't. Luck is often a by-product of hard work,
and it came in abundance to Scott Ryon. A surprised
woman who stood staring from her doorway at Ryon acknowledged that her daughter, Heather, matched the description. Somehow, she had missed the newspaper
coverage. Yes, Heather was at home, and would talk to
them.

Within the hour, Ryon had heard a vivid narrative of
Heather Crane's harrowing experience on a stormy night
in Old Town, including portrayals of "Germ" and his scary
buddy, "Cesar." The girl also provided a detailed description of the Western-style, long-barreled gun Cesar had
pointed at her. She had no trouble recognizing, from photo
laydowns, pictures of Cesar Barone and Leonard "Germ"
Darcell.

Now, if they could just find that damned gun. All the
descriptions and stories were helpful, but physical evidence
usually carries the day in murder trials.

Chapter 21

Lieutentant Ashenbrenner, along with her counterpart from the sheriff's office, Arlene Wittmayer, threw a stone at two birds on Tuesday, May 4, with another new release. The top priority was to find the .22 caliber weapon used to kill Chantee Woodman. Leonard Darcell's description of it would help, and they had the distorted slug taken from the victim's head. Now they needed the actual gun. The next chore was to request news media representatives to walk a tightrope between helping with public appeals, while not pressuring too much for information that might hinder the investigation. Ashenbrenner handed out the document which stated:

"Washington County Task Force investigators need the public's help in locating a handgun believed to be involved in the death of Chantee Woodman, whose body was found alongside Highway 26 on December 30.

"The handgun is described as a Ruger revolver with a shiny stainless steel finish. It is believed to be a model KNR-6 commonly referred to as a "single-six." The weapon has interchangeable cylinders and can fire .22 or .22 magnum caliber rounds. It is a traditional Western-style configuration with wooden grips and a six-inch barrel."

In the last paragraph, the bulletin appealed to reporters. "Media inquiries to investigators slow and inhibit the investigation. We appreciate the keen interest this case has generated but we will need to release future information in the form of written press releases. Please direct any further press inquiries to the above-listed public information officers."

Another woman who'd been exposed to the crescendo of news reports wanted to talk to Tom Robinson. He kept an appointment with her at a Carrows restaurant in Tigard. Choking back tears, she told him that she'd filed a missing person report on her forty-four-old boyfriend who ran a construction company. He'd vanished on April 20 after receiving some telephone threats. They'd been together for two and a half years, she sobbed, and she was pretty sure he'd been an informant for the DEA. A burglar had stolen all of his belongings and papers after he disappeared.

A picture took form in Robinson's mind in which she was probably the victim of a very devious con game. He cleared his throat in an attempt to coax her to get to the point, but didn't voice his question. What did this have to do with the Bryant case?

Well, she said, she'd been snooping around in her lover's vacant construction office, and she'd found a copy of the *Oregonian* newspaper dated March 18 which contained an article on the murder of Martha Bryant. Since the expansion of additional news coverage on the case, she'd figured out that Cesar Barone may have kidnapped her man to hold him for ransom, or something like that.

Had she ever met or heard of Barone before? No. Had her boyfriend ever mentioned the name? No.

As the conversation progressed, Robinson learned from her that the missing man had cleared out the faltering business' bank accounts before his mysterious disappearance. The sympathetic officer tactfully suggested to the whimpering woman that she'd possibly been deceived by her absent lover. Robinson tried to console her before he excused himself, but knew that he left behind a bewildered and disillusioned woman.

The next development sounded far more promising, so Michael O'Connell rode along with Robinson. They visited the stepfather of a man reportedly acquainted with Barone, and who had been employed at the same cabinet shop. Even more interesting, the caller stated that some guns had been stolen from him.

The middle-aged man told the officers that he'd questioned his stepson, who had denied any involvement with the murder of the nurse-midwife. The boy had a drug problem, said the distressed stepfather, and might have stolen

the guns to pay off a dealer. Responding to Robinson's
request for some details about the weapons, the man described two big rifles and two handguns. The latter included
a .45 caliber six-shot revolver and a .45 caliber pistol. No
.22s involved.

Twice the tipster had transported his wayward stepson
to the address on 224th Street where Barone lived, thus
his concern that his stepson might be involved in Barone's
alleged crimes.

Later, when the stepson came home, the officers questioned him. Yeah, he'd worked with Cesar and "partied"
with him both in Cornelius and over at Ron Price's house.
They drank beer together and played pool. Cesar, he said,
liked talking about his Army experience and some drug
deals he'd made back in Florida. And the speaker had often
seen the 9 mm pistol Cesar usually carried with him in a
holster underneath his coat. One night, he said, they went
to a strip bar in Portland, the Calico Cat, and Cesar carried
the hidden gun into the place. That was late in December,
during that big snowstorm. No, the stepson said, he'd never
seen a Ruger .22 in Cesar's or Ron's possession.

Asked what he was doing on the night of October 8–9,
1992, the stepson said he couldn't remember. He'd been
unemployed at the time, and the days just ran together in
his memory.

While the connection to Cesar Barone at first sounded
like it had potential interest, neither Robinson nor O'Connell could see any link to the murder investigation. They
had both developed extraordinarily accurate intuitions and
could usually recognize when someone was lying, or when
a hunch needed to be followed. This guy wasn't involved
in the murders. They knew that they'd followed just one
more fork in the stream that went dry.

The partially burned house where Barone had lived with
Ron Price was finally vacated and the owner considered
the advisability of trying to repair it or simply demolish it.
He was leaning toward the latter alternative. Tom Robinson got wind of it and decided to have another look
around the property. Hoping to find a .22 used to kill
Chantee Woodman, Robinson drove to the address once
more and joined a demolition crew inspecting the grounds.

Even though Scott Ryon had used a metal detector during the last search warrant, it still seemed feasible to Robinson that they may have overlooked it somewhere. Kicking through overgrown grass and trash surrounding the charred house, he noticed a vent tube for the septic tank. It looked big enough to drop a handgun into, where it could slip down and be lost in the muck below. Not a pleasant thought, but certainly a possibility. The demolition crew chief wanted to help, and told Robinson that when they started the job, they'd keep their eyes open for the missing gun.

His workday had nearly ended when Robinson received a call that offered another prospect for finding the Western-style Ruger .22 revolver. A detective from the Regional Organized Crime and Narcotics (ROCN) team told Robinson of a confidential reliable informant, called a CRI by officers. The guy might have some helpful information. The CRI had been associating with Troy Masters, Barone's cellmate, and had heard Masters speak of the murder confessions by Barone.

Robinson mentioned that it would be very helpful if the guy had any scoop on a missing Ruger .22 revolver. The officer checked with his CRI, and told Robinson that the man said he was present when Karen Masters had exploded in fury at her husband Troy because he'd sold a .22 stainless steel revolver for drug money. She had insisted that Troy get the gun back, which he did. The CRI nosed around and found out the gun was currently stored in a locked cabinet owned by a heroin addict friend of Masters.

Once again, though, Robinson's hopes for finding the missing .22 revolver were dashed when the weapon described by the CRI turned out to be the wrong one.

The first legal skirmishes that would eventually develop into a full-scale war of litigation ignited in early May. Defense attorney Keith Rogers represented Barone on the burglary and sex offenses, while attorneys Griffith Steinke and Laura Graser had been appointed on April 30 to represent him on the murder charges. The latter two immediately sent letters to the DA and to the sheriff conveying the wish that their client have no further conversations with "the State."

Barone, though, decided to take some independent action without bothering to inform his legal counsel. He wanted to complain about an allegation that one of the cops had released his family's phone number and address to the press. The accusation turned out to be untrue, but Cesar wanted to make his complaint known, so he wrote a "kite," a letter from prison, and managed to have it delivered to the sheriff.

In the first paragraph, Barone accused the officer, then proceeded to express his grievance:

> "I am not guilty of any crimes, Sir. My family and I are both afraid that the people who really committed this crime are free at this time, and therefore a threat to my family's well being. Especially to those people who are too ignorant to see if a person is really guilty of a crime or not before they pass judgment, just because the press splashes you across the news.
> "Sir, I would like to know what recourse I can take to ensure my loved ones' well being."
> > Thank you,
> > Cesar F. Barone
> > F Block

Because Barone had initiated the complaint, Michael O'Connell and Larry McKinney walked to his cell door and spoke to him through the bars about the accusation. In a conversation that lasted maybe two or three minutes, Barone reiterated his complaint, expressed his anger about the breach of confidence, and growled that the house where he used to live with Ron Price had been "firebombed."

O'Connell reminded Barone that he and McKinney were detectives, so if he wanted to talk, they'd have to reinform him of his Miranda rights. They read the universally familiar words to him, and he said he understood. That accomplished, O'Connell asked him a few questions about the issue, said he'd look into it, and the two investigators departed.

The traditional stuff hit the fan. His lawyers filed a complaint with the court that Barone's Miranda rights had been violated when the detectives talked to the defendant with no defense attorney present. The court heard oral arguments and agreed with the defense.

DDA Roger Hanlon prepared a written motion requesting the court to reverse its preliminary findings. In the document, Hanlon defined the issue in the form of a question: "Were the statements by the defendant on May 5, 1993, to Detective O'Connell freely and voluntarily made after an intelligent, knowing and voluntary waiver of his state and federal constitutional rights?"

Barone, Hanlon argued, knew from years of experience about his rights to counsel during any discussion with law enforcement officials. Not only that, but O'Connell had spelled them out again. "It is undisputed in this case that [Barone] initiated contact by sending out a 'kite,' " Hanlon wrote. "When a defendant initiates a discussion, as here, it must also appear that defendant intended to waive his right to counsel."

Hanlon's persuasive presentation at least resulted in the judge taking the matter under consideration. It wasn't a pivotal issue that would determine Barone's guilt or innocence, just a warning shot of the artillery barrage that would be coming soon.

The more important hearing came on Tuesday, May 11, when the grand jury handed down a second indictment, this one charging Cesar Barone with first-degree murder in the death of Chantee Woodman. If he could be convicted, he'd be eligible for the death penalty since the charge also accused him of trying to rape her and of killing her to prevent the possibility of her ever identifying him. In speaking with reporters about the indictment, DA Scott Upham chose not to divulge the name of Barone's "associate," the man alleged to be with Barone the night they'd picked up the redhaired girl. Upham said, "The matter of the accomplice, if any, is still under consideration by this grand jury." The newshounds did, however, wheedle an acknowledgment from investigators that Barone "is still a person of interest" in some unsolved murders of elderly women in the county.

*   *   *

Barone's defense attorneys may have convinced him to keep his mouth shut around investigators, but he seemed unable to apply the advice to conversation with his fellow inmates. Another informant came forward to express his outrage. His buddy had been Barone's cellmate, he said, and had passed on to him some "sickening" confessions about "numerous murders and rapes" Cesar had committed.

The informant's pal had observed Barone during a telecast of breaking news on April 28. Cesar, he said, became excited talking about the news story which told of his being indicted for murder. Then, Barone had decided to entertain his cellmate with a vivid account of his adventures: He said he lived on the same block as an "older woman." Even though he was living with his girlfriend, he reportedly said, he went over to the woman's apartment and "partied with her." After leaving for a while, he went back and she died of asphyxiation. There was something in his story about a bathtub, according to the informant.

The deplorable confessions from Barone made the cellmate's "skin crawl." Barone had exhibited the same kind of excitement, the informant thought, when the newscaster mentioned a woman named Schmidt.

The task force reviewed the informant's statement, and while it helped convince them that Barone was guilty of serial murder, the details were not specific enough to be used as evidence. They were also second-hand hearsay, which no judge would allow a jury to hear.

It would be far more helpful if an informant would cite particulars which could be corroborated by physical evidence.

That help came in the person of Leonard Benjamin Darcell III on May 11, 1993.

Darcell had earlier accepted the offer of Scott Ryon and Larry McKinney to take a ride and talk about the death of Chantee Woodman. Wearing a jail-issue orange jumpsuit and shiny, stainless steel handcuffs, Darcell crawled into the passenger seat of an unmarked car, driven by Ryon, with McKinney in the backseat accompanied by Alan Watson, and a video camera. The whole session would be recorded.

With Darcell nervously chain-smoking and verbally sketching the hours leading up to meeting Chantee Woodman, the foursome motored to Portland and pulled over to the curb close to the Satyricon nightclub. Darcell finished his narrative about the "redhead girl" who lucked out when Cesar dropped her off in a parking lot.

Stammering, yet trying to use his most impressive vocabulary, Darcell described the rainy night, how he'd seen Woodman, whom he would continually call "Chantel," sitting at a bus stop being approached by a black guy. After he'd rescued her from the stranger, he said, she accepted his invitation for a ride and hopped into the passenger seat beside Cesar. Some of the details were foggy to Darcell, he explained, because he'd been drinking beer all evening. His voice took on the whiny twang of a man in trouble.

Referring to picking up women, McKinney asked, "Do you do this a lot?"

"Yeah. I'm a good Samaritan."

"Did you point a gun at her?"

"NO!" with a disgusted sound.

"Did Barone point a gun at her?"

"No." Not quite so resolute this time.

"What happened when she got in the car?"

"She asked us to take her home."

Waffling about the seating arrangement in the Hyundai that night, Darcell couldn't be positive if Woodman was in the front seat, or backseat. He also began expressing doubt about which of the two men convinced Woodman to get into the car.

Ryon and McKinney had seen this type of behavior before. Cons tried it all the time—trying to paint a fuzzy, blurred picture so they couldn't be pinned to their own statements in court.

"Okay, let's start over. Was she in the nightclub or outside of it?"

"The Satyricon was dead, man, and it was dead on the streets." Finally, Darcell said she was outside.

"What was her condition?"

"She appeared intoxicated. She was walking—odd, real loose in her conversation, really friendly, you know."

"Was her voice slurred?"

"I don't think so."

"But you think she was drunk?"

"Yeah." He recalled her getting into the Hyundai and giving them directions to where she lived.

Ryon started the car again with Darcell pointing the way, trying to guide the detectives through the same route he and Barone had used that night. After several wrong turns, Darcell admitted his confusion. Even for a sober motorist, in full daylight, Portland is not the easiest city in which to drive. One-way streets can destroy plans to circle a block, other thoroughfares are for buses only, and the angle of all the streets where they intersect with Burnside can vex the best of drivers.

Darcell spoke of his fear of being stopped by a cop and busted for his parole violation. That's what occupied his mind while Barone drove that night, he said, not in which direction they were moving. And they never got to her house. Instead, she'd accepted their invitation to go to a party.

Over the western hills of Portland, where upscale mansions occupy the view sites, Ryon blended into traffic on Highway 26. Ten miles later he exited at Cornell Road and headed toward Hillsboro. Darcell recalled Barone pointing out a video store where he had spent time as a kid. Still not sure of the exact route they'd taken, Darcell did recall being on 209th Street and going through Hillsboro. He said, "We went from Portland to Cornelius, about an hour. She knew we were going to Cornelius." When it became obvious to the officers that Barone hadn't used the most direct route, McKinney asked, "Were you trying to keep her from knowing the route you were taking?"

With exaggerated sarcasm, and perhaps trying to convince the authority figures in the car that he was not a "gutter punk," Darcell replied at the top of his vocabulary level. "Given my enhanced enlightenment of the situation today, that's very possibly a possibility." He should have stopped there, but he had to go a little over the top. "I was—very low capacity. I wasn't thinking at all. My thoughts had no conjecture."

Not impressed, McKinney asked again if Darcell had seen Barone threaten Woodman with a gun. "No," Darcell snapped. "I never saw him point the gun at her in the car." He added, though, that he had seen Barone flash the gun when they first walked into the house.

"Was she still drunk?"

"She had three or four beers in the car, but I wasn't counting. I don't count how many drinks other people have unless I'm drinking with heavy drinkers and I'm trying to make sure they don't get more than me." His attempt at humor failed to tickle any funny bones.

Trying to recall just how much beer all three of them had consumed, Darcell said that Cesar had bought a case and that about half of it had been consumed by the time they reached Cornelius. "I was death-drinking that night," he said, and explained, "what that means, it means I keep drinking until I pass out."

Scott Ryon shook his head, and drove through the western city limits of Hillsboro toward the Cornelius house where Barone had shared quarters with Darcell.

The detectives were anxious to hear Darcell's version of how Chantee Woodman had endured the last night of her life.

Chapter 22

Scott Ryon steered into the driveway of the two-story house where Barone and Darcell had lived. Because Matilda Gardner now occupied the ground floor there, and the officers did not wish to bother her, they didn't plan to go inside. Instead, they would sit in the car and listen to Darcell verbally take them through the sordid events of those early morning hours of the previous December.

Darcell resumed his narrative after a period of thoughtful silence. "Me and Chantel headed for the kitchen. I saw Cesar remove the gun from his pocket then go in the bedroom. I thought he was putting it away."

Darcell and Woodman had rummaged through the kitchen in search of something to eat. Cesar joined them, carrying the gun in his hand. "We sat down at a table and he shoved it over to me. I just shoved it right back. I didn't want it."

"Why did you think he wanted you to take it?"

"I don't know. It gave me a slight cause to be alarmed."

McKinney spoke up. "You told me you'd had an argument with Cesar, something about backing his play." Darcell said that had happened before they met Woodman.

Ryon asked, "What did you think was going to happen to that girl?"

"Nuttin'," Darcell sulked. With the exception of a tendency to whine, he was generally articulate, but kept pronouncing the word nothing as "nuttin'."

From the backseat came the impatient voice of McKinney. "Don't tell us that, Len—"

Darcell interrupted in a loud, rapid volley. "I didn't know Cesar was going to shoot that girl. I was cocky. . . .

It was none of my doing, man. I wouldn't back Cesar doing that shit."

"You did back him."

Darcell became sullen. He lit another cigarette, grumbling, "I didn't back him."

"You're the one who made a suggestion to take her to Jones Creek," McKinney said, reminding Darcell of a comment he'd made earlier.

"Yeah," Darcell said, again swallowing his words, "after he told us he was going . . . we're talking about peace, love . . ." he drifted off to an inaudible groan. The cops weren't buying his drama, so he spoke out loud again. "Hey, but I wouldn't back my own father's play . . ."

"You knew what it meant when he shoved that gun at you," Ryon barked.

"I didn't want nuttin' to do with that gun."

"Own up to it. Don't lie . . . Was Cesar challenging you?"

"Maybe. I brushed it off, shined him on."

Silence filled the car. Darcell knew he needed to take another tack. He changed the subject back to the first girl Cesar had menaced that night. "After we dropped off the redhead, I told him off. I said we were friends, but don't ever do that again. That's crazy. I was pissed off."

Returning the focus to Woodman, McKinney asked, "So you had sex with her?"

"Yeah, in the back room with no windows. Let's go inside," Darcell challenged. "I'll show you everything."

"No," McKinney barked, unequivocal, leaving no room for argument. The officers had seen the interior and refused to risk upsetting Matilda Gardner any more. She'd endured enough. Darcell sulked for a moment, then spoke again. During the sex with Woodman, he recalled, Barone came into the room. "Yeah, he started talking shit, didn't think it was very fair. It was his money, his beer, his house. He griped that I was being rude and out of line for making off with the girl."

"You knew Cesar was getting weird. You knew what happened with the redhead. How could you have sex with Chantel?"

Darcell sniffed, took a deep drag from his cigarette. "It

didn't start out that way. I didn't have sex planned. We were just talking and listening to the radio. I wanted to crash. And I wanted her to sleep in the same bed with me. I knew she was getting freaked about Cesar, 'cause I was . . ."

"Why not take her out of there?"

Sounding impatient, Darcell snorted, "Where would we go?" He took a couple of deep breaths, looked out at free people driving by on a nice spring day, and brought himself back to his own dismal reality. "So, we laid down, crashed. I wish I wouldn't have had sex with her. It was the misunderstanding of the century, man, of my life."

"You said she didn't want you touching her breasts, and her leg hurt?"

"Yeah, and she said she was tired, too."

Incredulous, McKinney asked, "And now she feels like sex?"

"Guess so."

"Doesn't that seem odd to you?"

"Yes and no. I've had some weird experiences right here in this house."

"Did she ask you to protect her?"

Darcell thought about that one for a moment. "She asked if Cesar was all there. Then she kept on kissing me back." Recalling that he'd been in a fight two days before they went searching for women in Portland, and probably didn't look exactly like Sir Galahad that night, he hastened to add, "I still had a black eye, some stitches."

"You told us a while ago that she said she didn't feel like having sex."

"I know, but we kept kissing. She gave me the typical excuses, said she had a headache, and was tired. You hear that all the time, especially when you have sex with a lot of girls you meet the same day."

The autopsy of Woodman's body had revealed she'd been anally penetrated. One of the officers asked Darnell if he'd had anal sex with her. "No," he said, "just straight vaginal sex in the missionary position. She just laid there and let it happen. It got real hot under the sleeping bag. But she was real dry. She was breathing hard, and stuff. I asked her if she was all right. I had this other girlfriend who was always dry, even when super turned on."

"How did you convince her to have sex with you?"

"It wasn't real hard. I didn't have to twist her arm."

"She didn't fight you off?"

"Nah."

"What happened when you finished with her?"

"Cesar came back in. I got up for a smoke. We had our shirts back on. We were sittin' on the bed, and he came in and started going on about it was really unfair."

"Did he have the gun?"

"No."

"Did he act angry?"

"Yes, really angry."

"You sure he didn't have the gun?"

"I'm not sure. Maybe he had it on and off." All three of them returned to the kitchen, Darcell said. "Cesar grabbed her in the kitchen and Chantel got really upset. She was crying and saying 'No.' She said she wanted to go home, and acted real scared. Anyone would have been. I started losing faith in my ability to control Cesar."

Had Darcell started to sober up and realize the danger? "No, that started earlier, when Cesar said he wanted to have sex with her."

"Then what happened?"

"I think it must have been about five or six in the morning. I told her, 'Okay, I'll take you to Portland, when the bus starts to run.' She said she didn't have bus fare. I was tired and didn't want to go to Portland. I'd just had sex and wanted to go to sleep."

"So what did she do?"

"I tried to get her to go to bed to get some sleep, but she wanted to go home. I offered her a couple of dollars and told her the bus stop was right over there." He pointed across the street. "The bus might have been running by then. But she didn't want to go by herself. It made me feel obligated to take her home. I got dressed, and asked Cesar for the keys 'cause I didn't want to hassle with a bus."

McKinney frowned, wondering why Darcell would gamble on driving forty miles while still drunk and why he'd take a chance insulting Cesar by asking to use his car to take the woman away from him. "Did you see the risk there?"

"Yeah," Darcell groaned. He needed a break, some time to organize his thoughts. He announced an urgent need to use a restroom. The officers recognized the ploy and ignored it, so Darcell resumed his narration. "Cesar said I was really rude. Chantel picked up her thermos bottle, she was dressed by then, like she was going to leave. Then Cesar got us backed up to the counter. That's when he had the pistol in his hand. He started arguing about it was his gas, and he was footin' the bill, that I was rude. He said she should be nice to him. He kinda' said it to me, for her benefit."

Darcell's speech picked up speed, became more agitated. "I argued with him, and told him he was way out of line. I'd never said that to Cesar before, but I was standing up to him. We were getting ready to fight, getting to the point where my brain short-circuited, getting pissed off, getting close to my temper where I stop thinking. Then, all of a sudden, I reminded myself that he had a gun in his hand. I'm getting ready to kick him in the nuts, take out his knees or sumpin'."

Pausing to take a breath and light up another cigarette, Darcell again looked longingly out the window at cars zipping by, people going where they wanted to go. Freedom he'd now give anything to have again. Brought out of his reverie by a question from the backseat, Darcell spoke again. "I tell him she's not going to have sex with him. Then Chantel put her hand on my arm, tells me to be cool, everything's going to be all right. She said, 'This has happened to me before.' Cesar said she was being smart."

Chagrin darkened Darcell's face. He said that Cesar and Chantel walked out of the kitchen toward his bedroom and Cesar was gloating. "They go into the corner bedroom, where Cesar slept. I followed as far as the living room. She said nuttin', just walked with him. He had the gun in his hand. There wasn't any door to his room, just a blanket nailed over the archway."

McKinney asked if Darcell could see what took place in there. No, he said, but he could hear it when the girl hollered, "Take it easy," and sounded exasperated. "I sat in a chair next to the TV, and there was like a Nintendo game on." He'd tried to concentrate on that instead of the noise coming from the bedroom. "It bothered me a lot, it was grossly wrong."

"Why didn't you stop it? You said at one point he left the gun on the table where you could pick it up. That's why your fingerprints might be on it. So why didn't you pick it up and stop him?"

Darcell denied having said those words. "Nah. I don't recall that."

"Was there a telephone there?"

"Sure. Two or three of them."

"Did you think she was being raped?"

"Yeah."

"You didn't call 911 to report it?"

"I wish I would have."

"Were you backing Cesar's play?"

Darcell raised his voice again. *"No.* I was wanted. I was concerned for my own safety. Where would I go. The cops all knew me."

"So what happened?"

"I couldn't handle it. I went to the other bedroom, then to the kitchen. Straightened up, did the dishes. Just put stuff away."

Silence loomed inside the car. All three officers had heard rationalizations during their careers, but this one made their jaws flex. This guy is hearing the rape of a woman. He professes to be concerned about her welfare. And he's cleaning up the kitchen? One of them asked, "Were you still living there then?" Darcell said he wasn't, and blithely continued, claiming he picked up the beer cans and kept himself occupied.

"Could you still hear noises from the bedroom?"

He could hear something, Darcell muttered, but the noises were "more relaxed." It seemed to be over, finished. Cesar's voice still sounded like he was "gloating," saying "I knew you'd see it my way." Chantel lifted the blanket hanging over the bedroom entry, and came out with Barone behind her. Cesar said, "It's all cool now. I'll take her home."

Expressing indignation, Darcell said, "I grabbed my

leather jacket. Cesar wanted me to stay there and said he would take her to Portland. I wanted to go with them." He claimed he planned to see that she suffered no more harm. As they left, Cesar pulled on a pair of driving gloves.

"Did Cesar have a gun in his hand? You told me before that he had a gun in her back."

"Yeah. As we came out of the house, he grabbed her by the hair. He told her to close her eyes, he'd guide her to the car." According to Darcell, Cesar didn't want the woman to be able to describe the house, which could barely be seen in the predawn, cloudy darkness. "He kept referring to 'us guys' like I'm backing his play, but if I had, I would have stayed in the house. I didn't want to let them out of my sight. I wanted to make sure she made it to Portland." They all climbed in the Hyundai, Darcell said. He sat in the rear seat again. Cesar backed the car out and then turned west instead of toward Portland. "I thought, *wait a minute*. I hoped maybe he was going to the 7-Eleven for some cigarettes or something."

Darcell had reached the point in his story where Barone had driven away from the house, so Ryon again started the unmarked car and drove westward, asking Darcell to direct him along the same route Cesar had used that night. But Darcell again expressed confusion about the exact roads. He did recall, though, that Cesar had the gun poked in Chantel's ribs while he drove. They stopped at a red traffic signal, he said, and Cesar threatened her by saying if she tried to get out or run he'd "plug her."

Darcell recalled asking Barone, "Where are we going?" Cesar told him they were going to the ocean. When Darcell wanted to know why, Barone replied they were going to drop her off for a long walk so she could think about whether or not to give them up to the police. I thought that was "cool," Darcell told the officers, because she'd at least be safe.

With Ryon trying to guess which of the few available routes Cesar had taken, and finally heading north on Nehalem Highway, Route 47, toward the Sunset Highway, Darcell rambled on "I was trying to think of a way everybody could get out of this. I didn't think that someone might die, just hoped that everything would work out."

"What was the girl doing?"

"She said walking was just fine and promised she wouldn't talk to the police." The three officers could imagine the terror she must have started to feel, just hoping and praying to get out of that car and escape with her life.

Ryon asked for directions again, and Darcell said he thought they'd entered a four-lane highway. During the wild ride that night, he said, "Cesar had a gun either on his lap or in her ribs most of the way." Looking out the window as they passed through the small community of Banks, Darcell said he recalled seeing the town that night. He snickered, "Just blink your eyes and you'd miss it." At the edge of the hamlet, Ryon wheeled north onto the Sunset Highway.

Recalling his conversation with the captive woman, Darcell said, "I told her it was a desolate area and it would be a long walk. She asked intelligent questions, like how far would it be and what kind of people were around."

Cesar drove quite a distance, Darcell said, and at some point on the highway, Barone announced, "This is far enough." He pulled over to the side of the road and made a U-turn by an embankment.

Darcell pointed out the site where Cesar had turned around, so Ryon also made a U-turn. At Darcell's directions, Ryon pulled over to the right where the shoulder was wide enough to allow parking. A thick forest of Sitka spruce and fir trees lined both sides of the road, which had narrowed to two lanes. The trees hid a steep vertical stone cliff on the opposite side of the highway. Ryon had parked just short of a metal guardrail on the right side which disappeared around a curve 150 yards ahead. Except for the occasional car or truck whizzing by, the woods which gave off the clean aroma of Christmas trees, were silent.

The four men all emerged from the police car and stood where the body of Chantee Woodman had been found on a dismal, icy morning, over four months ago.

Pointing and gesturing, Darcell said, "Cesar told her to get out of the car. I got out to get in the front seat." He'd whispered to the girl, Darcell said, instructing her to walk toward Tillamook because it was closer than Forest Grove. "I wanted to tell her to use local roads, but before I could

do it, Cesar got out. I told her to start walking, but Cesar
gave her a push to the rear of the car. He walked around
there with her, behind the car, and he had a gun pointed
at her. He told her not to go to the police. I said, 'Okay,
let her walk.' Cesar nodded. I said, 'Let's go.' I turned
around to get in the car and the door was still open.''

Animated, trying to illustrate with his hands and arms
but hindered by the handcuffs, Darcell mimed getting into
the Hyundai. Passing motorists gawked wide-eyed at the
orange-clad, cuffed and chained man demonstrating some
incomprehensible thing on the remote highway. "I heard a
smack," Darcell said, "like she got hit." Darcell said he
turned to see what was going on. "Barone was close to her,
intimidating her, pointing a gun at her with his left hand.
She was pumping her hands up and down. He hit her two
more times with his right fist. He said sumpin' to her, don't
go to the cops or this is what will happen to you."

As Darcell remembered it, Barone had yelled at her,
"Look at me!" Then, Darcell said, she was trying to push
the gun away from her face, crying, and "losing it." "Cesar
kept telling her, 'This is how it will feel, remember it.' "

The whine disappeared from Darcell's voice while he described the cruel treatment. "She kept looking down and
towards me. Cesar hit her again, the third time. I took two
steps forward, watching that gun. She was choking, sobbing,
pleading, crying, and said she wouldn't go to the police."
Darcell quoted the terrified captive as saying, "Please don't.
I have so much to live for."

According to Darcell, Cesar then said, "Everything's
going to be okay." He comforted her, Darcell said, by putting his hand on her shoulder and pointing the gun away.
"Don't be scared, trust me," Cesar reportedly said. Woodman whispered a weak "Okay."

When Cesar yelled from behind the car, "All right, let's
go," Darcell recalled, he agreed and started to climb back
in.

"I had one foot in the car when I heard a gunshot." He
leaped out and stood where the woman was in his view.
"She dropped to her knees, then onto her side." Darcell
recalled yelling something but he couldn't remember what.
"Cesar looked at me. I was just standing here." Darcell

pointed out the spot to the officers exactly where he'd stood that morning.

"Cesar grabbed her by her foot and drug her toward the woods off the shoulder of the road. She tumbled, rolled down. I followed them, staring down at her. It was dark and wet. The ground was soft and I slid." Darcell swallowed hard and mumbled, "Oh, man."

Cesar, Darcell said, stood up on the highway's edge. "I looked at him. I said, 'She alright? Oh, my God!' Cesar started talking about she's dead. I asked how did he know for sure."

The next comment, as Darcell quoted it, made the officers' stomachs tighten. Barone reportedly said, "I'm always sure of my shots."

Darcell recalled how it affected him. "I got it in my head that those shots—he could plug me. So I climbed back in the car. We jumped in and left."

In the car with Cesar, en route back to Cornelius, Darcell said, he was appalled at Cesar's behavior. "Cesar was jubilant, cheering, pumping his fist in the air and yelling, 'Yeah,' and 'Whoa, did you see it?' "

"He said he'd never felt so good in his life. He was flexing his arms. He asked me how I felt. I felt sick. He said, 'What are you talking about? Talk to me.' But I was quiet. It was just about dawn, really raining, but I had to roll down the window to get some fresh air to keep from puking. The clouds hid the sunrise. I just stared straight ahead."

Recalling the long ride back, Darcell said he spoke to Cesar. "I told him that he was going to get caught. He looked at me in disbelief and asked how. I told him I didn't know. He said, 'There's no connection to me and her. The police can't connect us.' I asked him, 'What about ballistics? They have ways.' I asked about the bullet, and he said they'd never find it."

Darcell told the officers he would always remember what Cesar said next. "It gets easier each time. You gotta try it next time." Cesar expanded on that, Darcell recalled, by saying, "The first one is the hardest. That makes number five," and raised his hand with five fingers extended. Cesar really seemed to get a big rush out of it, Darcell said.

When Cesar got them back to the house, Darcell recalled, he was in a trancelike state. "I just concentrated on putting one foot in front of the other." Cesar had given him "unnerving" looks, Darcell said.

As if in deep thought, Darcell told the detectives that he thought Cesar was trying to make him feel like an accomplice. But instead, he just felt sick. "He called me Germ, and asked if I was gonna' freak out on him. I said I wouldn't. Cesar replied, 'That's good. You're just as much involved and we'd both take the fall.' I believed it. You don't see things like that every day."

His voice softening to a philosophical tone, Darcell said, "I felt very guilty that she died. I'd tried to be strong for her, but she died. I told Cesar she wasn't the type to go to the police. I had an ex-girlfriend who had been raped several times, and she never went to the cops. I was trying to plant ideas in Cesar's head to drop her off. I would have stayed with her except my backpack was in Cesar's house."

The rationalization sounded foolish to the detectives. Darcell didn't seem to notice. "I didn't want her to get hurt at all. I tried to stay between her and Cesar."

Ryon, McKinney and Watson stared at him. Looking off into the distance, Darcell said softly, "It didn't work, man."

Chapter 23

One of Betty Williams's four sons, still grieving over his mother's ignominious death in her bathtub, scanned through a newspaper in the second week of May. A hazy notion formed in his mind, took shape, and materialized into focus. He turned to his father and asked, "This can't be the gun they're looking for on this case, can it?" He referred to the revolver police had photographed under Betty's desk on the morning her body was discovered. Family members had subsequently packed it away among her possessions.

The next day he handed the silver-plated, long-barreled Western-style Ruger revolver, along with three rounds of loose magnum ammunition, to his brother, who telephoned Sergeant Mark Christy.

It didn't take Christy long to trace the weapon's serial number 26119949 to the original owner, who produced a bill of sale showing he'd sold it to a cabinet-shop owner named Andy Tremaine. Tremaine had put it in the possession of Cesar Barone, and still fumed over never having recovered it from the ex-employee. *Good Lord,* thought Christy, *the damn thing has been right here all the time.* Barone had made a monumental error leaving it in William's apartment the night she died. He must have been sweating bullets the whole time wondering when it would be traced.

Christy was right. Barone had fretted for months about his hasty oversight. And he'd almost lucked out. Fortunately, Betty's son finally connected the weapon to the search. The revolver had one empty chamber and five rounds of live ammunition. The one missing round had apparently been fired point blank under the chin of Chantee Woodman on December 29, 1992.

Christy and O'Connell sent the ammunition to the OSP crime lab to be compared to the shell casing Darcell had tossed onto the roof of the shed, plus another shell that had turned up in Barone's closet on the ground floor of the two-story Cornelius house. Criminalist Chris Johnson would also see if he could match the slug taken from Woodman's head to the .22 Ruger.

When Leonard Darcell took the long ride up Sunset Highway with the three officers, he may have told some truths, but they regarded some portions of his tale as self-serving distortion and exaggeration. The trio agreed that he was probably more deeply involved in the rape and murder than he cared to admit.

The grand jury saw it that way, too. Before May ended, they indicted Darcell, charging him with one count of felony murder involving the use of a firearm. The press release stated that Darcell was probably not the shooter in the Woodman case, but his participation in her kidnapping was enough to try him for murder. Newspapers announced that Darcell had been released "by mistake" from jail the previous December, prior to Woodman's death, and had ignored a summons to return.

During the ride with the officers, Darcell indignantly asserted his innocence in the killing. He had written a letter to his father expressing those same denials and self-pity just one day before he first prophetically said to detectives, "Hold on, you guys. I'm going to tell you something that will probably change the rest of my life."

In that letter to his father, dated April 27, 1993, he wrote, "Nothing in the world, no amount of preparation, no degree of discipline, no quantity of love or lack of such could have prepared me for what I saw happen on the night of December 29, or the decision that was put to me on December 31. When the man I called friend, the man who I had seen extinguish a human life with no degree of remorse, the man who I had introduced to my family as 'friend,' the man I trusted to dance with my sister looked me dead in the eyes and pretty much implied "Never utter a word *or else.*" In fact, the exact quote was 'Be cool, or I'll come to Seattle and shoot you, too.' "

His main concern in the decisions he'd been forced to make that night, and in the weeks following, Darcell wrote, was for his family and their safety. He'd given serious consideration to going to the police, he claimed. But he'd heard Barone frequently boast of having many "Ranger" buddies who would "back his play, right or wrong." Darcell apparently interpreted that to mean that if he informed authorities about the events surrounding the death of Chantee Woodman, Barone would send his former military cronies to execute Darcell or members of his family. Because of that, Darcell said, he'd fled north, to Seattle, and gone into hiding for the express purpose of preventing his relatives from being harmed. He denied that his violation of parole had anything to do with it.

"In Mr. Barone," he wrote, "I had encountered a sense of evil that nothing in the world could ever have prepared me to deal with." Barone had demanded complete silence, so Darcell had no choice but to comply. He hinted of his guilt about anyone who had suffered as a result of his failure to speak out, but expressed gratitude that investigators had alleviated it to some degree by telling him that no one had lost their lives because of his "inability to act."

Darcell's written words denied any culpability for Woodman's death. He also said that Barone raped her that night. After that, Darcell said, he worried that Barone might take her life so he pleaded on her behalf for Barone to spare her. Of course, he wrote nothing about consuming so many beers that night, "death drinking," as he'd told the detectives. And he didn't mention helping to get Chantee Woodman drunk and having sex with her. He'd confessed to the officers that Woodman had made "typical excuses" not to have sex with him, but he'd ignored her because "you hear that all the time from girls you meet the same day." Those words couldn't be found in the letter.

"Maybe I didn't try hard enough," he wrote. "Maybe I should have attempted to forcibly disarm Mr. Barone." Equivocating about that possibility, he rationalized that it probably would have been an unwise choice considering Barone's "Special Forces" training.

Moving on to his family relationships, Darcell assured his father that none of his relatives should feel any guilt over his errors. He'd been raised to accept personal responsibility, he said, and was willing to do that. Citing the rape of an elderly victim, Darcell wondered if it possibly could have been avoided if he'd gone to the police. He begged God's forgiveness if his inaction had contributed to the crime. And the specter of a young woman's death, he said, would haunt him forever. His innocence had been shattered by it, and it would motivate him to be as productive with the rest of his life as possible, driving him to accomplish something good. "May I do the Lord's will from now on, and not my own."

Darcell didn't mention whose will it was that he'd promised Woodman, at five or six that fateful morning, to take her home on the bus when it started running, but backed out a short time later by offering her "a couple of dollars" to go home by herself. His noble instincts didn't appear to be operational when they were needed.

Painting a grim verbal picture, Darcell described his feelings as he sat in a jail cell writing the letter. He said he was innocent of any crime, but guilty in his own heart. If his death would make it right, he wrote, he would gladly forfeit his life. People in the justice system often hear that expression, but recognize that it usually sounds as hollow as the similar spurious claim that "I'd give my life if it would bring the victim back."

In prison, being branded as an informer, a "snitch," is often a condemnation to death. But, Darcell wrote, he had no fear of such a reputation. "I am not scared of death. Earth is a very painful place to live in these final days." Following those statements, he changed direction by saying that he'd really prefer to survive so he could be a living memorial to Chantee Woodman.

The letter failed to recall Darcell's answers to questions the officers had asked him about what he was doing while Barone had Woodman in the bedroom. He'd been so concerned about her safety that he occupied himself playing with a Nintendo game. 'Was there a telephone in the house?' a detective had asked. Yes, two or three of them, but Darcell had elected not to use them. What had he done then? Gone to the kitchen, straightened up, and washed dishes. While Barone held down and raped the woman Darcell had convinced to get in the car with them in Portland.

Darcell wound up his six-page hand-printed message by asking his family to be strong and to believe that he was going to do everything he could to make "this mess" right in the eyes of God and the world. With more references to the power of faith and religion, he ended the letter.

Investigators who later read the words doubted their sincerity. To them it sounded more like something a streetwise con might prepare for his lawyer to use in pleading for a lesser sentence, pointing to it as a declaration of remorse.

Darcell still faced trial for the part he played in the murder of Chantee Woodman. If he sincerely meant what he wrote, he'd have the opportunity to testify and express the same sorrow to a jury.

The Washington County grand jury heard testimony from members of the investigative task force along with informants Troy Masters, Dave Sparks, and Wayne Fallon. District Attorney Scott Upham pointed to the .22 revolver recently recovered from Betty Williams's family, and told jurors it had been originally found in the apartment of Betty Lou Williams. Cesar Barone had admitted being the last person to see her alive. The implication was clear; Barone had threatened her with the weapon to force her into sexual acts.

On June 10, the grand jury issued a third indictment against Barone, this one charging him with the felony murder of Betty Williams. DA Upham later told reporters that Barone "literally scared her to death." The charge against Barone accused him of causing Williams's death while attempting to rape her.

Williams's family felt renewed pain. The grief they'd experienced from losing her the previous January now turned to puzzling anger. A daughter-in-law, wondering why anyone would want to hurt Williams, said, "Betty was a real trusting person. She didn't have any enemies."

Sergeant Mark Christy, who hadn't been able to dismiss the suspicious circumstances of Williams's death, didn't want any fanfare, but he'd been convinced for some time that Cesar Barone had cost the woman her life. Ever since Cesar's girlfriend, Denise Nichols, had admitted to Christy that she and Cesar had been in Williams's apartment drinking with her on the night of her death, Christy had visualized Cesar taking Denise home, just a few yards away, then returning to Williams's apartment to force her to satisfy him sexually. The woman's weakened heart hadn't been able to withstand the perverted sexual assault. Christy had been right, and Barone would face a murder trial for his cruelty.

Another newspaper reader saw Cesar Barone's photograph, took a closer look, and felt her heart trying to pound its way out of her chest. "My God," she blurted, "that's the guy I saw at Margaret Schmidt's house!" Just a few days before the elderly crippled woman's nude body had been found on her bed, the reader had paid a call to Margaret to see how she was doing. The kindly sexagenarian had become quite adept at using her walker despite her obesity, and the visitor had left her in good spirits. As she left, she noticed, but paid little attention to, a young man hanging around. Now she recognized the man as Cesar Barone. Within moments, the woman was on the phone to report her discovery.

Yet another inmate came forward to report his conversations with Barone in C-tank, and how the murder suspect had admitted his sexual attacks on elderly women.

In the Washington County courthouse, Judge Michael McElligott had tried as long as possible to respect the wishes of the police investigators and the district attorney. They'd wanted to keep search warrants affidavits, which contained investigation details and names, sealed from the public and press until several critical facets of the job were completed. Releasing the information too soon could damage chances to find people and evidence. The judge had agreed and ordered the documents sealed.

Unhappy with that decision, attorneys for the news media had appealed. Despite the modified "gag" order, a television crew had been spotted at Ron Price's residence on 224th Street filming the interior of the scorched house. As soon as they'd finished, the reporter with them came to DA Scott Upham's office. His receptionist buzzed Upham to inform him that the reporter was saying if Upham wouldn't agree to speak about the investigation, the search warrants would be published.

Describing the incident, Upham would later say, "I went out and spoke with the reporter. She asked me to confirm certain things. I said, 'I can't do that.' She said that she'd spoken to her lawyer and he'd informed her they had the authority to publish that information." It didn't seem to matter that it had been sealed by the court. Upham replied to the reporter, saying, "Well, if you do that, you're going to be running afoul of the sealing orders and perhaps some criminal statutes." She left. That evening the television station showed some of the film clips of the burned house, and reported that Mr. Barone was wanted in connection with the disappearance of eight women. They also said a search warrant showed that two guns taken from the home had been used to kill Martha Bryant. A newspaper repeated the information the next day and noted that the television station didn't specify where they'd obtained sealed court documents.

In a court hearing on the matter, Scott Upham complained about the reporter to Judge McElligott. He said, "One of the women mentioned in the warrant was contacted on May thirteenth by the same individual and apparently the same cameraman. Now, this woman is eighty-two years old. She's the listed sex crime victim in a pending case involving Cesar Barone."

Upham said that Detective O'Connell had responded to a complaint by the elderly woman about the reporter's intrusion. The DA read the officer's report to the judge. In it, O'Connell stated the victim heard a car pull up to the side of her house. She thought it was a hair stylist arriving at her appointed time. When she went to the door, she saw the news crew standing there. Media people had already been bothering her over the phone. She pleaded that she didn't want any more publicity. But the reporter told her she'd have to go on camera, and if she didn't, they'd have to broadcast her real name on television. At last, the victim consented to be filmed only if they promised not to show her face.

Upham told the judge that he was concerned about safety and privacy issues, or subjecting witnesses to intimidation which could have a negative impact on trial testimony. "There has been an intense press involvement in this particular case, like a feeding frenzy almost, where people are going around trying to one-up one another, and I think it's a perfectly valid reason you can take into consideration . . ."

Judge McElligott swung the sword of Solomon in making his decision to unseal the affidavits already leaked and to retain the clamps on other unreleased documents. The *Oregonian* ran an article on May 25, reporting that: "The previously sealed warrant information was released by Judge Michael J. McElligott after KPTV (12) and The *Oregonian* sought disclosure. Other information was kept sealed so as not to compromise investigations by the county's homicide task force."

Few inmates have offended their cellmates as universally as did Cesar Barone. In late June, Michael O'Connell heard from another outraged convict who wanted to talk about Barone.

The con had asked Barone why he'd told other inmates about his crimes. Cesar, the informant said, didn't think they would tell on him. "Did you do what they're accusing you of?" the new cellmate asked.

"Yes," Barone reportedly answered.

"Man, you just hung yourself."

Cesar looked depressed. According to the con, he offered to set his new companion up with a woman he knew. "How about setting me up with your ex-wife, or her mother?" The con asked, half jesting. Cesar answered that her his ex-wife was too sophisticated for the con, and that her mother was dead and buried. The con interpreted that to mean the mother-in-law had been killed and buried in the backyard somewhere.

When the crimes hit the newspapers, the informant told O'Connell, Barone got scared and started yelling that they had the wrong guy. But that didn't dampen Cesar's raging

hormones. One afternoon, the con saw Cesar walk back
into his cell after a visit from his female attorney. The two
men got into a conversation in which Cesar allegedly said
that the attorney was "fine" and he wanted to have sex
with her.

"It's not right for you to talk about her that way," the
informant claimed he said, "she's your lawyer and she's
trying to protect you." But Barone, he said, continued to
talk about her in sexual terms.

One night, the informant recalled, Cesar was let out of
his cell to use the phone. According to the con, Cesar
turned toward him, smirking, and said he was going to call
his female attorney and talk dirty to her. "At least Cesar
laughed after he said it."

The informant said that Barone was angry with the guy
he used to rent from, Ron Price, because Price had failed
to follow instructions Cesar had given for setting the house
on fire, hadn't done it the way he'd been told to do it.

Barone had told his cellmate about being in the Army
and his involvement in the Panama invasion. He bragged,
the con said, about helping to capture Manuel Noriega and
that he'd killed people in Panama with guns as well as with
his bare hands.

The weird thing was, the informant told O'Connell, that
when Cesar talked about killing people, his face would
light up.

In the first week of July, O'Connell found a man who'd
worked with Barone in a cabinet shop. The man told
O'Connell that he and Barone had been drinking one night
in a Portland topless bar, when Barone made some strange
comments. As the ex-coworker recalled it, Barone said he'd
once shot a girl in the head because she'd attempted to rob
him. She'd used a .25 caliber semiautomatic pistol, so he'd
been forced to shoot her.

Barone had also confessed, the tipster said, that he had
used Andy Tremaine's .22 Ruger to kill someone, then had
placed the weapon back in Tremaine's truck.

O'Connell listened, recorded the statement in a report,
and filed it in a thick binder.

*   *   *

Detectives Roger Mussler and Derald Riggleman turned up one last informant who was in jail, but had not been a cellmate of Cesar Barone. George Demory readily admitted his reason for being in the slammer. "I'm here for two bank robberies, and I ain't expecting no favors."

The detectives asked him what he wanted to talk about. Demory said, "My wife was pregnant, we were on welfare, and she went to Healthy Start. That midwife, Martha Bryant was assigned to help her. She treated my wife wonderful. She only cared about bringing life into this world, not taking it."

He'd met Cesar Barone, he said, towards the end of October. "It was my wife's birthday. I wanted to order her some cake. So I called her from a Kmart. I'd been drinking. She says, 'I told you time and time again that I'm not bringing the baby around if you're gonna have alcohol on your breath.' She hung up on me."

Demory said that made him mad, so he drove to a bar close to the Sunset Highway. He had a couple of drinks, shot some pool, and returned to his bar stool. A man he would later know was Cesar Barone sat down next to him. "We got to talkin'. I said I was from Hillsboro." Barone said he was too, "So we went over and sat in a booth together."

They'd ordered some more drinks, Demory said, and he told Barone his troubles. "I said 'My wife lives in Portland and the bitch hung up.' Then I said, 'I'd like to smash her in the face.' But it was the booze talkin'."

Barone's next remarks, as the informant recalled, startled him. "He said, 'Where does she live in Hillsboro? I'll take care of the bitch for you.' I thought it was just chitchat. But he says, 'I'll pop a couple of caps in her.' I guess he meant he'd shoot her."

At the officers' request, Demory did his best to describe Barone. "He had on white pants and a polo shirt. I asked him if he worked in a hospital. He told me he didn't, but he was a certified nursing assistant. What a coincidence! So am I."

The two men had resumed the conversation about Demory's wife, with Barone still hinting he'd take care of the problem. Barone said he "done it" before, which Demory

interpreted as meaning killed before. "I thought he was
bragging. He mentioned he'd 'shot the bitches off the road.'
And he said he had a six-shooter. Offered to sell it."

The bar session lasted more than two hours before each
man went his own way. But that wasn't the last time Demory saw Barone.

About three or four weeks after Christmas, the informant
said, he was in a Portland tavern on Burnside and 20th
Street. "It was a rough crowd in there. Somebody tapped
me on the shoulder and said, 'Remember me?' It was
Cesar. He said he'd lost that pistol. The gun was gone and
he could never get it back. He told me he was thinking of
doing some burglaries. He was gonna use the trick of reading obituary columns." Demory referred to an old scam
used by burglars. They'd read the obits in newspapers, list
the names of people who died, and look up the addresses.
That would allow easy access to the deceased person's
home since there was a good chance it would be unat-
tended with the surviving occupants staying elsewhere while
grieving or attending a funeral.

During their renewed conversation, Demory stated, Barone told him that he'd scared one woman to death. The
next comment, according to Demory, made him sick. Barone reportedly said, "I used to terrorize the bitch by telling
her I was gonna take her eyes out with my hand." The
informant demonstrated, making a gouging motion with
his thumbs.

"I just learned, on television, that his whole name is
Cesar Barone. I heard it at the bar, but I couldn't remember it. I do recall asking him if he was Italian or something.
He had an odd answer. He said, 'You'd be surprised where
this name came from.' He told me he'd whacked a couple
of bitches."

Asked about his general impression of Barone, Demory
said, "He seemed like an isolated loner."

The detectives thanked Demory for his statement, then
headed back to Hillsboro. At headquarters, Mussler typed
up the report, inserted it in another bulging folder, which
he placed in a bookcase nearly overflowing with three
shelves of thick binders related to the case against Cesar
Francesco Barone.

PART FOUR

Trials
and
Tribulations

Chapter 24

Inside the Oregon State Penitentiary, in Salem, a new man joined the sixteen others sitting in cells on death row. Douglas Franklin Wright, known widely among convicts as "the Animal," had spent most of his adult life in prison for everything from sexually fondling a five-year-old boy to robbery, kidnapping, and murder. Incredibly, he'd been paroled several times, despite the serious crimes. He spent his prison time buffing his powerful body to perfection.

Convicted of killing three of the four homeless men whose bodies were discovered on the Warm Springs Indian Reservation, Wright would receive no more paroles. The judge had ordered him to die for his crimes. Wright didn't seem to care. He was quoted as saying, "There's no doubt in my mind if you paroled me or released me today, I'd probably do well for a while, then I'd probably start killing people again, or I'd be robbing or stealing or whatever." Once an extraordinarily handsome man, the ex-Marine would tell a reporter, "I've always had a desire to kill people and I chose to do it. I don't make no excuses for my behavior and if anybody deserves to be executed or locked up for the rest of their life, it's me."

Detective Michael Walley of the Fort Lauderdale PD, who had been with the homicide team since 1981, took a sip of coffee and absentmindedly scanned through his newspaper. An article about some murders all the way across the country, in Oregon, caught his attention. A man identified as Cesar Barone, an unfamiliar name to Walley, had been charged with killing several women. With mild interest, Walley skimmed through the story, then came to a name that froze the movement of his widening eyes. His

mouth gaping open, Walley craned his neck to get closer
to the page.

Back in November 1979, Walley had still been a uni-
formed patrol officer. In the early morning of November
29 of that year, he'd been the first unit dispatched to a
crime scene that he'd never forget. In a neat little home,
he found the body of a pitiful little woman named Alice
Stock, age seventy-three, who had been savagely raped and
murdered. When detectives took over, he left the scene,
but followed the progress of the case. A young man named
Adolph "Jimmy" Rode had been suspected of killing the
woman after being released from jail, three years after he'd
terrorized her with a knife. A shoe print outside Stock's
bedroom window had characteristics similar to shoes worn
by Rode, but charges had never been filed in view of the
evidence shortage. The case had troubled Walley for fourteen years.

Now, in the article, there was that name leaping off the
page, Adolph Rode, calling himself Cesar Barone! He'd
moved to the Pacific Northwest following his release from
Florida State prison. Women in Washington County, some
of them elderly like Alice Stock, were being raped and
murdered, and Barone had been accused of being the killer.

An excited Mike Walley showed the article to his boss,
and convinced him to reopen the murder case of Alice
Stock. Detective Robert Williams, who had arrested Rode
in 1977 on burglary charges, teamed up with Walley to
tackle the job. Together, they flew to Portland in mid-Au-
gust 1993, and drove over to Hillsboro to meet a youthful-
appearing, energetic sheriff's detective named Michael
O'Connell.

After briefing the Florida sleuths, O'Connell accompanied them on visits to four informants who willingly repeated the narratives they'd given to the Washington
County task force.

Following the departure of the two Florida investigators,
O'Connell told reporters that the pair had "found things
to help with their cases" but explained that he could neither divulge any names of people interviewed nor reveal
specific facts uncovered.

*   *   *

Before Cesar Barone faced a judge and jury, O'Connell would make reciprocal visits to Florida for the purpose of examining the crimes for which Barone, aka Rode, had been convicted in that state.

At a seemingly endless series of court hearings, the murder trial dates for Barone were repeatedly pushed into the future. The charges for raping elderly women who had survived to testify against him would have to be dealt with first, though, tentatively in February 1994.

Meanwhile, two weeks before Christmas, 1993, Leonard Darcell sat in a courtroom to face charges related to his involvement in the death of Chantee Woodman early one year earlier. It took five days to select a jury from Washington County residents who'd been flooded with news reports on the case. Would the jurors see Darcell as a cold-blooded killer, or a weak-willed stooge manipulated into a dreadful situation by Cesar Barone?

With Judge Alan C. Bonebrake presiding, Prosecutor Robert Hermann stood up and faced the jury to deliver his opening statement.

At age forty-four, Bob Hermann had the calm dignity and appearance of a senator or governor of the state. One might guess that he'd grown up in the surroundings of affluent luxury, considering his elegant bearing, but he laughed at that notion. "No," he said, "I was born in Providence Hospital in Portland on the last day of February 1949, and grew up out on the edge of the Multnomah School District. There were a lot of rich kids in my high school, but I wasn't one of them. I always had to get rides with the guys who had cars." Hermann's family included two older brothers who helped motivate and develop his athletic skills, so he went out for football, basketball, and track in high school, and lettered in all three. After graduation in 1967, he attended Willamette University in Salem where he earned his degree in 1971, while a bloody, controversial war raged in Vietnam.

Having drawn a relatively low military draft lottery number, #271, Hermann faced the distinct probability of being inducted into the Army. The alternative of attending graduate school grew even more appealing. By the time he took his law degree in 1974, the Vietnam conflict had ended, so Hermann spent a leisurely half-year traveling around the country before accepting the Hillsboro job as a prosecutor.

While still in law school, Hermann had clerked for the Washington County DA, and as a certified law student, handled a few low-level cases for college credit. "I loved the whole courtroom atmosphere," he'd later admit. He points with pride to one of his most interesting murder cases in 1985. A New Zealand citizen who lived in Portland, and was a member of the police reserve, had shot his wife to death. The accused man came to court with an elaborate defense story, claiming he'd mistaken the victim for a burglar, grabbed a gun, aimed it, and it went off by accident. Hermann discovered the individual had carried out a similar shooting in New Zealand in which the victim survived, and had used the same excuse! After the Oregon jury convicted the defendant, the state supreme court heard appeals and subsequently upheld the verdict. The case changed laws relating to evidence admissibility.

In 1982, Hermann took over the duties of chief deputy DA, which put him in charge of the grand jury system and supervision of attorneys handling felony cases. By late 1993, he'd handled seventeen murder cases. Off the job, most of his time was spent with his wife and two daughters, but he maintained his involvement in athletics including playing and coaching basketball and softball, and participation in a national slow-pitch tournament.

The jury listened attentively as Bob Hermann, clear and articulate, told them that Leonard Darcell's participation in the kidnapping of Chantee Woodman made him equally culpable for her death. Darcell had given several statements to investigators and in each version he'd subtly changed details about his own involvement, which Hermann pointed to as demonstrating a consciousness of guilt. The prosecutor promised the jury they'd see a videotape of Darcell taking three officers on a step-by-step re-creation of the kidnap, rape, and murder of Woodman.

Defense attorney Charles Fryer requested that the jurors listen carefully to witnesses who would testify that Darcell feared for his life as the result of threats made to him by the real killer, Cesar Barone. Could the defendant do anything else? You couldn't convict him for murder because he hadn't worked up enough courage to risk his own life to save the victim, or for shading the truth when he finally spoke out to the police.

A succession of witnesses took the stand, including investigators, forensic experts, and people who knew both the victim and the defendant. A nervous Heather Crane spoke in a birdlike voice describing the fear she experienced in the little white car with Cesar and "Germ." A man people called "Doc" told how the two men had shown up at his house in the early morning hours of December 29. Investigators Scott Ryon and Larry McKinney verbally took the jurors from the body discovery scene to the arrest of two suspects, and a myriad of subsequent fact-finding efforts.

And the panel of twelve weighers of fact did, indeed, watch the videotape of Darcell's last trip up the Sunset Highway.

After almost a week of testimony and evidence presentation, Hermann summed up his case. He explained to jurors that if they agreed that Darcell had been involved in Woodman's kidnaping, even if they thought her death was accidental, then they must find him guilty of felony murder. Defender Fryer appealed to them to not penalize Darcell for being unable to predict that Barone, the "bad guy," would kill Woodman, and that guilt by association wouldn't be a just outcome.

The jurors deliberated almost sixteen hours before handing in their verdict. As Hermann had said, Leonard Darcell was guilty of kidnapping and felony murder.

Hoping for a lenient sentence, Charles Fryer raised issues of mitigation in a written report. He referred to the "skinhead girl" Heather Crane had mentioned in quoting Darcell. As she testified, Darcell had told Barone that it would be okay to do sexual things to "that skinhead girl." Fryer noted that Darcell had returned from San Francisco shortly before Christmas, 1992, where he'd befriended a skinhead prostitute. She had complained to Len that her pimps were taking all her trick money, so he tried unsuccessfully to intervene. It earned him a severe beating, while she stood by saying nothing. Afterwards, Darcell had a very low opinion of her, and told Barone about it. Thus, it would have been okay to sexually assault the prostitute who hadn't defended him, but not Heather Crane. Darcell's defense of Crane, Fryer argued, should be recognized in determining a sentence. Fryer also held that when Barone gave Darcell the spent bullet casing as a souvenir, he'd intentionally placed it where authorities could later find it.

As mitigating factors in Darcell's defense, Fryer wrote, "The offense was principally accomplished by another and the defendant exhibited extreme caution or concern for the victim." It was obvious, said Fryer, that Darcell placed himself at great risk when he insisted on accompanying Barone on the ride from Cornelius. Finally, said Fryer, "Defendant has been diagnosed by an Oregon State Prison psychiatrist as suffering from Post Traumatic Stress Disorder as a result of what happened on the night Mr. Barone killed Ms. Woodman. . . . Mr. Darcell feels extremely guilty about what happened to Ms. Woodman and about his inability to foresee and prevent her death."

Judge Bonebrake examined all the reports and solemnly listened to oral arguments. On March 4, 1994, he read aloud the sentence he'd imposed for kidnapping, ordering the defendant to be ". . . committed to the legal and physical custody of the Corrections Department of the State of Oregon for a minimum of 10 years without any possibility of parole. . . ." For the murder conviction, Bonebrake said, "It is further ordered that . . . the defendant be committed for a minimum term of an additional 10 years (total 20 years) without possibility of parole . . . work release, or any form of temporary leave or employment at a forest or work camp."

Leonard Darcell would be behind bars for no less than twenty years.

While Barone waited for his February trial on the rape and burglary charges, he received some more bad news. On Monday morning, January 10, officials in the Washington County jail handed him an indictment. A grand jury in

Broward County, Florida, had finally decided to charge Barone with the 1979 murder of Alice Stock. Florida would have to wait for the pending February trial plus the frequently postponed murder trial he faced for killing Martha Bryant, Margaret Schmidt, Betty Williams, and Chantee Woodman. The DA had chosen to hold off on charging Barone with murdering Elizabeth Wasson or Joyce Scarbrough, since very little evidence had surfaced on either case.

If Florida ever managed to bring Barone to justice, he might have serious reason to worry. No one had been executed in Oregon since 1962, but Florida had a considerably different track record. In addition to Ted Bundy, thirty men had been electrocuted since reinstatement of Florida's death penalty in 1976.

Deputy DA Roger Hanlon drew the duty of prosecuting Barone in the trial for rape, burglary and theft. Standing a little over six-two, and a solid 195 pounds, Hanlon hailed from Boston, Massachusetts, where he spent his first nineteen years. Born twelve days before Christmas in 1952, the son of an FBI agent, Hanlon's roguish eyes sparkled when he recalled his boyhood summers on Cape Cod. He'd usually leave school a few days early to maximize the amount of time on the cape where scuba diving, water skiing, sailing and long days on the sunny beaches made life worth living.

Following high school, he moved to another magnificent beach town on the opposite corner of the nation, San Diego, California, to attend San Diego State College. He earned a degree in criminal justice administration there in 1976. Not quite ready to don a suit and tie, and still mightily attracted to the sun and sand, he moved to Huntington Beach, 100 miles up the California coast. There he worked at various jobs, sometimes laboring in the construction industry. Another move followed in 1984 to Manhattan Beach, where outdoor beach volleyball, which would eventually become an Olympic Games event, was in its infancy. The surf, sun, and sand crowd populated apartments and condos along the strand, separated from the golden beach only by a paved path, eight feet wide, were a constant flow of skaters, joggers, and sun worshipers passed in parade.

Out in the rolling surf, wet-suited youth bobbed from dawn to dusk waiting for the perfect wave. At night, the crowds congregated up the hill in three or four popular bar-restaurants. Roger Hanlon lived smack in the middle of it, on the 4400 block of the Strand until 1985.

That year, he finally listened to the longstanding call of a law career, transplanted to Lewis and Clark University in Portland, and took his law degree in 1988. In the interim, during a trip to Ireland, he met a stunning colleen whose Irish brogue, traffic-stopping beauty, billowing red hair, and tolerance of his sly sense of humor, changed his life. Accepting the responsibilities that come with marriage, he took a job with the Washington County DA.

With one murder trial under his belt, which had ended in a plea bargain, Hanlon accepted the challenge of prosecuting Cesar Barone in the rape-burglary-theft trial.

Chapter 25

The Honorable Gayle A. Nachtigal, judge of the circuit court, Washington County, after swearing in the jury, twisted her chair toward Roger Hanlon and gave permission for the prosecution to proceed with opening statements.

Hanlon captivated the jury with his remarkable skill at telling a story. His statement, presented in a folksy yet intelligent narrative, created a clear picture of the accusations against Barone.

The defense attorney, Keith Rogers, no slouch himself in delivering a spellbinding tale, completed his opener, and waited for Hanlon's first witnesses.

After police officers testified, Matilda Gardner took the stand to unfold her recollections of living above Barone in the two-story Cornelius house. They'd been courteous to each other, she said, and sometimes talked about the flowers outside. When he'd asked to use the phone that day, one year ago, she hadn't even hesitated. Of course he could use it. And then when he said he needed to use the bathroom, she'd accommodated him. She couldn't believe what happened next, she said, trying to fight back the tears. Wielding a knife, he'd forced her to partially disrobe, and had tried to rape her. Matilda's obvious pain at reliving the horror touched gallery observers, who glanced at jurors' faces, wondering if they felt the same empathy. Jurors are never instructed to remain expressionless, but somehow it's a universal truth that they automatically adopt poker faces.

Next on the stand came spunky little Sarah Ross, now eighty-three years old. She'd intentionally dressed in the same shirt and shoes she'd worn when Barone conned his way into her house and tried to attack her. When Hanlon asked her about kicking the assailant in the shin, Sarah took off one of her shoes, held it up, and said, "How would you like to get hit with that hard rubber?"

She'd pressed her necklace alarm button, she told the jury, and informed Barone the police were on their way. He'd fled with her purse, which was later found in the Tualatin riverbed.

The elderly woman who had dreamed of Christmas past while she lay in a nursing home entered the courtroom in a wheelchair. Multiple sclerosis had paralyzed her from the waist down. One of the jurors whose eyes were downcast when the crippled victim's chair rolled to a stop, looked up and gasped an audible, "Oh, my God!" Observers felt goose bumps. From her wheelchair, the woman testified about how frightened she'd been when a man entered her room and put his hand inside her nightgown to fondle her breasts.

Barone's onetime girlfriend, Denise Nichols, took the stand to report that Cesar had stolen her VCR, a ring, a TV, and cash. Barone glanced up from the defendant's table once or twice at her, but showed no emotion.

Ron Price, spruced up to the best of his ability for the court appearance, said Barone had pressured him to help sell the electronic items. Instead, he croaked, he'd returned them to Denise. As a result, Barone had threatened him by saying, "You'd better watch your back."

Next, Roger Hanlon called Sheila Hawkins, who informed the jury that she and Barone had lived together for a period of time. Barone had tried to convince her to lie to the police to provide him an alibi for the time period in which Matilda Gardner was assaulted.

When Hanlon rested the prosecution's case, Cesar Barone faced a big decision. More often than not, defendants decline the opportunity to testify in their own behalf. Defense attorneys deny it, but many of them prefer that their clients not take the stand because it opens up too many possibilities for the prosecutor to bring out unfavorable issues. Cesar Barone felt confident that he could withstand such a challenge, and swaggered to the witness chair on Monday, February 21.

Keith Rogers first asked Barone to state his age, and

the witness said he was thirty-three. Did he know Matilda Gardner? Yes, approximately two years, in a neighborly relationship, just speaking in passing. Barone described the help he'd once given when the woman's daughter suffered an epileptic seizure.

The defense attorney asked Barone to tell the jury what happened on the morning of February 13, 1993, involving Ms. Gardner.

Barone cleared his throat and spoke with the trace of a southern drawl. "I'd been out most of the night with some friends, and we [had] all eaten breakfast at Shari's and left and we went down to a place in Cornelius, I mean in Forest Grove. . . . and I played some pinball there. I had done that on a number of occasions because they stay open twenty-four hours. I stopped by approximately eight o'clock in the morning because I knew she was always up early. And my intentions were to ask her about part of a bed. This is a footboard that fit on the bottom of a bed that I had given to my roommate."

Roger Hanlon checked his notes. In a previous version of the story, Barone had reportedly said it was a headboard. Defender Rogers also recognized the discrepancy and asked, "Was it a footboard or a headboard?"

"The footboard," Barone replied. "The piece that goes down on the foot of the bed, and sort of like there's metal brackets that just sort of fit into slots. It wasn't a big piece of furniture or anything like that."

To the defense attorney's questions, Barone said he'd previously moved from the house, wanted to leave instructions about the footboard, and also just wanted to say hello since he was in the neighborhood. Rogers asked, "What happened when you went to the door?"

"Well, she had like—almost like a horn that's on the door and it's real loud." He'd pushed the button and Gardner came to the entry. "Before I even had a chance to say anything, she says, 'Oh, hi Cesar,' real gregarious like."

"Was anything said about allergies or her eyes?"

"She had said, because she had known about my training in the medical field, was talking about her allergies, her eyes watery and red. And I was speaking to her, and I leaned forward, maybe a half a foot or whatever, to look into her eyes, and they were all red and watery. And I asked, you know, I said, well, maybe if she tried taking some Benadryl to combat the allergy."

"What happened next?"

"Then she leaned forward and tried kissing me." A nearly inaudible groan rumbled through the gallery.

"What . . . did you do in response?"

"I leaned back, because we never had that kind of relationship. She never led on to that kind of thing happening."

"What did you do?"

"I was like, what was that about? I asked her what that was about, and she laughed, and I had laughed because I thought—I didn't know what it was."

"And did she say anything about a friend coming over?"

". . . I didn't hear no names. She said a fat lady was coming over to get some bears."

"Did you know what she was talking about at all?" Barone didn't. "Did she invite you to come over later?"

"She did. She asked me at that time if I wanted to have sex, and I said I had things to do that morning. And she said, 'Well somebody is coming over to get some bears.' And I said—she goes, 'Well, can you come back this afternoon?' And I said okay, and at that point I left."

"Did you have any intention of coming back in the afternoon?" No, he said, he didn't. Rogers asked where Barone went after that. To Denise Nichols's apartment, Barone replied. And he'd later told Sheila Hawkins about the odd encounter, saying it happened after he'd been crabbing in Tillamook. The defender wanted to know why he'd bother to tell Sheila that.

"I was still trying to establish a relationship with Sheila and I was at Denise's house when I called." Gallery observers needed a program to keep all these women in Barone's life sorted out.

Rogers tried to help along those lines, but even more knots appeared in the tangled web when Barone said he wanted the relationship with Sheila and didn't want Denise to be involved in the picture. After a few questions about time frames that revealed little of importance, Rogers asked if Barone had ever been at a nursing home in Forest Grove. He referred to a facility where a helpless woman had been fondled and someone matching Barone's description had been seen trying to steal a television set. Barone acknowledged having been there several times, with Sheila, to visit an elderly male patient he knew, and at other times in search of a woman he'd met in a bar. She'd told him that she worked in the nursing home, but his attempts to find her there had been unsuccessful.

Regarding his fingerprints found on a window in a patient's room, Barone had an explanation for that, too. He claimed that during a visit he'd noticed the screen was bent away from the window and he had tried to push it back into place.

But he absolutely denied being at the home on that December morning when the woman was molested and the television theft attempt had been made. The defense attorney nodded with satisfaction and sat down, so Roger Hanlon stood to question the witness. First, he established that Barone had been convicted of a 1977 burglary in Florida. And another one in 1980. And a prison escape attempt in 1981.

"Were you convicted of aggravated battery of a policewoman in Dixie County, Florida, in 1984?"

"No," Barone snapped.

Unfazed, Hanlon asked, "What were you convicted of in March 1984, in Dixie County, Florida?"

"Strong-arm battery of a police officer." Same difference to the jury, but technically correct. Hanlon made sure the jury knew that all of the convictions were felonies.

After the judge dealt with a couple of objections, Hanlon wanted a description of the woman Barone claimed he'd met in a bar and tried to visit at the nursing home.

"Her name was Cheri or Cheryl. She was five-eight, 125 pounds, blonde hair, middle-of-the-back length, small-boned. She had two kids." Rolling out the stats as if he'd memorized them.

Hanlon asked if he'd given the description to anyone at the nursing home in his attempt to find her. Yes, Barone said, he had. Hanlon shot back, "And did they identify her for you?"

"Yes."

"What's her last name, Mr. Barone?"

"I have no idea. I don't recall her last name at all."

"They gave it to you though?"

"I don't recall if it was of any importance." The words were delivered in a flippant manner with commensurate body language.

"I thought you said they gave you her last name."

"They recalled who I was talking about and they said she no longer worked there."

"Didn't you just testify that they gave you her last name?"

"I don't recall if they gave me her last name. I don't remember. They might have."

Hanlon refused to let it go. He wanted the jury to share his belief that the woman never existed, but had been dreamed up by Barone as an excuse to hang around the nursing home. "That's not the question. Didn't you just testify they gave you the last name?" Barone insisted that he didn't recall. And Hanlon still pounded away. "Mr. Barone, listen to the question. Didn't you testify just a minute ago, and we'll have it read back if need be, that they gave you her last name?" Barone finally agreed he might have said that. Hanlon had made his point, so he moved on. "How many times did you visit the patient you knew at the nursing home?"

"Approximately five, four or five times."

"How long have you known him?" Barone said he'd met the man and his wife in the summer of 1992. Hanlon launched a barrage of questions intended to throw doubt on that relationship, too, then suddenly jumped back to the window screen Barone had pushed back into place. "Can you explain why you recall such a minor event?"

With what appeared to be an effort to remain impassive, Barone answered, "I'm sort of a busybody. When things are hanging down, I'll push them back up or move them out of the way, pick trash up. That's just the way I am." At that point, Hanlon probably should have whipped out some photographs of the squalor and clutter in the interior of the Ron Price house where Barone had lived during his last few weeks of freedom. Of course Price would have been blamed.

Hanlon took another tack, though. "When did you first

learn that your fingerprint was found on the window of room number one?"

"Oh, maybe six months ago, five or six months ago." He'd learned it through a police report.

"Okay. So some seven months after you were there, you were able to remember when it was you were there, mid-December, and you remembered pushing up a screen on window number one? Is that correct?"

Squirming ever so slightly, Barone answered, "I've had a lot of time to think about this."

Hanlon held up a knife and sheath, and elicited from Barone an admission they were his, but he wouldn't agree that he'd left them at Ron Price's house. No, he said, he hadn't told Price to remove them from the house, either. Nor would he say he'd asked Price to torch the place.

"On the morning of the thirteenth, what time did you arrive at Denise Nichols's home?"

"I'm not sure of the exact time. I just went from Matilda's house over to Denise's apartment." Hanlon ran Barone through events of the preceding night again and wanted to know if he could name any of the people at the party he said he'd attended. "No, not offhand," Barone muttered. And he said the only thing he drank at the gathering was Cokes. But he'd dropped by a bar afterward and had a couple of "screwdrivers."

"Did you tell Sheila Hawkins that Ms. Gardner tried to kiss you and tell you to come back that afternoon for sex?"

"I told her that later."

"Why didn't you tell her that day?" Hanlon referred to the morning after the attempted sexual assault, when Sheila had called Barone and asked him to bring her some Advil.

"Because I—why embarrass people, you know? They're already saying things that are not true, or whatever, so there's no need for me to say that. The truth would come out." Roger Hanlon turned his back to the defendant and smiled. He certainly hoped the truth would come out.

"So who's saying things that aren't true, Mr. Barone?"

"Ms. Gardner."

"Pretty uncommon experience for a fifty-nine-year-old neighbor to try to kiss you and tell you to come back for sex?"

"Sure. It has never happened to me before." He hadn't told Denise about it either, because it was "kind of embarrassing, actually."

Hanlon turned up the heat a notch. "Did you tell Wayne Fallon in the jail that you like old women with big tits?"

His face flushing, Barone tried evasive action. "I never liked Wayne Fallon, so I never talked to him."

"I didn't ask you whether you liked him." Hanlon repeated the question.

"No, I did not."

"Did you tell another inmate that you liked women, old women, with big tits?"

"No, I did not."

"Does Wayne Fallon have some kind of ax to grind with you?"

"Yes. Him and a couple other people—they thought they were bullies. I've never sat well with bullies. I—they were going to beat up [another inmate] and I told them . . . to beat up somebody that wasn't old, somebody that could defend himself." Barone described the targeted victim as out of shape. "He was always complaining about a bad back. Complaining, you know, he was scared that they were going to hurt him. And so I—him and I would play cards all the time, cribbage, and I said they weren't going to beat him up. And Fallon was instigating, trying to get the other guy to beat him up. And then I caught Fallon stealing candy out of their cells, and that was another thing, reason, why I had nothing to say to the guy, much less confide in him."

"Mr. Barone, do you know what a kite is?"

"Yes. It's a request slip. Any type of activity that may, you know, person in jail wants to be involved in, maybe be moved, be—do something, get involved in one of the programs, to go to the law library, haircut, talk to a supervisor."

"Did your cellmate know that you were protecting him from Mr. Fallon?"

"Yes, he did."

"Were you aware that the man you were protecting kited out of your cell block because he wanted to get away from you, that he was afraid of you?"

Barone allowed himself a little smirk. "I think if you look at the records you would see that I was removed out of the cell block before he was."

Sighing audibly, Hanlon said, "The question was, were you aware that he sent out a kite requesting to get away from you?"

"No, I'm not aware of that. I know that just before I left, as I was going out the door, he handed me his phone number. I didn't think that was indicative of being afraid of somebody . . ."

When Hanlon asked again about the relationship with Ms. Gardner, Barone turned to Judge Nachtigal and said, "Your honor, can I ask my attorney one thing real quick about something?" The judge's answer wasn't complex. No. Appearing embarrassed, Barone apologized. To the next questions, he claimed he'd never held a knife to the woman's throat, nor had he dropped his pants and demanded oral sex.

"You never put her on the ground and told her you were going to rape her?"

"No, I did not."

"You never climbed on top of her with her clothes off and your clothes off?

"No, I did not."

"During the time you lived on North Fourth, did you ever park your vehicle on the other side of Baseline, south of the railroad tracks?"

"Yes, I did."

"Why, Mr. Barone?"

"I didn't want to be associated, you know, Denise—with Denise Nichols, because Denise lived across the street from where I was living with Sheila and I didn't need to add to the complications, so it's easier for me to park my car down the street, half a block away, and walk to the house."

The answer pleased Hanlon because it not only sounded like an alibi for parking away from the two-story house when Barone wanted to rape Matilda Gardner, but it also revealed the devious behavior of Barone in juggling his relationships with women. Hanlon asked a series of questions about some requests Barone may have made of various acquaintances to provide falsified statements of his whereabouts during the assault. He unequivocally denied doing such an underhanded thing.

Reminding Barone of the morning he was arrested at a bar, Hanlon asked, "Do you remember the officer asking you if your car was in the parking lot?"

"Yes, he asked me how I got there."

"What did you tell him?"

"I said I got dropped off by friends."

"Where was your car that morning?"

"In front of the parking lot." The implication of Barone's lie was clear to observers. If Barone had been dropped off by friends he probably could not have been at Matilda Gardner's house, alone. Also, he probably didn't want the police to look inside the Toyota where they might have found some guns and knives. His failure to tell the truth sounded like consciousness of guilt.

Barone had made a series of statements to Sergeant Mark Christy after the arrest. Hanlon asked, "Did you tell him Ms. Gardner tried to kiss you that morning?"

"I said nothing of the kind."

"Why not, Mr. Barone?"

"Because I knew the truth would come out in the long run." Hanlon verified the defendant had been told by Sergeant Christy that he was suspected of burglary, rape, and sodomy. He asked Barone, "You left out the part about her coming on to you?"

"Yes."

"Are you trying to say that was just an oversight on your part?"

"No, because it was—I had the impression that if I spoke with Sergeant Christy, you know, was up front with him, told him what happened or whatever, related my side of the thing, just that nothing happened, that he was going to let me go."

"Well, wouldn't it have best served your interests, then, if the only thing that happened that morning was that an old woman came on to you, why wouldn't you have told Sergeant Christy about that."

"I didn't think it had any relevance."

"You were being accused of rape and—attempted rape

and attempted sodomy and burglary of that very woman in that very residence, Mr. Barone."

"I said I didn't do it. I mean what more can I say? At that time he came out with the charges, he said, you know, 'Did you do this?' And I said, 'No, I did not.' And, you know, I'm thinking, well, she's maybe mad because I didn't come over there. I had no idea when they went and spoke with her or anything like that. He didn't say, 'You went over there at eight o'clock this morning and we were over there at eight-fifteen or eight-thirty.' He did not say, 'If you went over there that evening,' or did not say, 'If you went over there three or four days later.'"

The convoluted rambling didn't make a lot of sense to observers. Hanlon asked, "How would that have changed your answer to Sergeant Christy?"

"If it had been three or four days later, I could have thought, well, maybe she was mad because I didn't come back over. I had no idea."

Having shown the jury Barone's failure to tell the police his version of the confrontation with Matilda Gardner, Hanlon now brought out an obvious lie the defendant had told. Sergeant Christy had asked Barone if he was in fact the man who'd been known in Florida as Adolph Rode, who had a record of felony convictions. "You denied it, didn't you?" Hanlon asked.

Barone stammered for a moment. "I just—I denied it, yes, I did."

Jurors' faces remained blank, but Hanlon felt confident they understood the nature of this man.

Keith Rogers's redirect examination of his client lasted less than one minute. He established that Barone had legally changed his name from Adolph Rode, and that he was only sixteen when he'd faced his first burglary charge, and nineteen when he'd been charged with attempted burglary of an automobile.

Following final arguments by both sides, and the reading of jury instructions by Judge Nachtigal, the jury filed into their deliberation room to weigh the facts and make a decision.

Chapter 26

After deliberating for no more than three hours, the jury returned and handed their verdicts to a clerk. They'd found Cesar Barone guilty in fourteen of the charges, all of them in the first degree, including burglary, theft, attempted sodomy and attempted rape, but had not found enough evidence to convict him of snatching Sarah Ross's purse, or of stealing a VCR and TV from Denise Nichols. The latter two items had been returned to her by Ron Price.

Roger Hanlon urged Judge Nachtigal to hand down maximum possible sentences for the multiple convictions. Barone still faced a murder trial, but there was certainly no guarantee that he'd be condemned for killing the four women, or any of them. Hanlon wanted to be sure Barone would stay behind bars as long as possible.

Judge Nachtigal heard appeals and motions from both sides, then announced her decision: Barone must be confined to the Oregon state penitentiary system to serve consecutive terms for the attempted sexual abuse of the paralyzed female patient and of attempting to burglarize the nursing home, for attempting to rape Matilda Gardner, for stealing Denise Nichols's cash and her ring, and for the attempted assault of Sarah Ross.

Commenting on the cruel nature of Barone's crimes, a stern-faced Nachtigal said, "You're a predatory individual and you are an extreme danger to this community." She spoke for nearly five minutes enumerating the number of months to be served on each count and cited five "compelling reasons for an upward departure" to be applied to the sentences: (1) the particular vulnerability of the victims; (2) the threat of violence toward victims and witnesses; (3) persistent involvement in similar offenses; (4) the use of a weapon; and (5) The degree of harm or loss to victims was significantly greater than typical for such offenses.

Consistent with Roger Hanlon's recommendation, Judge Nachtigal exercised her legal option to apply the "upward departure." In layman's language that meant she *doubled* the maximum terms provided for in state guidelines! Barone would be locked in prison for more than forty-four years! Nachtigal said, "I certainly hope you serve every single day of it."

If Barone ever could find a way to legally shorten his years behind bars and walked out of prison earlier than the prescribed term, he would be required to register as a sex offender, could never have direct or indirect contact with Matilda Gardner, would be prohibited from contact with minors without permission of a parole officer, and could not possess any "printed, photographed, or recorded materials that he may use for purpose of his deviant sexual arousal."

One thing Cesar Barone learned from the trial; he would think twice before ever again taking the witness stand. In his pending trial for murder, he would not testify in his own behalf.

Barone's appointed attorneys for the forthcoming murder trial, Griffith C. Steinke and Laura Graser, had already plunged headlong into the task of defending him. Steinke had once been an ITT employee and minister for a small church. A staunch opponent of capital punishment, he'd had only one client sentenced to death. Graser had once been a prosecutor in the Washington County DA's office.

One week after Judge Nachtigal had slammed Barone with a sentence exceeding four decades in prison, another judge had also made an important decision. The Honorable Michael J. McElligott, Washington County circuit judge, announced that the charges against Barone for murdering Martha Bryant, Chantee Woodman, Betty Williams, and Margaret Schmidt would be consolidated into one single trial, scheduled to commence on October 25, 1994.

A motion had already been put before the judge for a change of venue. Objecting to the broad television and newspaper interest in the case, one of the defenders wrote,

"This extensive news coverage and rampant speculation by
the media about the alleged crimes of the defendant is so
recent and pervasive, that it would be impossible to guarantee that the defendant could get a fair trial. . . . We ask
for this change of venue to protect the Defendant's right
to fair trial."

Judge McElligott expressed the opinion that Washington
County residents could be objective in determining the guilt
or innocence of Mr. Barone.

Because of the unprecedented complexity of handling a
fourfold prosecution, two deputy district attorneys would
share the duties. Bob Hermann would be joined by
Roger Hanlon.

District Attorney Scott Upham might have personally
tackled the case, but every minute of his time would be
consumed in a courtroom down the hall from Judge McElligott's. A local businessman had been accused of killing his
attorney wife, and the story had caught the imagination of
news media reporters. Upham would prosecute the prolonged and complex case.

Hermann and Hanlon launched themselves into intensive
preparation for the Barone trial, with a scant five months
to assemble all the evidence, contact hundreds of potential
witnesses, and prepare to cope with a torrent of legal motions the defense would surely unleash.

One of the primary worries troubling the prosecution
team was the hearsay evidence a motley array of jail informants would present to the jury. These guys were not exactly Boy Scouts, and it might be difficult for the twelve
citizens, good and true, to place much credence in their
stories. In the case of Betty Williams, the defense would
no doubt insist that she died of natural causes, and there
was no murder to even be considered. The Reebok shoe
print left at Margaret Schmidt's house contained characteristics similar to the shoe recovered from Ron Price's
charred house where Barone had lived, but that would be
challenged by defense experts. In the Woodman case, it
didn't appear that Len Darcell would testify, and the videotape taken during his trip to the crime scene could be interpreted as self-serving. The prosecutors still waited for DNA

lab results to see if it was Martha Bryant's blood found in the little .22 revolver barrel, which had allegedly been in Barone's possession. Additional tests were in the pipeline to determine if bloodstains in the Chevrolet backseat matched Bryant's DNA pattern. If so, that would be the strongest physical evidence available. Both Bob and Roger knew Barone had committed the murders, but convincing a jury, beyond a reasonable doubt, would be no day at the beach.

One strategy the defense team worked hard to implement was to convince Judge McElligott to sever the trial into two, three, or even four trials. That could mean delays, reluctant witnesses, more opportunity for reversible errors, and most important of all, no overlap of evidence. In other words, if the case against Barone was weak in the murder of Margaret Schmidt, for example, the defenders might stand a better chance of acquittal on that charge in a separate trial. Thus, they could avoid the risk of the jury in a consolidated trial finding him guilty of any one of the murders because they might believe he committed the other three.

To convince the judge to consider severance, attorney Laura Glaser prepared supporting documentation for the motion. In it, she stated:

"These four murders are about as different as murders can be. The Bryant case involved an unknown confederate. Bryant and the defendant did not know each other." Graser also pointed out that the nurse-midwife was killed on a Friday, Bryant was in her forties and not obese, she was driving a car, and was shot in the temple.

Woodman, Graser wrote, was killed on a Wednesday, involved accomplice Darcell (who could not have been present at the Bryant killing) and the victim was only in her twenties. No blood or DNA evidence could link Barone to the case, and the victim was shot under the chin.

Williams, who'd died of a heart attack, wasn't murdered at all, Graser contended. The woman was a friend of the defendant and she died of natural causes brought on by poor health, not gunshots. There was no evidence of a sexual assault. No accomplice. Graser alleged that Williams had died "apparently while sitting on the toilet having a bowel movement."

Schmidt, according to Graser, was obese, elderly, and a total stranger to the defendant. No accomplice. No blood evidence, only an ambiguous shoe print. A complete contrast to the other cases.

The only major similarity in the four cases, Graser wrote, was that all the victims were women. "Beyond that, the state has charged or suggested in press conferences that there were sexual offenses, but the state cannot bootstrap joinder by the language it uses in the indictment or during press conferences. There is physical evidence showing an obvious sexual assault in the Bryant and Schmidt cases, but there is no such evidence [relating to the defendant] in the other two." Graser also pointed out that each homicide took place in a different location and that, as the state admitted, three different guns were used in the Bryant and Woodman cases, but no guns in the other two. "These homicides are very different, and the only reason to try them together is the minor gain in judicial economy and the impermissible 'gain' of creating great prejudice against the defendant."

Some taxpayers might have quarreled with Graser's use of the term "minor gain in judicial economy." Trials are enormously expensive, and getting a bargain four for the price of one would probably appeal very strongly to a large segment of the people who pay the bills.

Judge McElligott listened, examined the merits of the arguments, and took it under consideration.

In September, a private investigator for the defense interviewed Carlos Romero in the Oregon state penitentiary. Much of what Romero said agreed with statements he'd made seventeen months earlier to Tom Robinson, with one noticeable exception. The PI reported the informant seemed to be waffling on who had possession of his .22 revolver at the time of the Bryant murder. Romero suggested, the PI said, that Barone could not have had it at that time.

According to Romero, the PI said, the Woodman murder case had some holes in it, too. Leonard Darcell, he reported, had talked to Romero and had told him a story that differed from what he had told the police. For one thing, Barone, Darcell, and Woodman had all been using cocaine on the night she died. Romero also wanted to be sure the police did not think that his gun was the one used to shoot Woodman.

Bob Hermann and Roger Hanlon took a second look at the defense motion to sever the trials. Maybe the proposal had some merit. There also might be some advantages for the prosecution. They would be treading through a minefield of legal traps by trying all four cases at once, and a single reversible error would force them into repeating the entire process. In separate proceedings, each verdict would stand on its own. In early October, they stood before Judge McElligott and agreed with the defense team. "Let's sever the trials."

The judge, a tall thin man with black hair swept forward into four or five stiletto-shaped locks on his forehead, round wire-frame glasses, and creases like parentheses on either side of his unsmiling mouth, was a person who tolerated no nonsense in his courtroom. Prone to sudden animated movements of his long arms, and generous with scathing redress of anyone straying from proper decorum or procedure, McElligott's style kept attorneys alert. They understood that it was not a good idea to risk being subjected to his wrath. But two lawyers who'd tried a number of cases in front of McElligott's bench whispered to a journalist, "He's really a good guy."

The judge nodded at the prosecutors' reasoning regarding the severance, and on Monday, October 10, two years and one day after Martha Bryant had been abducted and shot to death, he ruled that at least two trials would be held. The Martha Bryant case would be first, still scheduled for October 26, and McElligott would rule later on splitting up the other three. The judge also said he'd appoint a separate team of attorneys to represent Barone for the subsequent trial, or trials.

Additional motions had been presented to McElligott, as well. A prison corrections officer had offered to testify about a confession Barone allegedly made. The officer said he'd overheard the defendant state that he'd admit to the

murder of Chantee Woodman, but in regards to the death
of Martha Bryant, he'd drag his feet every inch of the way,
and the state would have to prove its case. Laura Graser
leaped to her feet and said no such admission had ever
been made by her client. It didn't matter, McElligott said.
To allow that into evidence would breach the lawyer-client
privilege, therefore it won't be heard in his courtroom.

Neither would the jury be told about the acquaintance-
ship between Cesar Barone and the late Ted Bundy. The
matter was irrelevant to Barone's guilt or innocence. In any
case, Barone not only denied killing anyone, he also denied
that he'd ever met Bundy.

The postponements and delays came to an end in the
last week of October when Judge McElligott arranged to
summon 1,500 candidates for jury service. The citizens lined
up in the chilly autumn weather to file one by one through
a security portal where coins, keys, belt buckles, or metal
weapons would set off an alarm.

Narrowed down to a manageable few hundred, then doz-
ens the panelists sat quietly in the courtroom while the
voir dire process began in earnest. Griffith Steinke and
Laura Graser framed questions meant to identify potential
jurors' attitudes about the death penalty. Both sides would
wage a battle to seat jurors inclined to favor or dislike
imposing capital punishment. They also needed individuals
who would not be seriously inconvenienced by a trial that
might last into 1995.

All the leftover Thanksgiving turkey had been consumed
over the long holiday when the trial of Cesar Barone, accused of murdering Martha Bryant, got underway on Monday, November 28. In the modern, rectangular courtroom
with soft-hued walls and indirect lighting in the high ceiling,
the jury of seven women and four men sat in gray uphol-
stered swivel chairs. Victims' family members and reporters
filled the three rows of gallery seats, directly behind Bob
Hermann and Roger Hanlon at their prosecution table. The
defense table, placed at a forty-five-degree angle to their
right, was equipped with three chairs. Laura Graser, a
pleasant-appearing woman with a kindly expression,

dressed primly in a ruffled white blouse and a dark suit, was seated on the left end. Griffith Steinke, early forties, wearing rimless glasses and frown lines across his broad forehead, his light brown hair thinning at the top, occupied the center chair, and Cesar Barone, clad in a dark suit, large-collared shirt, and patterned tie, sat to the far right. At the head of the room, elevated above everyone, his head haloed by a large circle emblazoned with the words STATE OF OREGON, 1859, Judge McElligott surveyed the assembly. He swore in the jury, and signaled the prosecution to start the proceedings.

Prosecutor Robert Hermann stood to deliver his opening remarks. Following introductory comments and explanation of the charges, Hermann told the attentive jurors they would see evidence and hear witnesses to convince them, beyond a reasonable doubt, that Cesar Barone was guilty of aggravated murder. There was one witness who wouldn't be able to testify, though, he said. "Quite bluntly and quite obviously, you will not hear from Martha Bryant, so you will not hear testimony from the victim as to who her kidnapper was."

Hermann laid out the sequence of events in the predawn hours of October 8, 1992, describing Bryant's delivery of a baby in Tuality Hospital, her compassionate aid to the new mother, and her departure at almost three that morning. "You're going to learn that Martha Bryant was a living human being, a little less than a month past her forty-first birthday. And you're going to learn from the evidence that she headed out Cornell Road on her way home, and you will see that her car was literally blown off the road by gunfire . . . She was taken, whether from the car or by getting out and trying to get away, she was taken from that scene. You'll learn that she was shot in the back while in the car . . . and taken from that location down to 231st."

Dead quiet in the courtroom. All eyes riveted on the elegant speaker. "You will see and conclude that it was a brutal, enormous assault on her vehicle and ultimately on her person . . . that there was an attempt to sexually assault her. And most likely because of the condition she was in from the gunshot wound and probably the battle she put up to keep from being taken against her will, she wasn't much use to her assailant. And then you will learn that she was executed, a gunshot wound to the right temple of her head." Hermann spoke the word "executed" with slow, clear articulation. "And you will learn that wasn't enough. Her body was displayed. She was left in the middle of the highway for everybody to see that came along."

With a slight pause to let the horror sink in, Hermann made eye contact with each juror, and held up a chart of the crime scene. After mentioning witnesses who'd heard the gunshots and seen a muscle car drive away, the prosecutor turned to the autopsy of Bryant's body. The wound to her temple, he said, was the type "you would expect there might be blow-back in the barrel of the gun because of the close proximity of the shot." The bloodstains, he said, were similar to Bryant's, but could not be absolutely matched with samples from her.

Hermann told of the massive investigation and the efforts of police to track down a suspect. Finally, in April 1993, he said, the defendant had told jail inmates of his involvement and revealed details that could only be known by the killer. The muscle car he'd used was also tracked down and hauled in. Bloodstains in the back seat were subjected to DNA tests. Hermann gave the jurors a brief explanation of RFLP and PCR testing processes, information the whole world would hear about one year later in the nationally televised trial of O.J. Simpson in Los Angeles. The blood in Barone's backseat, Herman said, "revealed a DNA pattern identical to Martha Bryant's." The criminalist involved would testify that "this particular pattern is found in less than one in ten billion DNA patterns."

More evidence had been found in Martha Bryant's underwear, Hermann revealed. A pubic hair lifted from her underpants "was similar to" a pubic hair sample taken from Cesar Barone. The 9 mm semiautomatic pistol used to shoot up the Volkswagen had been recovered during a search of Barone's residence, and the .22 caliber execution revolver, owned by a friend of Barone's, had been in the suspect's possession when Bryant was killed.

Through Hermann's words, the jury learned that two different traffic officers had encountered Barone that night, nor far from the crime scene. A variety of witnesses would give the jury all the details, Hermann said, and wound down by telling the jurors, "When you are through with it all, the conclusion will be inescapable that this man sitting here in the courtroom is the man that is guilty and responsible for executing Martha Bryant. Thank you."

Every juror turned slightly to glance at Cesar Barone, who sat stiffly in a suit and tie, his salt and pepper hair trimmed and brushed back, and his face decorated with a new pair of eyeglasses. Observers thought he looked smug and confident.

Before releasing the jurors for a lunch break, the judge gave the standard admonition not to discuss the case among themselves or with anyone else and not to draw any conclusions yet. He would repeat those words often during the next few weeks.

With everyone reassembled, sleepy from too much lunch and the warmth of the courtroom, Griffith Steinke greeted the jurors with his first smile, and reiterated the importance of not reaching any conclusion about the case until they'd heard all the evidence.

That evidence, he hoped, would lead them to find his client not guilty. Nothing the prosecutor had discussed, he said, would point to Cesar Barone as the one who murdered Martha Bryant. "Not only do we not know who fired the bullet that killed Martha Bryant, be we don't know if it was done as an execution or as a matter of rage on the spot."

Steinke emphasized that one of the witnesses had reported hearing two male voices near the Volkswagen. He told the jurors that the evidence he presented would prove that one of the men present that night stayed at the wheel of his car and yelled orders at the other man who stood next to the Volkswagen. Creating a word picture of the fusillade of shots slamming into Bryant's moving car, Steinke pointed out that it would been extremely difficult for the perpetrator to drive at those speeds, control the car, and fire bullets into another car. The prosecutor, Steinke suggested, while tilting his head in the direction of Bob

Hermann, had not presented an accurate account of what happened that night. The case against Barone was clearly exaggerated.

His voice shaking with indignation, Steinke challenged the "one in ten billion" chance, according to DNA tests, that the blood in the Chevrolet belonged to Bryant. The guns used could have been in the possession of several different people, he hinted, and the allegation that Bryant's body had been deliberately displayed in the middle of the road was nothing but conjecture.

Finally, Steinke lashed out at the use of inmates whose stories cannot be trusted, and whose details did not match the facts of the case. "It's our job to keep the government honest," he said.

In an unusual move that morning, Judge McElligott instructed the bailiff to take the jurors to a yellow school bus waiting outside. They traveled a few blocks to the storage facility where they walked slowly around the bullet-riddled green Volkswagen, examining it in awed silence. As soon as each juror, plus the six alternates, completed the inspection, they climbed back into the bus for a trip northeast of town, along Cornell road. After a stop at the site where Martha Bryant's Volkswagen had bounced to a tragic halt, the jurors rode another short distance to the spot where Martha's body had been found. The eighteen people, wearing jackets to ward off the autumn morning chill, hands in pockets, walked slowly in single file along both sides of the road, creating their own mental images of the horror-filled night two years before.

Chapter 27

During the remainder of the opening day and a portion of the second day, Tuesday, testimony from police officers established a chronology of events: the flood of 911 calls reporting gunshots, the discovery of a stalled Volkswagen riddled with bullets, and a search for evidence that turned up a handful of spent 9 mm shells.

Jurors learned how the mortally wounded Martha Bryant was seen by startled predawn motorists who told of discovering her sprawled in the middle of 231st Street. One of the witnesses expressed to the jury his shock and described how he raced eighty miles per hour to a phone to call for emergency help.

After lunch, Julia Florea, a registered nurse who worked for LifeFlight, the helicopter service, took the stand and filled the courtroom with pain. "Our initial information was that we had a female who had a gunshot wound to her chest, that they were attempting to manage her airway and were having some difficulty. When I got out of the helicopter and got over to where the patient was, I saw . . . she was having some difficulty breathing and she was doing what we call posturing. She was not conscious, but every time she would have any stimuli, she would turn her arms inward and clenched her teeth, and so they were unable to get an airway down into her mouth because they couldn't get her mouth open."

By injecting relaxant drugs, Florea managed to "intubate" the patient, then helped "logroll" her onto a board for transport in the chopper. Asked about Bryant's clothing, the nurse described what she saw. "Her pants and underwear were down around her knees. I remember she was wearing purple socks and she had Birkenstocks on. Her blouse was laying underneath her. We had cut pieces of it back, and I saw the gunshot wound to her chest. And upon looking at her, I knew that she probably had a gunshot wound to the head someplace, just by her appearance, but nobody had located it until we got there." Florea told of accompanying Bryant on the flight, to the trauma room, and was with her until the end. She told the jury that the patient never recovered consciousness.

Griffith Steinke asked for more information about the difficulty in breathing mentioned by Florea. The witness said, "Her respiratory rate was very shallow and slow. She had blood in her nose and mouth." The patient made "moaning, gurgling sounds . . . and her legs were rigidly extended, with her toes pointed."

Everyone in the room seemed to exhale when Julia Florea stepped down.

Almost before the next witness was seated, Griffith Steinke rose, asking the court's permission to reverse the usual order by asking questions before the prosecution started examination. The defense wanted to prevent gory autopsy photographs from being shown to the jury. Judge McElligott disagreed, finding that although the photos were unpleasant, they were a necessary element of the prosecution's case and were not prejudicial.

Pathologist Karen Gunson testified that the cause of Martha Bryant's death was a gunshot wound to the head. In the doctor's detailed narrative of autopsy procedures, she first described the wound, then said, "Once we look at this injury, we then want to find the path of this bullet through the body, so we pull back the scalp and remove the skull to see where the bullet goes. And when we did that, we found there was gunpowder blown into the soft tissue beneath the scalp, between the scalp and the skull. The reason this is important is because these findings indicate this is a contact wound." With the use of full-color photos, she demonstrated the path of the bullet through the brain and how the deadly missile wound up behind the cheekbone.

Jurors' faces remained stoic even though some of them may have felt queasy from the ghastly photos. Dr. Gunson described the back and chest wounds, and injuries the victim had sustained on her face and body, where lacerations, bruises, and contusions could be clearly seen. There was also an abrasion in the vagina.

Before asking about the additional injuries, Hermann wanted to be certain the jury understood what "intubation" meant, since the previous witness had used the term in describing efforts to clear Bryant's air passages. Dr. Gunson defined it as "just placing a tube through the mouth into the trachea, or the breathing tube, in order to assist the patient to breathe."

One minor injury, but important, was a fractured, bloody fingernail. Gunson explained that she'd paid particular attention to it "because Ms. Bryant was a nurse-midwife, and . . . they do have contact with patients, so they often are very careful about fingernails and so forth, because they're dealing with delivering babies." The badly broken fingernail, then, probably resulted from being assaulted.

A jailhouse informant, who was on Hermann's list of witnesses yet to be called, had used the term "sucking sound" in quoting Barone's description of the noise made when the woman from the Volkswagen tried to breathe after being shot. Herman wanted the jury to hear a professional opinion in advance, so he asked Dr. Gunson, "Would a person suffering that type of a wound ever make a kind of sucking sound?"

Gunson said, "Certainly could because there is a communication between the outside air and the chest or lung itself. So many times when that occurs, there's something called a sucking chest wound, where there is free interchange of air from the outside into the chest itself, and it sounds like a sucking noise when that occurs." Hermann looked into the faces of jurors as if to transmit a message to remember that point.

Referring to the multitude of additional wounds on the victim, Hermann asked the doctor if she was able to offer an opinion whether those injuries were consistent with someone being thrown out of a moving vehicle?

The pathologist said no. A fall from a moving car would cause "brush-burn abrasions where they slide along the concrete or asphalt." Hermann hoped the jury perceived the implication that the injuries then, came from a severe beating by the assailant. Next, he asked about the contact bullet wound. "Are you familiar with the term 'blow-back?' "

"Yes, sir. Blow-back is where blood or brain tissue is actually sucked into the barrel of the weapon that is held tight to the head, and we see that in contact gunshot wounds, precisely because the weapon is held tight to the head."

With that gory image in the minds of the jurors, Hermann sat down.

Steinke immediately attacked the "thrown from a moving vehicle" comments with an excellent question. "What about being dropped from a standing vehicle?" Gunson admitted the distinct possibility the wounds could have been caused in that manner. But Steinke's next query didn't work quite so well. Could the bullet wound in the victim's back be from a ricochet slug?

"No, sir. The wound has a round, punched-out appearance. Ricochets, or what we call atypical gunshot wounds, are irregular in shape and size." And it hadn't passed through metal or glass, either. That left only one alternative, that the bullet must have had a clear path from the weapon muzzle to Martha Bryant's back. It wasn't difficult to picture the terrified woman twisting and bending away from flying glass shattered by the first salvo. With the window glass eliminated, there were no obstacles in the path of the bullet that hit her.

Steinke regained some ground on the subject of the injury to the victim's vagina. Gunson said she'd examined the abrasion under a microscope and found inflammatory white blood cells in it, meaning that it was "hours old." The doctor couldn't say how many hours, adding, "I certainly cannot say that it's associated with this particular incident." Steinke drove the issue home by eliciting from the doctor an agreement that the abrasion might even have been two or three days old.

The next two witnesses lived in the neighborhood on the west side of the long driveway where Bryant's Volkswagen came to a stop. One man had heard noises then caught a glimpse of the rectangular taillights on an older American-made vehicle. The second witness was Gloria Thomas, who had heard a commotion outside, and had looked out her second-story bedroom window. She'd seen a man standing at the VW driver's door, heard muffled words, and a few minutes later watched a muscle car drive away. Her initial report to the police had included the mention of two men's voices.

In her testimony, she recalled hearing the gunshots and peering out into the moonlit night where she saw the cars and the man. Hermann asked, "In terms of the voices, how would you describe—I think you used the word 'yelling.' How would you describe them?"

Gloria spoke confidently. "I can tell you that it was definitely male in tone that I heard. The person did not have a high-pitched voice. It was very low and very, very, short sentences, and very loud, extremely loud . . ."

"And how about the other voice?"

"I only heard a male voice, I mean a male voice in tone."

"Were you able to distinguish or did you perceive, from what you heard, did you distinguish that there was more than one voice?"

"No. I couldn't tell like from what directions—At the time, I thought that the person was either inside the car or very near the car, the person that I heard talking, and it was a male voice." And she could never distinguish any of the words spoken.

Hermann spent some time having Gloria use a chart to demonstrate her vantage point and the location of both vehicles. She was "adamant" that the suspect car was a Chevrolet. She saw it clearly as it backed out all the way across Cornell, turned eastward, and vanished. Recalling the subsequent trip to Portland used-car lots with Detective O'Connell to search for a vehicle that resembled the one she'd seen, Gloria said she hadn't found an exact duplicate of the car.

Somewhat gingerly, Hermann returned her attention to the man she'd seen from her bedroom window. "Did you indicate to the police, at one point, that your impression was that the man you saw got into the passenger side of the suspect car?"

"Initially, yes."

"But you've testified today that he got in the driver's side?"

"Yes." Hermann wanted to know what changed her mind. She answered, "I can just keep seeing the thing over and over in my head, again and again. And the person I saw did not get in the passenger side, they got in the driver's side. I remember telling that to the detective, that I did see the person get in the driver's side, probably four months later. I mean, I was certain of that at that time." Hermann spotlighted the time frame in which Gloria had changed her story pointing out that it was prior to March 15, long before any suspect had been identified in the case.

Once more Hermann asked her to describe the man she'd seen. Gloria's voice resonated with certainty. "The person was probably mid to late twenties, medium build, dark-colored hair. The hair stood up, because I could see light through it." He'd walked around the front of the car, in front of the headlight beams, and she got a pretty good look at him.

It was time for the afternoon break, and Hermann needed to check with the judge before he asked the next question. With the jury out, he told McElligott he was going to ask Thomas to look at a photo taken of Barone, in jail, before he had his hair neatly trimmed, and ask her if it was consistent with the suspect's hair she'd seen that night. Judge McElligott twisted toward Steinke and said, "And your objection is going to be . . . that the person is wearing jail clothing?"

"Two objections," Steinke said. "One, he's in jail clothing, and two, he's present in the courtroom and she can look at him right here."

McElligott didn't have to use his years of legal training to make his ruling, just some common sense. He suggested that the photo be trimmed to excise the jail clothing, got nods from Hermann, and overruled Steinke's objection. The defender forced a smile, and requested the break be extended to fifteen minutes so he could go get a Coke. McElligott made that ruling in Steinke's favor.

Back in front of the jury, Hermann held up the photo and asked the witness if anything in it was consistent with the person she'd seen. She answered literally, "It's a male, first of all, and the hairstyle and the fact that it goes up and away from the face. . . . The hair is consistent with what I saw." She couldn't, though, make a positive identification of the man she'd seen.

When Grif Steinke cross-examined her, he treaded softly. "I have some difficult questions to ask you and I'll try to do it as gently as possible. Over the course of time, your story has changed in some significant respects; is that correct?"

Sounding defensive, Gloria Thomas insisted that her story had changed in only one important segment, and that was the suspect entering his vehicle on the driver's side rather than the passenger side. Steinke reminded her that in her first report, Gloria had said she'd heard "two different male voices in a short, abrupt conversation." Steinke asked, "Did you tell the officer that you believed that the other voice was coming from the driver's seat of the vehicle and giving orders to the one standing outside?"

"Yes."

"I want to ask you if this is what you told Officer Martin," Steinke said as he held up a document and read from it. "Thomas said that she had been having dreams concerning the homicide . . ." The defender looked up, then back to the police report, which indicated the woman's dreams may have influenced her to alter her statement.

Frowning, the witness said she couldn't recall the conversation with Officer Martin, but didn't think she'd been dreaming. "I mean, I can visualize the whole thing over in my head. I wouldn't say that's a dream."

As late as January 1993, Steinke reminded her, she'd still been talking to the police about hearing a second male voice. Thomas became evasive, circling around details of what she'd heard and when, but finally acknowledged initially thinking she'd heard two male voices. She was sure about her recollection today, though, she insisted. "I heard—and this is exactly what I heard. I heard shouting and I heard command-type words coming out of someone's mouth. It sounded like someone was responding. And that's exactly what I told them."

The issue bounced back and forth for another ten minutes before Steinke felt he'd made his point. Hermann asked a few redirect questions, then released the drained young woman.

On the trial's third day, Wednesday morning, Michelle LaChance described her association with Martha Bryant as a midwife and how she'd helped deliver the baby in the early morning of October 9, then left the hospital not long after Bryant had departed. As she drove home, she said, she noticed some activity on Cornell Road. "I was very tired. I had a window open to try and stay awake. I was looking out the left side of the car and saw three or four police cars and a lot of broken glass and I thought to myself something had happened. I kind of wanted to make it home. And I didn't see her car."

Another midwife, Debbie Duran-Snell, in response to Hermann's request, described Martha's voice as "low and throaty." If the jury chose to believe there were two possible male voices heard at the stalled Volkswagen, Hermann planted the possibility that one of them was actually Martha Bryant.

Duran-Snell recalled for the jury a frightful experience she'd endured two nights before Martha's death. A man, she said, was lurking outside the hospital exit right around midnight, in an area reserved for doctors and nurses. After hesitating until he moved out of sight, she hurried to her van, jumped in, locked the doors and saw him again standing nearby. En route home, a car pulled closely behind her, then alongside. She couldn't see the driver, but the car looked similar to descriptions she later heard of the suspect car in the Bryant murder. When Caesar Barone was arrested, she recognized the newspaper photo of him as the man she'd seen staring at her in the hospital parking lot.

The testimony was presented over Grif Steinke's objections that it was highly prejudicial against his client. Out of the jury's hearing, Judge McElligott explained to both lawyers, "I kind of assume that the state wants that prejudice. The question is whether it's fair or unfair. . . . You don't offer evidence unless you expect it to be prejudicial. That's the whole idea. It's whether it's unfairly prejudicial because it asks for speculation to occur rather than inference to occur." After hearing more explanation from each side, he ruled the testimony would be allowed.

The first day of December brought threatening dark clouds over Washington County, contrasting with sparkling strings of Christmas lights and colorful decorations along Main Street near the Hillsboro courthouse. Exhaling vaporized breath, employees, attorneys, reporters, jurors, and court watchers scurried into the warm building each morning. On Tuesday, the heavens opened up and the howling downpour caused a temporary postponement of the trial.

When Judge McElligott's courtroom resumed business, evidence mounted day by day against Cesar Barone with testimony from investigators, forensic experts, and his acquaintances. The defendant didn't feel much like celebrating on his thirty-fourth birthday that week, nor on December 5 when his ex-wife took the stand.

The jury paid close attention as she told how they'd met through a personal ad, their subsequent marriage, and his military experience during which he'd mailed home from Panama a 9 mm semiautomatic pistol.

Barone wore glasses as he sat at the defense table, and Hermann suspected they were for effect rather than improved vision. He asked Kathi if Cesar had ever worn glasses before. She recalled that for a short period prior to his joining the Army, he'd used some for close-up work in the cabinet shop, but lost them and never acquired replacements. Her testimony that day was short, but she'd be recalled several more times.

After Michael O'Connell related how he and Tom Robinson had collected a pubic hair from Barone, a forensics expert reported that the hair found on Bryant's underwear was "consistent with Cesar Barone's pubic hair standards and ranges." Not as powerful as fingerprint evidence, he admitted, but a very strong indicator. On cross, Steinke narrowed the possibility a trifle by getting an admission from the expert that sometimes hairs are "cross-transferred" by other means than sexual assaults.

Rain pounded Hillsboro, soaking Christmas shoppers and snarling traffic, but the windowless courtroom was sequestered from the weather and holiday spirit as the real-life drama blocked everything else from the participants' minds.

Criminalist Chris Johnson of the OSP crime lab, who had spent scores of hours on the case, told jurors that bullet fragments found in the VW and the empty cartridges found in the vicinity, had been fired from Barone's 9 mm pistol. The slug found in Bryant's head could have been fired by the .22 revolver Barone reported had in his possession at the time, but the damage to the distorted piece of metal precluded positive identification.

Another OSP scientist led the jury through extremely technical explanations of DNA evidence before telling them the blood in the backseat of Barone's Chevy Chevelle matched only one person in ten billion, nearly twice the earth's population, and that person was Martha Bryant.

Ray Cardenas, Barone's old buddy who'd joined him for a skiing trip at Mount Hood and a long string of other social encounters, made it obvious he didn't enjoy his day on the stand. With a pained expression, he reluctantly spoke of drinking with Barone on the night of October 8 at a couple of joints, then taking him home before 2:30 A.M.

Sheila Hawkins recalled Cesar coming home about that time, but leaving again a few minutes later after rummaging around in the bedroom and taking something with him. It was nearly two hours before he returned. Asked about the Chevy Cesar'd been driving, Sheila said he sold it a few weeks later, and claimed he lost most of the money when it blew out of his pocket while riding a motorcycle. Her testimony brought the first look of dismay on Barone's face when she said he'd gained a lot of weight since they lived together, and looked about fifty pounds heavier. At the break, he whispered to a bailiff that he'd only gained fifteen pounds.

Barone's former boss at the cabinet shop, Andy Tremaine, and his wife were appalled at Cesar's behavior when he showed up at the shop after Bryant's death, she testified. The defendant, she said, discussed the murder reports in an animated manner. "He seemed very upbeat, excitable, and almost happy. He was hyper. There was lots of pacing and hand motions, and he was talking real loud." In the weeks afterward, the witness said, Barone became very moody and easily angered. "He acted as if he was concealing something."

Jurors and spectators were treated to a show when Troy Masters, still bearing the appearance of a rock musician, swaggered to the stand. During his testimony, he waved, gestured, grinned, and imitated the sounds of rapid gunfire when describing Barone's boasting regarding the murder. "He popped caps at her car numerous times, pop, pop, pop-pop-pop." And in describing the mortal wound to her temple, Masters formed the shape of a pistol with his hand, put the forefinger to his own temple, and voiced a sharp "Boom." The attorneys worded questions to Masters with care, avoiding any reference to the other three murders Barone stood accused of. The witness would have to wait until the upcoming trial to share Barone's confessions about those killings.

Barone had bragged about the murder within earshot, too, of ex-inmate Wayne Fallon, who testified next. Now out of prison and working full time, Fallon said he'd never heard anything like Barone's appalling confession before in his life. "It's something that's not easy to forget." The jury also heard about the "sucking" sounds Barone had reportedly described in reference to Bryant's pitiful attempts to keep breathing.

Ron Price took long, gangly steps to the stand, plopped down, and stammered to the jury that he'd burned his own house in an attempt to destroy evidence because Barone had ordered it and had threatened to kill Price if it wasn't put to the torch.

Both Tom Robinson and Michael O'Connell spent hours in the witness chair describing the complex and frustrating months of investigation that finally led to Cesàr Barone. Following their testimony, Bob Hermann called DNA expert Bruce Weir (who would testify eight months later in the O.J. Simpson trial) to reinforce the blood link between the stains on the backseat of Barone's car to Martha Bryant. Another DNA scientist informed the jury that the "blow-back" blood found in the .22 barrel stood a one-in-eight chance of coming from Martha Bryant. In other words, he said, about 12.7 percent of the North American population would also have similar blood.

With that, on Thursday, December 8, Bob Hermann rested the prosecution's case.

Chapter 28

Insiders worried that the defense presentation might take forever, considering the fact that Steinke and Graser had listed a staggering 123 potential witnesses to be called. It didn't turn out that way, though. Grif Steinke summoned no more than ten people, mostly to dispute the pivotal issue of Hermann's blood evidence.

The first defense witness was DNA expert Robert Thompson, who had built respected credentials as an employee of the OSP lab in Portland, and more recently had boosted his reputation through his work with the U. S. Bureau of Alcohol, Tobacco, and Firearms. Laura Graser framed questions designed to undermine the reliability of the OSP lab's calculations, supported by geneticist Bruce Weir, of the one-in-ten-billion figure linking backseat bloodstains to Martha Bryant. Speaking in self-assured terms, Thompson refuted the astronomical calculation with his own math and contended that perhaps three of six chromosome tests might tie the stains to Bryant, but three others were inconclusive. About the DNA results, which resemble bar charts, Thompson said, "I do not believe that is dark enough, clear enough, or distinct enough." He further asserted that there was a chance that the bloodstains had been left by someone else.

Gathering momentum, Steinke called Michael O'Connell back to the stand and demanded to know how many jail inmates had offered to inform on Barone. The total, O'Connell said, was eighteen. Had some of their stories conflicted with others? Of course they had. A few of them may have been fabricated for selfish purposes. O'Connell had put credence in the ones who possessed information previously unpublicized.

The key element spotlighted by the defense was the possible existence of an accomplice, which might be borne out by some of the inmates' stories. If Steinke and Graser could implant in the jurors' minds the possibility that two men had been present at Bryant's killing, the defenders would have a good chance of establishing reasonable doubt that Cesar Barone had pulled the trigger. No one, they held, could ever be certain which assailant had killed Bryant.

Steinke's next gambit startled observers. With the courtroom darkened, he slipped a videotape into the slot of a VCR. A touching scene in full color unfolded on the large television screen in front of the jury box. They watched Martha Bryant "catching" a baby! In her distinctive voice, Bryant coaxes the mother to push, and helps guide the infant's tiny body into independence from the mother. The compassionate midwife then assures the child is breathing normally before wrapping it in a blanket and handing the precious package to the new mom.

It became clear to spectators that Steinke and Graser wanted the jury to hear Bryant's speaking voice and to understand that her vocal tones probably wouldn't be mistaken for a man's. The words of the prosecution's own witness, Gloria Thomas, assumed monumental importance for the defense. In her first reports to the police, which the defense contended were more accurate than her later modified story, the sounds of two male voices suggested that Bryant had been abducted by a pair of men.

On that notion, Steinke announced, "The defense rests."

The issue of two men, and the cloud of doubt concerning which of them had fired the fatal shot, was stressed in Grif Steinke's final argument to the jury. He divided his talk into four segments he titled, "Red Herrings," "Let's Talk DNA," "How Many Were There?" and "Tales From the Jailhouse." Attacking the prosecution's use of jailhouse informants, Steinke stressed discrepancies in their stories, ripped DNA statistics, and once more appealed to jurors to see that they couldn't convict Barone beyond a reasonable doubt when the issue of two possible shooters had not been resolved.

Bob Hermann recapped highlights of his witnesses, stressed the reliability of blood evidence, and said, "This woman was executed by that man," pointing to Barone who sat like an army general in his chair. "He dumped her in the highway and he's damned proud of it." Speaking with a timbre of righteous indignation, he told the jurors that even if they ignored the informants' testimony, the evidence against Barone was still overwhelming. "The only way to find the defendant not guilty is if you lose track of your common sense and logic."

It took the jury ninety minutes to make a decision. Cesar F. Barone, they unanimously decreed, was guilty of aggravated murder. On all counts, kidnapping, attempted rape, and trying to conceal the crimes, all while in the course of murdering her, Barone was guilty.

Two of the female jurors later commented that they were impressed by DNA evidence regarding the blood in Barone's car. They also took the crimes personally, as voiced by one of them. "When you stop and think it could be any of us, especially women who are alone, it brings it back down to earth."

Each of the jury members knew they would be required to reconvene after the New Year holiday to sit through another round of testimony. This time they would have three choices; sending Barone to prison for the rest of his life with a chance of parole, locking him up forever without the possibility of parole, or sending him to death row.

For the penalty phrase, Roger Hanlon took center stage to present opening statements. "There are other victims of Mr. Barone, all of them women, most of them elderly," Hanlon said. "And as this extraordinary tale of hatred and death unfolds for you over the next two-and-a-half weeks, keep in mind that this is the Martha Bryant homicide." In this hearing, Hanlon would be able to lay out evidence prohibited in the guilt phase, such as history of previous crimes, Barone's own testimony in the previous year's rape trial, and elements of murder charges Barone still faced in the next trial. Hanlon gave brief verbal sketches of the Woodman, Williams, and Schmidt killings, plus the murder of Alice Stock in Florida. "Keep in mind the big picture," Hanlon advised the jurors, "as you hear these little stories about a rape here, an attempted rape there . . . and several murders here and there."

The defense team chose not to deliver opening statements until later.

Once again, the three women Barone had been convicted of sexually assaulting came into court and relived the terror they'd experienced. One sat in a wheelchair close to the jury box and spoke softly of being molested as she lay in a nursing home bed, paralyzed from the waist down.

Most of the witnesses from the guilt phase and from the previous trial returned to add vivid details to their previous testimony. Heather Crane introduced the jurors to the cold, wet streets of Portland's December night life and how Barone, with Darcell, had terrorized her. In addition, detectives and officers traveled across the country from Florida to paint a picture of Barone's early crimes. His ex-stepmother described how the youth, then known as Jimmy Rode, had raped her. And Barone's ex-wife, Kathi, filled in details of his lies, night forays, and conduct during their marriage.

While a string of witnesses revealed to jurors Barone's pathological behavior, he sat still, ramrod straight, and listened as if they were speaking of someone else. With his styled hair, glasses, and suit, he might have been an upwardly mobile manager in one of the local high-tech business organizations. But a female guard from the jail revealed another side of the defendant by telling how he'd lunged toward her, fists clenched, the previous October. She was positive he was trying to intimidate her. A cellmate testified that Barone had whispered of his plans, when he was released, that his next victim might be a woman from the jail staff. And guards had found a homemade ten-inch "shank" in his cell just a couple of months after he was arrested. One inmate told of a time when a group of men were watching a commercial on television featuring beautiful young women. Barone had scoffed at the girls, saying he'd take a seventy-year-old woman over those young things any time.

A Florida cellmate of Barone's recalled that "Jimmy Rode" had owned a collection of publications depicting explicit sexual acts with older women, and that he'd heard Barone confess to raping and strangling elderly women.

The informant mocked his old pal's clumsy efforts to adopt an Italian accent, his long stories of being from Milan, Italy, and claiming that his relative was an ambassador. Just a couple of days ago, the Florida inmate said, Barone had walked by his cell in the local jail, recognized him, and realizing he was there to testify, threatened, "I'll get you, I'll kill you if you do this."

When the prosecution rested, Steinke and Graser suffered a blow to their defense strategy. They had planned to put witnesses on the stand to report that Martha Bryant strongly opposed the death penalty. But Judge McElligott ruled that such testimony would be irrelevant and unrelated to Barone's background. Nor would the judge allow arguments on the merits of the death penalty, since that was a political issue for voters, not a matter for the jury to weigh. Steinke was devastated, complaining that the judge had taken away his strongest point of mitigation.

Still upset by the ruling, Steinke delivered his opening statement, declaring, "My client is a psychopath and we're going to prove that. . . . We're going to ask you to place Mr. Barone in prison for the rest of his life, but not to kill him." He suggested that Barone could be far more useful to society as a subject of behavioral study rather than as an executed felon.

In their effort to save Barone's life, Steinke and Graser brought his sister, Debbie, to Oregon along with three other Florida residents, to offer possible mitigating factors for the long history of criminal acts. Debbie hadn't seen her brother since he'd left Florida in 1987. When he was very young, she said, their mother took them to Miami where she became involved in a romance with a black man whom she later married. Asked about Jimmy's interests as a youth, Debbie said, "He was preoccupied with his looks. He was not a fighter. He was more of a flirter with girls."

Jimmy had anticipated starting a new life when he got out of prison, Debbie said, by moving to Oregon, getting married, and starting a new family.

A boyhood buddy of young Jimmy confirmed in his testimony that the stepmother had mistreated him. "She would ride him for anything, it didn't matter what." The childhood pal expressed the opinion that the stepmother just didn't like Jimmy. Even though testifying on Barone's behalf, the witness recalled once when they were hunting wild pigs together, and wounded one, Jimmy seemed to take an odd pleasure in slitting the animal's throat. Suggesting the possibility of Cesar having a split personality, the witness said his old pal would act like two people living in the same body during their telephone conversations. "I would talk to Cesar one time and Jimmy the next. It was like two different [people]." If they send Jimmy to death row and execute him, his friend said, "It would be kinda like wiping out a whole childhood . . . I speak for Jimmy. I don't know Cesar."

Cesar's mother had started a new family with the man she met, and later married, in Miami. One of the offspring, Barone's half sister, testified that he was well liked during the brief times she'd spent with him. She also revealed that when their mother died in 1991, Barone had inquired about any insurance money he might have coming.

On the issue of saving Barone's life so he could be a subject of psychological study, Steinke called a respected expert in cognitive and physiological psychology. Dr. Joel E. Alexander, head of the neurocognitive laboratory at Western Oregon State College, testified that Barone had a very high IQ, and would present a unique opportunity for detailed examination of a subject who'd apparently never suffered any brain injuries. Bob Hermann listened carefully to the doctor, and on cross-examination asked what guarantees existed that Barone would submit to the studies. The doctor had to admit there were none. Hermann also asked, "In your opinion, is he fully capable of killing again and again?"

Alexander didn't hesitate. "In my opinion, yes."

In closing arguments, Bob Hermann called the murder "Unprovoked, deliberate, brutal and senseless." He said, "I don't doubt that there's not one of you who can't close his eyes and envision the scene, who can't close your eyes and see the picture of the gunshot wound to Martha Bryant's head." He paused thoughtfully and added, "Every day, you saw another bit of pain, another tragedy, another horror story."

Defender Griffith Steinke emphasized that saving Barone and using him for study might save the lives of thousands. "There is greater good to be had than kill and be killed," he said, striding toward the seated defendant. Standing close to Barone, Steinke pointed at the defendant's head and enunciated, "Somewhere in this brain is the key. We need it alive to help unlock that key."

One reporter observed that some of the jurors didn't seem very receptive to that argument, as seen in their body language of crossed arms, closed eyes, and the swiveling of their squeaking chairs.

For the final time, the exhausted twelve jurors retired to their room to deliberate. While a storm raged outside, dropping four inches of rain during the past week, and causing mudslides in the county, the jurors sat down to consider a life and death matter. They spent almost exactly the same amount of time they'd used to decide that he was guilty of murder, ninety minutes, to resolve his fate. One of the panel would later reveal her thoughts. "I kept saying, please God, send us a cloud, send us something to save him."

After slowly filing back into the jury box, they delivered their verdict. Cesar Barone must face execution for killing Martha Bryant.

A female juror, age seventy-two, noted that she'd been influenced to vote for death because Barone never demonstrated the slightest sign of remorse. Also, she said, the vicious manner in which he'd battered and executed Martha Bryant had frightened her.

The next day, in front of a packed gallery section which included some of the jurors who'd returned to see the conclusion, Judge McElligott formally read the sentence. He added his own views, verbally lashing Barone for subjecting jurors, clerks, attorneys, and everyone else, to "despicable abomination after despicable abomination." He added, "If there is a case that calls for the death penalty, this is it." Recognizing that the condemned man might never face an executioner, the judge shook his head. With the knowledge that no one had been executed in Oregon since 1962, he commented to Barone, "Your chances of dying a natural death are better than your being executed in this state."

Wearing the standard orange jumpsuit of inmates, along with handcuffs and leg shackles, Barone had nothing to say when given the opportunity. Observers noticed that he also no longer wore the eyeglasses that had given him the look of respectability.

Within hours, officials whisked Barone off to Salem to his new quarters on death row.

The pending trial for murdering three other women had already been postponed several times, and now would have to wait nine more months.

Chapter 29

For the next trial, scheduled to start in mid-October 1995, Judge McElligott had appointed two attorneys, David Rich and another respected local lawyer to defend Barone against charges of murdering three women. A few weeks before the Bryant trial ended, Barone wrote a letter to the judge. In it, he expressed his satisfaction with Rich, but said about the other appointee, "It is my belief that he will not be able to adequately defend me . . . Because of the magnitude of the above entitled cases, it is my belief that my legal needs require a much higher level of experience and know-how." Barone requested an immediate replacement.

Taxpayers might wonder about a convicted murderer's right to pick and choose who will represent him in court; maybe thinking he's damn lucky to have any qualified attorney. But judges have to take a more objective view of constitutional rights and the probability of reversals by appeals courts. McElligott replaced the lawyer with a new one, William T. Lyons.

Gee, that worked so well, Barone apparently thought, *I might as well try for another dismissal.* This time he went after McElligott himself. Through his lawyers, Barone filed a motion requesting that the judge disqualify himself due to his alleged personal prejudice against the defendant. They reminded McElligott that he had chastised Barone in open court for subjecting everyone to "despicable abomination after despicable abomination."

Oh, and by the way, they suggested, let's get a change of venue, move this trial to another place where the jury pool hasn't been exposed to these prejudicial comments and all this negative publicity about the defendant.

Barone added his personal observations, writing, "It was

apparently not enough that Judge McElligott sentenced me to death. He lectured me and said many gratuitous and unwelcome comments about me."

After giving the motions due legal process, McElligott ruled against them. He also announced there would be a single consolidated trial for all three murders. Watchdogs of the public treasury agreed with that idea, since the first trial had dipped into the taxpayer's pocket for over a half-million dollars. Some citizens held the view that a second trial was a waste of time and money. The killer had already been convicted and sentenced to death. Why waste the money to do it all again? How many times can you execute one person?

Aside from the danger of an appeals court overturning the conviction, and risking the possibility of Barone walking out of prison, there were other good reasons to seek justice once more. Don't the families of the other three victims deserve consideration? Should they just be written off and forgotten?

Bob Hermann addressed the issue, saying, "We have three choices. One, do nothing with these three cases right now. But legally, he's entitled to a speedy prosecution. Two, we could dismiss them, which would not be, in our view, an appropriate resolution of these very serious cases. And three, our choice is to proceed and try them."

Officials in Florida would keep a sharp eye on the outcome of the trials, waiting to extradite Barone to face charges of murdering Alice Stock.

By the time another summer had slipped away, and the October date loomed in the face of Washington County citizens, most of the U.S. population had been saturated ad nauseam with the "trial of the century" of O.J. Simpson in Los Angeles. Television viewers, glued to their screens for weeks, learned more than they ever wanted to know about DNA evidence, accusations of police misconduct, alleged planted blood drops and gloves, racial imbalances, and clever lawyers. Stunned observers found out that a "mountain of evidence," did not necessarily lead to a guilty verdict.

Bob Hermann and Roger Hanlon knew they had nothing like a mountain of evidence to present in the murder cases of Schmidt, Williams, and Woodman.

As jury selection began in mid-October, defense attorneys Lyons and Rich inquired of prospective jurors their impressions of the Los Angeles trial. Many candidates said they'd paid little attention to it, calling it a circus. Most of them, though, had heard of the Martha Bryant case, prompting the defense team to repeat their motion for a change of venue. Bob Hermann argued that the jurors' knowledge of the case wasn't important. What mattered he said, was their ability to be fair and impartial. McElligott again denied the motion.

Cesar Barone may have learned something from the Los Angeles trial, too. By the time an all-white jury was seated in the first week of November, Barone raised an objection. For years, he'd been telling anyone who would listen that he was of noble Italian ancestry. Now, in November 1995, he'd changed his mind. He was part African-American, he announced. And since he had "a substantial" amount of black blood, he considered himself a member of a minority group, therefore he strongly objected to the racial makeup of the white jury who couldn't possibly give him a fair trial. Bob Hermann took the trouble to examine Barone's ancestry, and found that one of his grandfathers had immigrated from Italy at the turn of the century, while the other one came from northern Europe. The prosecutor described the effort as "a feeble attempt to create a nonexistent issue for appeal."

Judge McElligott patiently explained that the jury adequately reflected a cross section of the Washington County community, and ruled against the motion to make changes.

The trial kicked off on Monday, November 6, when the jurors, freshly groomed, coiffed, and wearing mostly new clothing, filed into the box and took their seats. Judge McElligott carefully explained to them that they must keep evidence separate in their minds for each of the three murders. To help with that segmentation, the prosecution would present each case separately. McElligott asked if the prosecution was ready to proceed.

Defender William "Tim" Lyons glanced up with a puzzled look on his face, looked quickly at his cocounsel David
Rich, who subtly nodded, then bent over to enter some
notes in his legal pad. Bob Hermann signaled to the judge
that he was ready.

For the first few days, most of the same cortege of witnesses who'd testified in the previous trial appeared again
to lead jurors through bloody, mind-boggling horror and
death. Leonard Darcell took the stand and tried to invoke
his constitutional rights not to testify. Judge McElligott
sagely explained to Darcell that he wouldn't be incriminat-
ing himself, therefore he was ordered to answer questions.
Darcell still refused despite the noble intentions he'd expressed in the letter to his father. McElligott found Darcell
in contempt of court, which didn't seem to bother him since
he'd been convicted of murder. He left the courtroom,
maintaining his silence.

It took two weeks of witness testimony and evidence presentation to inculcate jurors with the facts and passions
involved when the disabled Margaret Schmidt was raped
and strangled in April 1991; Chantee Woodman crumpled
to the forest floor with a bullet in her head two days before
the end of 1992; and Betty Williams's heart stopped during
a sexual assault on January 6, 1993.

Cesar Barone, his salt-and-pepper hair much grayer now
and pulled back into a ponytail, again sat straight-backed
and grim through two weeks of the process. Halfway
through the proceedings, on November 13, he tried to fire
his lawyers. "I'm afraid of them," Barone told Judge McElligott in his complaint about their defense tactics. He
wanted to get rid of them and handle the entire defense
himself.

"Nobody can represent themselves in a case this serious," McElligott said. He also ordered Barone to be present in court each day despite his stated preference not to
attend the sessions.

When the prosecution rested on Tuesday, November 21,
the defense announced that it would call no witnesses, and
also rested. If Barone was in the driver's seat of the strategy
planning, observers thought he needed a new chauffeur.

Judge McElligott allowed closing arguments to begin that same day.

In many trials, as seen in the big Los Angeles extravaganza, the closing arguments by attorneys can be exceptionally powerful. In the Hillsboro trial, Bob Hermann summarized the Woodman case, followed by Roger Hanlon delivering the prosecution's arguments in the Schmidt and Williams cases.

All three narratives should have been taped as examples of superior summations. Both attorneys presented the material in much the same manner as the final scenes in old mystery movies in which the detective assembles everyone in a parlor and tells them how each clue, each piece of the puzzle finally falls into place, solving the mystery, arresting the killer, and tidily wrapping up the story in a satisfying conclusion.

Hermann went first.

"Ladies and gentleman of the jury, we've got to go back a little ways in our minds to the evidence in the Woodman case, but I suspect that it doesn't take very long for you to remember the very chilling tale you heard from the witness stand regarding the death of Chantee Woodman." His clear articulation and poise would have impressed Sam Spade or Philip Marlowe, or even Perry Mason. Hermann voiced the caveat that twelve citizens must be convinced of Cesar Barone's guilt beyond a reasonable doubt and advised them to follow instructions the judge would read later.

Reminding them that Woodman was twenty-three at the time, he said, "Her fate was decided when she ran into Leonard Darcell, then twenty-four, still on this earth, and Cesar Barone, thirty-two, still on this earth, when she was taken from one place to another against her will, some twenty miles away from her home where she wanted to go that night, out to a lonely stretch of highway . . . and during that process, Mr. Barone and his partner sexually assaulted her. And then, if that weren't indignity enough, Mr. Barone eliminated her. He prevented her from ever, ever, telling you or anybody else the whole story of that evening. He deliberately and remorselessly executed this woman."

Spellbound, the jury absorbed every word of Hermann's

delivery. In the gallery, the usual coughs and squeaking chairs were absent, and only the prosecutor's words filled the room. "You know he stuck that long-barreled revolver under her chin, a revolver that's single action. You've got to cock it and then you have to pull the trigger. He sent the bullet up through her chin, up through her tongue, up through her palate, into her brain." He paused to take a long breath. "You'll never hear an explanation from her of how it was she got into that car, when it was she realized she was never going home, what she had to do to try to defend herself, to be subjected to sexual assaults, and whether she thought maybe there was a chance she was going to escape alive when she was out on that highway and Cesar Barone, sticking a gun under her chin, jabbing her with it, and asking her, 'You're going to be a good girl aren't you? You're not going to tell?' "

Making it clear to the jury that those events alone were enough to bring in a guilty verdict, Hermann said that Barone still wasn't satisfied. "He has to boast about it. He had to tell others and relive again and again the enjoyment of killing . . . And beyond that, he was excited, even sexually aroused by it. That's what you heard from witnesses." Letting those comments sink in, Hermann spent the next several minutes explaining technicalities of the law and defining the multiple counts in the charges against Barone. He reminded jurors of testimony they'd heard from officers Larry McKinney and Scott Ryon taking them through major steps of the investigation, and the statements by jailhouse informants that connected the evidence to Barone.

Hermann took the attentive jurors back in time to December 13, just a little over two weeks before the murder, when Andy Tremaine, Barone's boss at the cabinet shop, had entrusted him with the revolver, for safekeeping after a car accident. And three days after that, Barone had purchased a white Hyundai.

Leading the jurors along the chronological ride, Hermann's next stop was December 29, in a steakhouse restaurant-bar where Barone and Darcell tried to pick up a woman who was with her fifteen-year-old son. Rebuffed, they drove through the gathering storm to Portland, and found the young redhead, Heather Crane. The jurors had heard testimony from her, in which she admitted accepting the offer of a ride from "Germ." Barone had threatened her with that same revolver, trying to force her into a sexual act, and she'd been lucky to escape with her life. After leaving "Doc's" place, the predatory pair picked up Chantee Woodman on a lonely, freezing sidewalk in Old Town.

"And that's the last reported sighting of her until about seven hours later when she's found out on the Sunset Highway, dumped alongside the road, dead." Hermann described the arrival of investigators who found no identification on her except a phone number on a piece of paper. They did find pieces of her flesh clinging to boughs of trees.

Step by step, Hermann took his audience through the investigation, the gory facts of the autopsy, and the fact that certain bits of information were not released to the press.

Ironically, he pointed out, the gun was found and photographed in the apartment of Betty Williams, but investigators had no way of connecting it to Woodman's death.

Quoting criminalist Chris Johnson, Hermann said about the slug taken from the victim's head, "Well, it has obviously been damaged, to the point that we can't do any particular ballistics on it. But what I can tell you is that assuming, as Dr. Gunson told us, that she got all the fragments out, that it's either a .22 long rifle or a .22 magnum."

Moving back and forth with measured strides, like Paul Newman in *The Verdict*, Hermann said, "Well, we know from the evidence that on February 27, Cesar Barone goes to jail on unrelated matters." But Barone couldn't keep quiet. "He could not stop reliving the excitement of killing another human being, and he was mouthing off in jail."

Skipping the content of informants' statements for a few moments, Hermann took jurors to the search of the torched house. Investigators found a couple of berets that tended to corroborate the testimony of "Doc" who described Barone's berating of Darcell and telling him he hadn't earned the right to wear a beret. But more significant, Hermann said, was the box of .22 caliber magnum ammunition. Then, on April 19, Leonard Darcell turned up, also in jail, and had plenty to say. Now investigators know what kind of a

gun they're looking for, and they track it down to Andy
Tremaine who'd asked Barone to temporarily take care of
it for him. And Betty Williams's relatives hear about it,
and match it to the revolver found among her possessions.
When the bullet is recovered from the top of a shed, courtesy of Darcell, and it matches the gun and the bullets
recovered from the burned house where Barone had
lived . . . "The gun had five rounds still in it. It holds six."

Hermann fleshed out his narrative with the stunning revelations of the informants. "What did he tell Mr. Masters?
He told him that he put the gun under her chin, fired one
time. The victim was freaked-out, terrified, pleading . . .
that he beat her up. He wanted her to perform oral sex at
one point. She wouldn't do it right. He beat her about the
face." Now speaking rapid-fire, Hermann's voice rose. "Six-
inch long-barreled revolver. He described it to Masters as
a .45. Not enough for Mr. Barone to say 'I used a .22,'
because the first thing you think of, a .22, these little dinky
things. He said, 'This is a six-inch, long barreled.' This is a
Clint Eastwood . . . big time. He told Wayne Fallon, 'If
women get me off, they get beaten. If they don't get me
off, they get killed.' "

Slowing back to his usual pace of calm dignity, Hermann
suggested to the jurors they could look at the evidence in
several ways. They could examine it from an investigator's
point of view, or chronologically. They could even toss out
parts of it if they wished. "No matter how you do it, you
still have enough to convict Cesar Barone of aggravated
murder."

Checking the jurors' expressions, Hermann could see
they were still hanging on his every word. "Imagine, if you
will, when you ask yourself whether this was deliberate,
imagine, out on a lonely stretch of highway, just two guys
present and yourself. You've been sexually assaulted.
You've been taken against your will some twenty miles
from your home. And maybe you have to hope that you're
going to have to walk your way home after being beaten
about the face. Maybe you've got that thread of hope that
you're going to see the next day. And you're getting this
gun jabbed in your chin, hard enough to make puncture
wounds. And you've got Cesar Barone there saying,

'You're going to be a good girl. You're not going to tell.' And you're praying and you're pleading for your life. And imagine, if you possibly can, the coolness, the callousness, the sickness of somebody who would have that gun cocked back and pull the trigger.''

Leonard Darcell, Hermann said, had freaked out at seeing the girl killed, so Barone had pointed the gun at him and said, "You could be next."

Appealing to their common sense and logic, Hermann said, "There is no question in this case, well beyond a reasonable doubt, Cesar Barone was there, he took her against her will, with Mr. Darcell. They were both involved in sexually assaulting her, and Mr. Barone killed her. And there is no way he can walk away from these charges and his criminal responsibility."

With a brief nod, Hermann quietly said, "Thank you."

Chapter 30

Roger Hanlon stepped up to the lectern. Tall, brown hair thinning, his handsome face braced in a serious expression, but the eyes sparkling with a hint of mischief, he greeted the jurors.

Pointing to an enlarged photograph, Hanlon said, "This is Margaret Schmidt. And it will probably come as no surprise to any of you, as I discuss Margaret's murder with you here this morning, that I'm going to be talking about shoes. This case pretty much began with shoes, and when the investigation reached its conclusion, the case ended with shoes. So I'll be speaking about that with you this morning."

Hanlon described how a friend of Margaret had arrived early on January 8, noticed porch lights off, and entered the house through the kitchen door. "That's when we knew shoes were part of this case because she saw, in the kitchen, shoe prints made by somebody who'd traipsed through talcum powder." The woman had then discovered Margaret "spread-eagled and nude on the bed." When detectives arrived they'd also seen shoe prints in the bathroom, where a can of talcum powder had been knocked off the window ledge.

"So the investigation was off and running. Right there, day one, where are these shoes? Detective O'Connell went off on a fruitless mission that weekend, going to shoe stores, with nothing more than mental impressions of what those imprints looked like, and turning over shoes, looking for a Reebok shoe, because everyone knew it was a Reebok. You could read the word Reebok in the prints." Soon, the detective contacted shoe distributors and learned more details. He was looking for Reebok ERS 2000 running shoes. O'Connell took photos of a new pair.

The search, Hanlon said, extended through the county by all police personnel, at the jail, on the streets, even at the high school running track. In O'Connell's personal quest, he saw only one pair, on a kindergarten teacher. And even after Barone was arrested, in the ensuing months, the detective continued to watch and saw only two more being worn in public.

An expert had testified, Hanlon reminded the jurors, and revealed that 263,304 pairs of those shoes had been manufactured. "Now, what can we do to reduce that from such an unmanageable and useless number? Well, the first thing we can do is eliminate 79,332 pairs of them, for one very obvious reason. This homicide is a man's work." Referring to a color photo of Margaret's nude body on her bed, Hanlon said, "A woman did not do this. We know that, intuitively, and without any doubts in our minds. A woman could not have done this crime."

Subtracting the women's shoes from the total number manufactured left 183,972 pairs, Hanlon said. That could be reduced further because the prints proved the suspect's shoes were size eight and one-half. The manufacturer had given investigators a figure of 7.8 per cent as the number made in that size. So, Hanlon calculated, we are down to 14,350. "But we know that this crime was committed here in little old Washington County, Hillsboro, Oregon, and it's unlikely the perpetrator was from New York. He pronounced it "New Yawk" and apologized. "I sound like a New Yorker. I'm sorry."

"So now what we can do is, Reebok can tell us how many of these shoes came to Oregon. And the number is, in 1989, '90, '91, is 2,026 total men's shoes. And we'll throw in the state of Washington [Barone's wife, Kathi, had said he might have bought them in Tacoma], seeing how they're just across the river. We'll throw those in, 1,448 men's shoes." He applied the factor of 7.8 percent to reduce the number to the correct size, and came up with 271 in both states. Hanlon stole a glance at some of the jurors who appeared to be calculating right along with him on their notepads. "We can do a little more with that number, not a great deal more. But Reebok knows, generally speaking, that about three percent of all shipped shoes get stolen, damaged or returned due to defects." Now he'd arrived at 263.

Raising one of his feet off the floor, Hanlon said, "This shoe that I'm wearing is a Rockport, okay. And let's assume, if you will, it's a size eleven. And let's assume . . . that there are only 263 [pairs of] Rockport shoes with these particular outsoles, size eleven, in two states."

Surveying faces again to be sure he hadn't confused anyone, Hanlon asked, "How many of those 263 men with this shoe are murderers? Well, the answer is zero. We know that because murder is an uncommon crime. I can't tell you what the statistics are, but as you know, if we had one out of 263 people committing murders, we'd have all fled this country."

One observer mentally figured out Roger's question, and came up with about one million murders. Hanlon was right. That would be a horrible condition in which to live.

Hanlon illustrated it for doubters. "To give you some kind of analogy, if there were even just one murderer within every randomly selected 263 people, that would mean that when you go to a [Portland] Trailblazer's game down at the new Rose Garden, and you're sitting there amongst 20,000 Trailblazer fans, there would be eighty murderers in the room with you. Well, of course, that's not true." He allowed himself a devilish little smile. The purpose of the exercise, he said, was to point out the significance of the possession by Mr. Barone of an ERS Reebok 2000, in the correct size. "And it is significant when it is placed in conjunction with the other evidence." Another tight grin. "I mean, Reebok doesn't market their shoes as 'Two out of three killers prefer Reeboks.' This is a random sampling of men."

To link the shoes to other evidence, Hanlon reminded the jury that Barone had threatened Ron Price's life to persuade him to burn down the house and destroy anything that might point to Barone as the killer. And, of course, the police had found the Reeboks during the second search, on April 17, even after the house had been partially destroyed by fire. Hanlon emphasized that Price wore a size ten. "I think I observed at least one of you looking at the size of his feet as he walked off the witness stand."

In Hanlon's hands he held two photographs that Barone's ex-wife had given investigators, both of them picturing Barone wearing the Reeboks. Hanlon recalled for the jurors that an expert had testified who had actually worn a new pair of Reeboks for weeks, running and walking in them for 300 miles in an attempt to duplicate the wear seen on Barone's pair. The expert had examined and compared the most minute details. He'd identified tiny nicks on the sole lugs, which showed up in the talcum powder prints. Despite all his work, though, the scientist could not say Barone's shoe was positively the one that made the print. The best he could do was say "It's most probably the shoe."

Hanlon took a deep breath, and said, "Well, at this point I could probably stop and say, based on that evidence, you can find the defendant guilty beyond a reasonable doubt. This is his shoe. The defendant is guilty. But that would ignore an abundance of other evidence." The prosecutor referred to the testimony of Troy Masters.

He quoted the charismatic, tough convict as saying, "Well, yeah, we met in the jail and started doing push-ups together. I was a bit of a bully and demanded paperwork. . . . and then he started talking to me about all kinds of things, things that made me go and tell my . . . wife." Hanlon said the wife contacted authorities, leading Detective O'Connell to interviews with Mr. Masters. Slipping into quasi-quotes of the convict again, Hanson said, ". . . The defendant spoke of an elderly woman with a walker. He was telling me all about her. He was pretty excited about it, talked about these things consistently. By his actions and by the way he looked, he was very excited. His physical features changed, his eyes changed, his breathing got faster as he recounted these things. He touched his dick and stuff like that. He made no attempt to conceal it. It was obvious to everybody what was going on. He told me he 'did' this lady."

Hanlon explained that according to Masters, the lady lived in Hillsboro, was an old woman in a nightgown who used a walker. And "did" this lady meant Barone killed her.

Another inmate, Dave Sparks, had corroborated the story, Hanlon said, and had also mentioned an old lady using a walker who'd been killed. Barone had admitted to Sparks that he'd sexually assaulted the woman. And to cellmate Wayne Fallon, Barone had said he liked "older women with big tits." Hanlon told the jurors the informants had volunteered the information to the police because Barone's wild confessions had gone too far over the top, even for these men. "They have mothers and grandmothers, and they weren't going to sit still and listen to this."

Just as his partner, Bob Hermann, had done, Hanlon took time out to explain the technicalities and definitions of the charges against Barone. He also made it clear that because the autopsy hadn't revealed any traces of semen in the victim's body, that did not rule out that she'd been raped. The pathologist had testified that "this was a sexual assault homicide."

Hanlon's next statement caused some observers to squirm uncomfortably. The pathologist "also noted that it took three minutes for Margaret to die!"

Anyone who stopped to think about it would realize that three minutes can be an eternity to a person being strangled or asphyxiated. Prosecutors sometimes, in closing arguments, ask the juries to stop and think about the crime for the minutes it takes to strangle someone to death. When that is done in a courtroom, even one minute of silence, while imagining the crime, stretches forever. Three minutes would be almost unendurable.

Hanlon didn't use that technique, but made the horror clear as he continued. "And what I would submit to you, ladies and gentleman, is that there can be no more an intentional and deliberate act than a smothering asphyxiation of a woman that takes three minutes to accomplish. And that is minimum. That is with a total occlusion of the artery carrying the blood up into the head, with total occlusion, barring the possibility that Margaret was able to, in her struggle, get her head out away from the pillow for a moment to gasp some air. With total occlusion it would take three minutes, with a person forcing that pillow and straddling her and perhaps using his forearm into her neck, she was . . . beseeching him, imploring him to stop. What would be more deliberate?"

Barone had been seen near Schmidt's home, according to witnesses, prior to the murder, Hanlon reminded the jurors. "What I submit to you, ladies and gentleman, is this: Mr. Barone knew this house. He'd even talked to Margaret Schmidt. He likes older women with large breasts. He went to this home on that night." Hanlon pointed to a diagram of the house. "You can almost picture this happening. He disabled the light bulb on the Fourth Street porch. He then went to the north side of the house to the window. And he needed to free up his hand, so he dropped the light bulb here. He pushed on the window. The nails prevented it from opening. The talcum powder on the window sill fell and spilled. The trampled ferns indicated there was some-one standing there.

"He proceeded to the west side and used a knife to cut the screen. He tried the window, left smudges on it. It didn't open because it was locked. Back on the east side, he found a shed where he could force the door partially open. He managed to squeeze through the narrow opening, and as he entered, he rubbed against a roll of vinyl, leaving a fresh sheen on the roll where the dust had been brushed off. From there, he was able to work his way into an en-closed porch hallway, and into the kitchen. In the dark house, he goes into the bathroom. Why? We don't know, never be able to figure that one out. But we know that he went in there because the imprints of the footwear are in the bathroom.

"The shoe prints then turn into the bedroom. Margaret Schmidt is murdered. The electric blanket is torn off the bed with sufficient force that it disengages the cord. Her nightgown, which is here in evidence, if you care to look at it, is torn or ripped from the ankles clear through to the top, leaving nothing but a few strands around Margaret's neck. Her panties are removed. And why in the would any-body would remove a woman's panties if he is not in-tending a sexual assault. . . . And this is how she's found, spread-eagled, nude, sexually assaulted and murdered.

Smothered, her blood spattered as she's aspirating blood
into her pillow, as she's being murdered.

"And then this man goes into the jail and he talks about
it. Why he would want to talk about it, why he was sexually
attracted to a woman like this is beyond explanation, but
that's what he did, ladies and gentlemen. The footprints
put him there. His statements put him there. The scene
speaks for itself. There is no question about it.

"As dark and sinister as it may sound, Cesar Barone
knew that his wife was coming to town on Saturday, the
twentieth. Mr. Barone had seen Margaret Schmidt and he
had something he wanted to do. And I mean it. As dark
and sinister, as macabre as that may sound, Mr. Barone
had something he needed to do before his wife got back;
and he took his last night out and this is what he did.

"And I can't explain to you why he did it, and you'll
never figure out why he did it, but that's not your job.
Your job is: Did he do it? And evidence that he did is
incontrovertible. It is unchallenged. It is indisputable. It is
all there for you. Mr. Barone is guilty of two counts of
aggravated murder for this horrible death of Margaret
Schmidt."

Chapter 31

Roger Hanlon's unpretentious, informative delivery of the circumstances surrounding Margaret Schmidt's murder had riveted the jury's attention, which reinforced, in the mind of cocounsel Bob Hermann, the wisdom of their prearranged agreement for Roger to also make the closing argument on the Betty Williams segment. It would be an obstacle-filled uphill battle considering the slim evidence and the strong possibility that the jury might reach a conclusion there'd been no murder at all.

As if speaking in confidence to each juror, Hanlon opened this portion of his talk in a calm, serious tone. "I want to speak with you now about the *murder* of Betty Williams. And this *was* a *murder*. It is something called a felony *murder*." He emphasized the pivotal word three times, trying to brand it in capital letters on twelve minds. "And it's important at the very outset here to explain to you and for you to understand what a felony murder is, because it is a murder of a very different breed, if you will." Two more repetitions of the "m" word.

Spelling out the specific legal definitions of the charges, Hanlon said, "The defendant was committing the crime of attempted rape in the first degree, which is sexual intercourse by the way of forcible compulsion; and in the course of, or in furtherance of committing the crime of attempted rape, Cesar Barone caused the death of a human being."

The word "intentional" he explained, was nowhere in the charges. "Felony murder is not an intentional killing. It is just the opposite." Hanlon drew the analogy of someone robbing a convenience store and using a gun to frighten the clerk. The robber accidentally drops the gun as he exits. It discharges, killing an innocent bystander. There was no intent to kill anyone, Hanlon said, but the concept of felony murder makes the perpetrator criminally responsible for the bystander's death.

To clarify the matter of attempted rape, Hanlon told the wide-eyed, attentive jurors that it needn't be proved that the rape was completed. If any sexual intercourse had taken place, even with the slightest of penetration, then forcible compulsion had occurred, meaning "physical force which overcomes the earnest resistance of the victim."

"I think the best way to review the testimony in this case is from the perspective of law enforcement and to look at what they knew, when they knew it, and to explain what they did. . . . Then go back and look at what the defendant knew, when he knew it, so that we're then able to conclude what he did."

An old rule for effective public speaking advises, "Tell 'em what you're going to tell 'em. Tell 'em. Then tell 'em what you told 'em." Introduction-body of speech-summary. Hanlon had the technique mastered in his personable, folksy style.

"Well, we need obviously, then, to start with the crime scene." Hanlon spoke of Williams's son searching for her that morning, his stunning discovery of her partially clothed body contorted into a humiliating position in the shallow water of her bathtub. Sergeant Mark Christy and his colleagues, Hanlon said, had found the circumstances suspicious, in view of the strangely disarrayed clothing, but no evidence turned up to confirm that it was murder.

Jumping ahead a little, Hanlon called attention to a question the defense had asked of the pathologist, Dr. Gunson: "Isn't it possible that she had a heart attack as she was seated on the john?" The doctor had answered "No, not really." She'd actually conceded that it was a possibility, but a very remote one considering the positioning of the body.

Back to the investigation, Hanlon recalled unusual circumstances such as an unlocked dead bolt, the normally barricaded backdoor not blocked, a bra lying on the living room floor, something missing from the top of her desk as indicated by the dust pattern, plus broken glass and scattered coins outside. And there was that Western-style revolver under her desk. But that meant nothing at the time. The victim hadn't been shot.

Hanlon acknowledged that Williams had been in very poor health, had a high blood-alcohol content, and actually did die of a heart attack. But Christy and Detective Mussler, he said, had to be scratching their heads, thinking, "it doesn't jibe with our experience. It doesn't jibe with what we saw there."

Sergeant Christy "has to go back and tell his chief, 'Chief, it's being declared a heart attack.' And the chief says, 'Tear down the crime scene.' 'Wait a minute, Chief. It doesn't jibe. It doesn't fit.' Well, the chief is a chief, and the officer is an officer, and the officer does what the chief says, and he goes and tears down the crime scene and the investigation ceases. For all intents and purposes, that's where it ended."

Scanning twelve faces, Hanlon shook his head. "Well, Sergeant Christy didn't let it go. Seven weeks later, on February twenty-seventh, he got an opportunity to speak to Mr. Barone," after the arrest on other charges. Sergeant Christy, Hanlon said, asked Barone, "Okay, by the way, where were you on Tuesday night, the fifth, into the early morning hours of Wednesday, the sixth, at the time Betty Williams was last seen alive?" And Barone admitted he was there, the last person to see Betty alive.

Now according to Barone's statement to the police, Hanlon said, he was in Williams's apartment with Denise Nichols, walked Nichols home, left her, and on his way out of the complex noticed Williams's door standing open. Barone claimed that he saw Betty sitting on the floor, drunk, so he courteously reached inside, flipped the lock, pulled the door closed, and left her safe and sound, alive and well.

With that, Hanlon said, the investigation hit the doldrums until April, when Troy Masters broke it wide open. Hanlon repeated Masters's report to O'Connell: "Cesar Barone is telling me about this thing that happened, and what he's telling me is that he was at an elderly lady's house drinking hard liquor. This woman got up to go to the bathroom, and Barone threatened her with a knife and raped her. In doing so, he scared her so bad, she had a heart attack. He could not get or maintain an erection . . . and he flopped the lady into the tub and filled it with water. He left her with her butt up in the air."

Barone expressed no sorrow, no remorse, Hanlon said. And the other inmate, Dave Sparks, told us the defendant had been visiting the lady, brought her some alcohol. Cesar knew her, was drinking with her. She had to go to the bathroom. He approached her in there, standing in front of her. She was scared. He was asking her to do sexual things.

Hanlon paused for a moment and said, "I'll come back to that word 'asking' in a minute."

According to Sparks, Hanlon said, the victim started to have a heart attack. Barone pushed her over into the bath-tub. He was trying to get her to perform oral sex. She was scared because he was terrorizing her. "Apparently, terrorizing is how Mr. Barone 'asked' Miss Williams to do sexual things, to do oral sex," Hanlon added.

Yet a third jailhouse informant had listened in disgust to Barone's boasting. "You heard from Wayne Fallon. Mr. Barone told him that he'd taken the woman in the bath-room. He was 'molesting' her." Fallon had tried to sugar-coat his words out of respect for the jury, Hanlon said, but when coaxed to be precise, the inmate had used Barone's own street language to describe having sexual intercourse with the woman from behind.

Hanlon reminded the jurors that Barone had started run-ning scared the very next morning because the crime-scene tape remained in place for over twenty-four hours. He'd hoped that the death would be declared natural and the cops would just drop the whole thing. And he knew he'd made a serious mistake. "What's that mistake? Barone left the gun there! The same gun he'd stolen from Andy Trem-aine, something that could point a finger directly at Barone as a killer. Can you imagine Mr. Barone's thoughts as he left that night in a hurry and he gets outside after pulling the door closed and locked behind him? He said, 'Oh, my God, I left Andy's gun. I made a mistake.' And he's still concerned about that mistake when he's talking to Dave Sparks months later."

Recalling testimony of jailhouse informant Sparks, Han-lon remarked, "Barone told the inmate that he didn't intentionally kill her. But Mr. Barone is not conversant in nonintentional felony murder."

When the investigation resumed as a direct result of the informants' statements, Hanlon said, detectives learned that Williams would normally have some money in the apartment that she'd earned from tips. There was none. She had a glass jar filled with coins. It was missing. And she should have had a plastic separator, which had made the imprint in the dust. It, too, was missing.

Discrepancies in Barone's various accounts of that night began showing up. To one person, he'd said Williams was sitting on the floor, to another, she was in a chair. To a female friend, Barone said he'd told Betty good night, but to Christy, he claimed he hadn't spoken to the victim. Inconsistencies like that can suggest a consciousness of guilt.

They also learned that Barone had brought a bottle of cheap rum to the victim. His fingerprints were on it, and it may have been the same square bottle he'd had with his pal, Ray Cardenas, up on Mount Hood, that two young women had described and Cardenas had mentioned in his testimony. On a table in Williams's apartment, Detective Mussler had spotted two glasses. They both appeared to contain rum and Coke drinks. One smelled of alcohol, one did not. Hanlon asked the rhetorical questions, "What's going on here, Mr. Barone? Are you plying this woman? Are you drinking Coke and making her drink rum so that you can assault her at knifepoint or at gunpoint?"

Ray Cardenas had testified about what Barone told him. In that account Barone had seen Betty dead in the bathroom. Another discrepancy. Andy Tremaine had described Cesar's hyper-excited state when he scurried into the cabinet shop to rave about the commotion up the street. A puzzled expression creased Hanlon's features. "Well, hold on here, folks. How in the world does Cesar Barone know to tell Andy Tremaine, hours before the autopsy was conducted, that the police thought it was a homicide and then concluded that it was a heart attack? That is probably the most curious statement made by Mr. Barone of all these inconsistent stories he's told everybody."

Making certain that no one was faulting the Cornelius PD for not realizing a murder had been committed, Hanlon asked, "What else could they do when the coroner tells you it's a heart attack, nonhomicide? If they're guilty of anything, I suppose it's just not having the vivid imagination of a Stephen King. You know, King might be able to write this script, but the police couldn't even begin to theorize that it was a death in the course of a sexual assault and an attempted robbery. But Cesar Barone, he thought of it."

And why was Barone making repeated calls from Denise Nichols's apartment to the police and trying to pry information from them about the autopsy results? He's got to know, that's why. And when he finds out it was a heart attack, "he's got to be as happy as a clam at that point."

Finally allowing his voice to show anger, Hanlon told the jury that Barone had admitted his crime to a number of people. "This is what the defendant confessed to. That he had sex with Williams from behind. And it's entirely consistent with what was found at the scene. This woman was thrown into the tub, in a position exactly like what he told Wayne Fallon. His admissions are corroborated by his confession to three different people. It's corroborated by the discrepancies in his statements to four other people. And it's consistent with crime-scene discoveries: the broken coin jar, missing money, unlocked dead bolt, and the condition of the victim's clothing."

Hanlon gathered his thoughts to make certain he hadn't omitted anything important, then moved to his final words, to tell 'em what he told 'em, to summarize his case. "There is a lot of corroboration here to support these confessions that the defendant made in jail . . . Just look at it, you view the whole picture, and this man is guilty. . . . This is sexual abuse in the first degree. It requires sexual contact by forcible compulsion. And remember, we don't need to prove a completed rape, only a substantial step, and that step is the one he took when he followed her from the living room into the bathroom. That was a substantial step, and so was using a knife, and disrobing her was a substantial step."

His voice indignant, Hanlon said that Barone had literally scared this woman to death. "And with that, the defendant is guilty of felony murder. And that's all I have to say on the matter of Betty Williams."

* * *

After lunch, defense attorney William Lyons stepped forward to summarize the case on behalf of Cesar Barone, in all three murders. First, he complimented Hermann and Hanlon on an excellent job in presenting their statements. "They have done it accurately and they have done it in a very comprehensive manner." It wouldn't make sense, Lyons said, to repeat all the facts of the cases, since those had been already covered in detail. "You are probably, at this point, shocked at what you have heard . . . you are distressed over what you have heard, and in a very, very real sense, although it may not be up there at the surface at this point in time, you are probably angry over what you have heard."

His strategy became clear. Give a little ground with compliments, then counterattack. "But these are not the types of things upon which we base our verdicts," Lyons growled. "We base our verdicts on the law . . . the evidence, and the inferences we can draw from the evidence . . . And with that in mind, I would like to talk to you about the Woodman case first."

The jailhouse informants had told their secondhand versions of what happened out there on Highway 26 that dark, stormy morning. But, Lyons said, "There were only three people that would have any clue as to what happened. One, of course, is dead." And, referring to Leonard Darcell, "One came in here and claimed he has rights and that he's not going to testify, not going to tell you what happened." In regard to Darcell's attempt to invoke the Fifth Amendment, Lyons said "he has rights against self-incrimination. And he firmly believes, to the point of refusing the judge's order, that if he does testify, if he does tell the truth, he is going to seriously incriminate himself."

Over at the prosecution table, Bob Hermann furiously scribbled on a yellow legal pad.

Pointing out that in order to find Barone guilty of killing Woodman, Lyons told the jury they would have to find that Barone had personally, himself, caused her death. After spending some time with definitions and examples, Lyons asked, "What evidence do we have at all that Mr. Barone was even out there on Highway 26? Chantee Woodman apparently went to a house with Mr. Barone and Mr. Darcell. Was she kidnapped at that point? Was this against her will at that point? Even Mr. Barone's words came to you through Mr. Masters and Mr. Fallon: 'We picked her up in a parking lot in downtown Portland.'

"We know from the evidence that Chantee Woodman, wisely or unwisely, will get into a car with a person who is not exactly a well-known acquaintance. She had met one fellow in a bar for just a matter of minutes the night before. I believe that was the fencing instructor . . ."

The two prosecutors realized exactly where Lyons was going. He would use Barone's own lies and exaggerations and turn them into an advantage. And he'd try to convince the jury of a strong probability that Darcell had killed Chantee Woodman.

Acknowledging Barone's bragging to jailhouse informants that he'd sexually assaulted Woodman, Lyons said, "There's no physical evidence any of the horrible things, sexually, that Mr. Barone claims were done. We do know, no doubt about it, that she had sexual relations with Leonard Darcell." DNA evidence had confirmed that. "But if you are going to violently rape a woman or sodomize a woman or subject her to unspeakable acts, there are going to be signs on her body . . . If you subject a woman forcibly to anal sex, for example . . . or to forcible intercourse, there will be signs of that.

"Mr. Darcell had sex with Chantee Woodman, and then we get into what Cesar Barone says happened: Took her out on Highway 26, threw her out of the car at fifty miles per hour. You know that's not true. Shot her with a .45 caliber or a .44 caliber. You know that's not true. Beat her so badly that her face was so swollen that she couldn't turn her face. You know that's not true. Threw her over a guardrail. You know that's not true. None of that is true."

Lyons alluded to testimony from detectives that Darcell told them Barone had given him the empty cartridge as a souvenir. Darcell claimed he threw it on top of a shed. Maybe Darcell was simply covering his own murderous tracks. "Mr. Barone has a tendency to take credit for things he didn't do . . . The evidence actually points to the fact that it was Leonard Darcell who was there and who caused the death of this woman he'd had sex with previously. He had the gun. He had the cartridge. He hid the cartridge."

Cesar Barone is not a normal man, Lyons said. "Anyone who likes to talk about these things, who gets the kind of satisfaction out of talking about these things is not normal. In order to convict Mr. Barone . . . you have to take his words at face value." And how could anyone do that in view of Barone's constant habit of lying?

"There is no evidence at all that he was even there," Lyons insisted. To hammer the point home, the attorney recalled the testimony of "Doc," who made it clear that Barone criticized Darcell. Was Darcell bent on proving himself to his pal? Darcell, after all, had refused to testify, exercising his right not to incriminate himself.

"There are too many questions," Lyons proclaimed. "Where did you get the cartridge, Leonard? Why did you hide it where you hid it? Tell us about the sexual relations you had with Chantee Woodman. And why is there no evidence that Cesar Barone had any sexual relations with her?"

Turning his back to the jury for a moment, Lyons spun to face them again. "Those are the things you need to think about. Within the context of the entire case the state has put on regarding Chantee Woodman, those are the questions that they can't answer."

Chapter 32

William Lyons hardly took time for a breath before he leaped into the next segment of his closing argument, the case involving the murder of Margaret Schmidt.

His first attack on the charges against Barone centered on the intent-to-rape issue. "We know that there was absolutely no physical evidence on the body of this sixty-one-year-old woman that anyone attempted to rape her or did anything that would give you that idea, other than the torn clothing and the underpants that were removed." To neutralize what he called an inference, Lyons cited a hypothesis: "Let's assume that Mr. Barone went in there with the intent to commit the crime of theft, goes into the bathroom to see what had fallen as the window was jiggled." Perhaps Lyons realized that using his client's name in the hypothetical wasn't a terrific idea, so he shifted gears. "And Mr. Barone or the perpetrator is standing there, and here's all this talcum powder. Look at those footprints. Suppose at that time the perpetrator hears Margaret Schmidt, "Who is in my house? Who is there?' [And he] runs a little bit, then into the bedroom, and kills her. And in the act of killing her, rips off her nightgown . . ."

Jurors looked puzzled. Was the attorney admitting Barone had done it? Was he trying to mitigate the horrible crime in some manner?" Lyons said, "The State has alleged burglary with the intent to commit rape. Unless you can find, beyond a reasonable doubt, that there was the intent to commit the crime of rape, you have to return a verdict of not guilty on that charge."

So, observers thought, the lawyer wasn't admitting anything, just trying to erase the word "aggravated" from the aggravated murder charge.

Lyons took another step along his convoluted path. "And, unless you can find, beyond a reasonable doubt, that this homicide, that this intentional killing was done to further the act of burglary with the intent to commit the crime of rape, then you have to acquit upon that charge."

The law is complex, and explanations of it are sometimes even more complex. Maybe that sharp lawyer down in Los Angeles had it right when he simplified his plea to the jury, "If it doesn't fit, you must acquit."

Suggesting a clear weakness in the inference that an attempted rape had occurred, Lyons asked, "Is it the only possible explanation? If you're attempting to rape someone, and in this case she's a large woman . . . and she's fighting and flailing about, that certainly would explain or could explain the ripped nightgown. How do you get the underwear off of this woman without them being ripped, if she is resisting and fighting?"

One observer wanted to jump up and say, "Sir, if you're holding a knife to the throat of a partly crippled woman, she may not be fighting and flailing. And she might do exactly what she's told to do." But the observer remained silent.

Lyons moved on posing another question. "Of all the witnesses you heard during the course of the Schmidt trial, who is the one you are immediately leery of? If you lived next door to Cesar Barone, and you came home and your mail was missing from your mailbox and you knocked on the door to ask, 'Cesar, have you seen my mail?' and he says, 'No,' would you believe him?"

The point Lyons wanted to make was that Barone was a liar. So, then, how could anyone believe the lies he told to the jailhouse informants. "He's a braggart, Mr. Barone is. He embellishes. He makes thing up." The prosecutor wondered how Barone had made up the parts of his confessions containing unpublished evidence. They also waited for the defense to tackle the shoeprint evidence. But Lyons sidestepped that issue like Michael Jordan putting a juke on a hapless guard. And not wearing Reeboks, either.

Lyons concluded his argument on the Schmidt murder by saying, "The facts, the evidence, in the Schmidt case do not support the allegations that the State has made in the charge of aggravated murder. Look very closely at it."

Shuffling some papers in front of him, Lyons raised his eyes to assure he had the attention of each juror. "Okay. I'm going to shift now and talk to you about the case involving Betty Williams. In this case, Mr. Barone is not charged with aggravated murder. The reason for that is obvious. There is no way under the sun, if you accept all the information and evidence . . . that Mr. Barone intentionally caused the death of Betty Williams. That takes it out of the realm of aggravated murder and into the realm of felony murder."

The distinction was important. The death penalty did not apply to felony murder.

The state, Lyons said, alleged that Barone, during the course of sexually abusing the victim, caused her death. And that Barone committed attempted rape. Once more, the defender asserted that Barone's stories should not be believed, and reminded jurors that the only evidence of sexual abuse or attempted rape came from informants, who had apparently believed Barone's wild tales. And how, Lyons wanted to know, could you believe informants who gave divergent accounts of what Barone had said?

"Betty Williams," Lyons declared, "spent the evening with Cesar Barone willingly, consensually." When Denise Nichols came over, he said, Barone hid in the background. "And Betty Williams is part of this game that is being played . . ." She winks at Denise. Is Cesar here? And then Cesar appears. There is absolutely no reason to suspect that Betty Williams and Cesar Barone were doing anything other than sitting around and drinking and talking at the time Denise arrived. That's clear.

"Mr. Barone, after leaving Denise's apartment comes back. We know he didn't force his way in. Nobody kicked the door in or anything of that sort." The drinking continued.

"Now Mr. Hanlon has suggested to you that Mr. Barone was plying her with liquor and forcing her to drink . . . I suggest that the evidence doesn't support that he was making a fifty-one-year-old woman drink against her will or that he was plying her with liquor. She drinks. You know from the evidence she likes to drink and she has a pretty substantial capacity for liquor . . . There is nothing untoward going on here.

"If a man is going to force a woman to engage in some sort of sexual relations with him . . . how do you get a woman's bra off and leave her sweater on? How can you do that? I know a woman can do that with a sweater on, but how would a man do it against her will? There's the bra on the living room floor, right in front of the couch. The inference there? Mr. Barone and Betty Williams were engaged in some sort of consensual activity.

"And this thing with the pants being down in a manner that suggests nonconsensual activity . . . that one leg is taken off in a totally normal manner. The other appears to be taken off in a somewhat different manner. But if that gives rise to the inference that someone was forcibly taking off Betty Williams's pants, I confess, the inference escapes me. I would submit it's to the contrary."

In her poor state of health, Lyons said, Betty Williams had a heart attack. Barone panicked and put her in the bathtub. To make it look like a drowning? Only a person in a panicky state would think that would work. But that was the effort. And we know Mr. Barone is a thief. He probably took her coin container. But, Lyons suggested, the defendant did not cause the death of Betty Williams.

"Well, ladies and gentlemen, that's really all I wanted to do, was to direct your attention towards the areas that I've discussed with you." Lyons said the prosecutors will be able to get up and offer rebuttal. It was his last time at bat. "I am asking you to use your common sense and logic . . . All the other things I've spoken about, I'm confident that you'll consider them and you'll do your job. Thank you."

Hermann and Hanlon would now have the opportunity to present rebuttal arguments, the final act of the drama. Then the judge would read instructions to the jury and send them to deliberations.

Reversing the order in which they'd presented closing arguments, Bob Hermann would talk about the Woodman and Schmidt cases, sandwiched around Hanlon's closing summary in the Williams murder.

Hermann stepped up first, greeted the jurors once more, and said he wouldn't drag them through all the evidence again, but he would refute some of Mr. Lyons's comments. One of the bulwarks of Lyons's argument was, "Don't believe anything Mr. Barone said, therefore you can't convict him . . . His client is a liar, by [Lyons's] own admission. And you might want to say to yourself, 'Geez, why would any . . . defense lawyer want to get up and admit their client was a liar? Well, desperate times take desperate means. Because . . . in trying to convince you that he's a bald-faced liar . . . is the only way that's going to cause enough confusion in your deliberations to give him some type of break, some type of lesser charge in this case.

"Now, let's talk a minute about Leonard Darcell . . . What counsel told you simply is not true. Mr. Darcell refused to testify and you heard the judge tell him he has no legal rights not to testify in this case. He had no Fifth Amendment rights not to testify. He was ordered to, refused, and was held in contempt of court . . . Was he protecting Mr. Barone? Was he protecting himself? Remember, this is the fellow that Mr. Barone told you, through witnesses, 'The kid freaked out. The kid was upset.' And he pointed a gun at him and told him, 'You could be next.'

"It's obvious that Mr. Barone had facts that only the killer knew." Hermann let that comment hang in the air for a moment to make sure the jurors appreciated its weight. "Mr. Barone is a liar, but even faced with the prospect of implicating himself in an aggravated murder, he never once mentions that Leonard Darcell was the killer. He describes himself doing the killing. He describes himself doing the killing. He describes how Darcell was freaked out about the killing. He describes beating this woman up . . .

"Another thing Mr. Lyons said, there is no evidence that this woman was the victim of any kind of forcible sexual assault; it could have been consensual." Holding up a photo of Woodman's battered features, Hermann said, "Well, I don't know about you, but just looking at her face, gunshot wound aside, it looks to me like that woman was beaten

severely about the face with numerous blows, with puncture
wounds under her chin. And furthermore, it's always a
good comeback, with a rape victim, to say, 'Hey, where is
the evidence of resistance?' Well, maybe somebody who
has a gun pointed at them would resist until the death, and
maybe they wouldn't. The law doesn't require a person
who is being subjected to rape or the threat of rape to say,
'See, I resisted. I only got shot once or I only got my face
beaten, only got my nose broken, but at least physically, I
can prove to you ladies and gentlemen of the jury that I
put up some sort of a fight.'

"We have his word that she was pleading for her life,
and he was jamming the gun up there. And we have the
facts, too. And we know a single gunshot wound, sure and
true, eliminated her from ever, ever, telling anybody
about anything.

"Well, I submit to you that Mr. Barone's statements to
you ring true. He made a mistake. He shouldn't have said
them. . . . He killed her so she'd never be in this courtroom.
And isn't it ironic his buddy wouldn't say the words, subjected himself to contempt of court, just as Mr. Barone had
planned he would . . . Isn't it ironic he convicted himself?

"Cesar Barone will get exactly what he deserves . . . and
that is, he'll be held legally responsible for her killing in all
four counts. Anything less in this case defies the law, and it
defies common sense in view of this evidence. Thank you."

Judge McElligott cleared his throat and said, "Mr. Hanlon is going to handle the rebuttal for the state in the case
involving Miss Schmidt. Mr. Hanlon?"

The tall prosecutor stood, shuffled his notes, and gripped
the lectern. He reminded the jurors that Lyons had said he
was not going to go over all the facts with them. "Well of
course he's not going to. If he had . . . all he would do is
hammer home to you the overwhelming amount of evidence to support a guilty verdict in Mr. Barone's having
killed, murdered Margaret Schmidt."

Hanlon's tone took on a touch of skepticism. "He tells
you, 'Mr. Barone could have been in that house, and he
could have been in there to steal, and he could have gone
into the bathroom and left those footprints, and then he

could have heard this woman awaken, and then he could have gone in there to murder her, and maybe it was accidental that the nightgown was torn from toe to neck.' This is wild-eyed conjecture, pure speculation. And he's hoping that you will adopt this, that you will misunderstand the evidence."

Stopping to take a breath, and perhaps calm his own anger, Hanlon said, "And that's all he can do . . . that's all the defense that could possibly be raised in this overwhelming abundance of evidence of the defendant's guilt." Now Hanlon openly mocked the defense: "Don't address the defendant's statements in jail other than to say, 'My client is a braggart and a liar.' Don't address the overwhelming evidence of the shoe prints. Just ignore it all and hope that you will ignore it, too."

After hitting lightly on a few of the issues Lyons had discussed, Hanlon reiterated gruesome details the informants had included in quoting Barone's confessions and ridiculed defense efforts to minimize it. "Don't be misled. Don't adopt this ridiculous myopic conjecture, speculation, guesswork, whatever you want to call it. Follow the evidence. Follow the hard evidence. Follow what the defendant said was happening."

The defendant had entered Margaret Schmidt's modest little house for the purpose of raping and killing her, Hanlon said. "Really, why else would he be there? There was nothing in that house worth stealing. He spotted her out on the porch where she sat, available for everybody in the neighborhood to see. He saw her, was interested, and went back, not in the daytime to steal or [commit a] strong-arm robbery, but under the stealth of darkness, in the middle of the night, as the woman lay sleeping . . . He was there to sexually assault her." The informants' stories contained reference to the walker, which had not been publicized, Hanlon said. They could only have known that from the killer.

"I'm tempted to get into something very theatrical, but I'm not going to. We need to prove to you that this was an intentional and deliberate killing. And you can envision Margaret Schmidt being awakened by the blankets being pulled off and this man on top of her, ripping her clothing away, pulling her panties off. She's struggling. She's a pretty helpless old woman, however. And you can imagine the force that would have been needed for this man, Cesar Barone, to get on top of her with a pillow, to use whatever necessary, his forearm, both forearms, the full weight of his body, whatever it took for three minutes. And I'm tempted to make you stare at the clock for three minutes and see how much you start squirming in your seats as you picture this helpless, defenseless woman, beseeching and imploring this man to let her live.

"Think about it. Three minutes he laid on top of this woman's face, choking the life out of her until he was successful. That is an intentional, deliberate, horrible death committed on a very nice . . . woman, well known to the neighbors, likes to sit and watch the neighborhood children come and go in the school, with her cats. He chose her because she is sexually exciting to him. He chose her for sexual purposes, and he raped her, attempted to rape her, and murdered her."

Cautioning the jury to carefully examine the complex verdict forms, which contained a variety of options, Hanlon asked them to be very careful. "And my last cautionary is this. Your function is to decide if the defendant did these things. Do not go in there and try to figure out why the defendant did these things. You will never come out of that jury deliberation room if you try to understand why Mr. Barone finds this old woman sexually attractive and why he'd want to smother her to death. You're no better suited to doing that than the four-hundred-dollars-an-hour psychiatrist that might want to try to figure this out. You're just not going to be able to do it. So keep your mind and attention focused on, 'Did he do it?' And that question is easy. Yes, he did it. Thank you."

For the final scene of the final act by the lawyers, Judge McElligott gave Bob Hermann center stage.

Speaking softly, Hermann said, "We've all heard of the concept of a person being scared to death. Is that medically sound?" He led the jury along the path of Dr. Gunson's testimony to suggest that it was quite possible. Tracing the investigation process again, and the multiple confessions informants and witnesses had attributed to Barone, Hermann said, "Now, this is a guy that you're asked to believe didn't attempt to sexually assault Betty Williams, precipitate that heart attack, even though there was property missing and even though his statements were inconsistent, just because he's a liar. Well, common sense and logic in this case is extremely important." Combine the admissions Barone made with the physical evidence, Hermann advised, and there could be only one conclusion.

It wasn't necessary to find that the death of Betty Williams had been intentionally caused, Hermann said, to find Barone guilty of murder. "It can be an accident. But if you're engaged in certain conduct defined by law, be it sexual abuse in the first degree or attempted rape, and your actions, because it's startling, frightening, causes that heart to misbeat and causes someone to die, then the law says you are guilty in this respect of felony murder and you have to suffer the consequences of your actions. And Cesar Barone, in this case of Williams, has told you himself, through the inmates, what he was up to, and he's guilty. Thank you."

The two defense attorneys huddled, compared notes, and began preparing a motion that same evening. Judge McElligott had made a remarkable error.

Chapter 33

With final arguments at last completed, Judge McElligott read the jury a long list of instructions previously worked out by the prosecutors and the defenders from a book of standard instructions. Mostly technical in nature, the guidelines are meant to help the jury understand what legalities apply to their verdicts. It was late in the afternoon when the twelve weighers of fact retired into their room to deliberate.

While they were out, the four attorneys caucused with the judge, and agreed that some detailed technical elements of the instructions needed further refining. Just as they finished rewording the definitions, the jury announced they'd reached verdicts in all counts, after less than two hours of deliberating. It caught the lawyers and judge completely off guard. Only one course of action could be taken.

Judge McElligott called the weary twelve back into the jury box where they expected to deliver their verdicts. Instead, the judge informed them that the instructions had been modified. He read the reworked words to them, and sent them trooping back to begin the process all over. They would have to reach verdicts within the revised guidelines.

It took the jurors nearly two more hours. The day had been exhausting, but at 10:15 P.M., they staggered back into the jury box and handed over their verdicts.

Hanlon and Hermann, with stubbles of beard darkening their grim faces, sat at the prosecution table, their thousands of pages of reference material stacked in boxes behind them. Rich and Lyons, at the defense table, looked concerned, but held an ace in the hole to ease their strain. Barone, at the far end of the table, rubbed a nervous finger against his compressed lips.

Judge McElligott surveyed the forms and nodded.

Cesar Francesco Barone was guilty on five counts of aggravated murder on the counts related to Chantee Woodman and Margaret Schmidt, and two counts of felony murder, with one extra count of murder, on the Betty Williams case. A penalty phase would be held the following week to decide if two more death sentences would be added to the one already hanging over his head for killing Martha Bryant. At least the jury would have a long holiday for Thanksgiving.

The two prosecutors congratulated themselves, took a deep breath, and launched preparations for the segment of the trial to decide Barone's fate. They worked all day Wednesday, enjoyed turkey with their families on Thursday, and met in Hermann's office on Friday to line up their penalty-phase strategy. They'd started to wrap up for the weekend when a colleague called late in the afternoon with a stunning rumor. They couldn't believe they hadn't noticed when it took place. Scrambling through transcripts of the trial, their hearts sank. The rumor was true!

In a brief moment eighteen days ago, after the jury had been selected, and prior to opening statements, a routine step people just took for granted should have been completed. But the critical step had been omitted from the proceedings.

Judge McElligott had forgotten to swear the jury in!

On the surface, it would appear to the layperson to be a harmless bureaucratic omission which had nothing to do with the guilt or innocence of Cesar Barone. But it had far greater implications.

As soon as Hermann and Hanlon rushed into McElligott's chambers that same evening to inform him, he blushed red, and wondered how it had happened. He couldn't think of any trial he'd ever heard of where a similar oversight had occurred. It was difficult to even imagine the results.

McElligott soon learned that defenders Rich and Lyons had noticed the failure instantly. Well, good Lord, why hadn't they brought it to his attention? He knew. The mistake could possibly cause an appeals court to overturn the entire trial.

The first order of business, of course, was to call a hearing of the lawyers. Then, when the penalty phase opened on Wednesday, November 29, McElligott would slap a ban-

dage on the open wound by swearing in the jury. Better
late than never.

On Tuesday morning at the hearing, none of the legal
experts could find a precedent for the unusual error. Jack
Morris, president of the Oregon Criminal Defense Association, said the swearing-in procedure was an essential element of the whole process, rooted in history. "It's
fundamental. It's not just a formality we can dispense with.
Sworn oaths are something we've incorporated as a society
into the most important of our affairs." Especially, he
added, if you have people deciding if someone lives or dies.

Was there an ethical obligation for the defense attorneys
to bring it to the judge's attention? The State Bar Ethics
Committee didn't think so. According to Lyons, the committee had said there was no obligation for them to report
the mistake. Lyons asked the judge to declare a mistrial
due to the error. No, McElligott snapped. The proceedings
would continue.

Cesar Barone, though, had remained silent long enough.
On Wednesday morning, as the penalty phase was about
to start, Barone angrily announced that he wanted no part
of it. Since McElligott had refused to nullify the trial over
the swearing-in omission, Barone growled, he would refuse
to participate, and wouldn't even remain in the courtroom.
If the judge forced him to stay, he promised to disrupt the
trial. "I'll object every time the prosecutor opens his
mouth," Barone threatened. "I have no desire to be here."
He'd turn his chair toward the wall and ignore the whole
farce. So back to the holding cell he went, escorted by
sheriff's deputies. He even declined the opportunity to
watch the trial via closed-circuit television.

The penalty phase lasted from November 29 to December 5. The only witnesses were called by the prosecution.
Barone's attorneys followed his instructions to call no one
to the stand. With the defendant back in the courtroom
once more, and his chair facing in the proper direction,
Judge McElligott asked him, personally, if he was sure
that's what he wanted when it might increase the chances
for the jury to come in with verdicts of death. Barone refused to look at the judge or to answer. Lyons stood up to

say, "This is his trial, your honor. This is his life." Not only did Barone decline to call witnesses, he wanted no closing arguments on his behalf. "I'm going to abide by those wishes," Lyons declared.

For the prosecution, Bob Hermann delivered a logical, yet impassioned review highlighting the important issues, concluding with an appeal to remember the long list of slaughtered women. He held photos of some of them in view of the jurors. "When you get back into the deliberation room—and it's a sad comment that I can't even hold these up in one hand, or even two hands—but maybe the better way to remember Cesar Barone's victims is not through the gory pictures of autopsies and gunshot wounds, but pictures of them as they were. And the reason we are here and the reason you are making your decision, and the reason Cesar Barone deserves the death penalty in both of these cases [Schmidt and Woodman] is because he killed these four human beings, and they will never have an opportunity to talk to you or face anyone else on this earth. And for that, Cesar Barone deserves the death penalty without question, in both of these cases. Thank you."

The jury retired, and returned one hour later.

Cesar Barone sat still as a stone. The only perceptible movement were his eyelids, blinking rapidly.

The defendant, Cesar Francesco Barone, is sentenced to 45 years in prison for the felony murder of Betty Williams.

For the aggravated murder of Chantee Woodman, Cesar Francesco Barone is sentenced to suffer the death penalty.

For the aggravated murder of Margaret Schmidt, Cesar Francesco Barone is sentenced to suffer the death penalty.

Two days after Cesar Barone's thirty-fifth birthday, deputies snapped handcuffs and leg shackles on him, and escorted him out, on his way to Salem, where he would join twenty other convicted killers. There had been no executions in Oregon for one-third of a century. One of the twenty men on death row would soon bring that long streak to an abrupt end.

PART FIVE

Why?

Chapter 34

All through the trials, for the investigators, for surviving victims, and for dead victims' families, a resounding question thundered through their lives. Why?

Why would a relatively handsome, physically healthy, intelligent young man have a morbid, destructive sexual appetite for elderly, disabled women? Why would he wish to rape and murder? Roger Hanlon warned the jurors not to ponder the question because that wasn't their duty. They would never finish the job in front of them, he said, if they tried to answer the question of why.

It searching for the "why?" it might be useful to first attempt to define the "what?" or classify the symptoms. The primary reference work for scientists involved in psychiatric diagnosis, analysis, and therapy is the *Diagnostic and Statistical Manual of Mental Disorders,* Fourth Edition (*DSM-IV*). A section of the book deals with antisocial personality disorder and lists criteria for identification of this behavioral syndrome. Cesar Barone seems to fit perfectly into this category of behavior, which is still sometimes referred to as a "sociopath."

Under the heading "Diagnostic Criteria for Antisocial Personality Disorder" is listed some of the following characteristics:

A. There is a pervasive pattern for and violation of the rights of others occurring since age 15 years, as indicated by three (or more) of the following:
   1. Failure to conform to social norms with respect to lawful behaviors as indicated by repeatedly performing acts that are grounds for arrest.
   2. Deceitfulness, as indicated by repeated lying, use of

aliases, or conning others for personal profit or
pleasure

3. Irritability and aggressiveness, as indicated by repeated physical fights or assaults

4. Reckless disregard for safety of self or others

5. Consistent irresponsibility, as indicated by failure to
sustain consistent work behavior or honor financial
obligations

6. Lack of remorse, as indicated by being indifferent
to or rationalizing having hurt, mistreated, or stolen
from another

B. The individual is at least eighteen years of age.

C. There is evidence of conduct disorder with onset before age fifteen years.

In the absence of empirical study of the individual, one
cannot make a reliable diagnosis, but Cesar Barone, by
these definitions, would certainly appear to be a classic example of the antisocial personality-disorder syndrome.

Saul Stolzberg, a renowned Southern California psychotherapist who has intensively studied the deviant behavior
of murderers and is conversant with the history of nearly
every known serial killer, made some observations. Without
the advantage of interviewing Barone, but from examining
what is known about his conduct and crimes, and from trial
records, Stolzberg wrote:

It would certainly seem that there would have to have
been some severe emotional trauma when Cesar's parents
separated during his early childhood. It is quite likely
that there may well have been tremendous feelings of
abandonment, rage, and anger at his mother's leaving the
family. His father may have also intensified those feelings
with his own rage and anger directed toward his wife,
Cesar's mother. Problems had to be readily apparent in
his family when Cesar's . . . stepmother recommended
counseling but the father did not pursue it.

As in all serial rapists and murderers, the perpetrator
operates in a world of power, control, and domination.
This too is the case with Mr. Barone. The early onset of
loss and abandonment of his mother, and the subsequent

death of his brother, intensified these emotions. The rape and strangulation of his ex-stepmother occurred within a month of his brother's death, which may well have triggered the event.

His mind-set seems to have been almost exclusively surrogate mother figures, including his ex-stepmother. As an adult, his rapes, sexual assaults, and murders seem to be more preoccupied with older women such as he might view his mother—vulnerable and over whom he was able to maintain an inordinate amount of power, control, and dominance.

Symbolically, by executing his victims with a bullet in the temple, or under the chin, or by strangulation, he is exercising the ultimate level of that power.

As with most psychopathic and sociopathic cases there is no remorse, coupled with considerable manipulation of people and various systems.

Stolzberg's observations would turn out to be remarkably similar to the opinions expressed by another expert.

In the Martha Bryant murder trial, penalty phase, the defense summoned perhaps the most respected, knowledgeable, and highly recognizable authority on serial murders in the country. Dr. Jack Levin, who is a professor of sociology and criminology at Northeastern University in Boston, has appeared frequently on the major television talk shows, often with Geraldo Rivera. His curly light hair and drooping mustache became familiar on the tube when he was regularly called upon to analyze the circus of the century in the O. J. Simpson trial. Levin, along with his colleague, James Alan Fox, also a favorite guest and friend of Geraldo Rivera, have co-authored several books on the subject of killers.

On January 27, 1995, Jack Levin settled in the witness chair in Judge McElligott's courtroom to answer questions put to him by defense attorney Griffith Steinke. It took quite some time for the expert to present his curriculum vitae, or résumé, of his remarkable accomplishments and qualifications that qualified him to testify as an expert.

Steinke said, "I'm going to be asking you some questions

about your research and also about Mr. Barone in particular, and I would like you to assume, hypothetically, that the following is in evidence." With that prologue, the legal word usage in which an attorney frames the background information about which he plans to ask questions, Steinke outlined a general biographical sketch of Cesar Barone's life history and his crimes. He pointed out that Barone had been convicted of murdering Martha Bryant, and also stood accused of killing Margaret Schmidt, Betty Williams, and Chantee Woodman, for which he was scheduled to be tried in October 1995. In Florida Barone had been indicted for the murder of Alice Stock.

Having made that introduction, Steinke gave Levin the opportunity to describe research he'd done with inmates at various prisons. There is often a tendency for expert witnesses to sound like classroom lecturers. Not Jack Levin. His enthusiasm for his subject took on its own energy, resounding through the courtroom with veritable authority.

With the eloquence of a person who loved his work, Levin reeled off examples of personally interviewing some of the most notorious serial killers on record. He'd traveled to Canada to visit Clifford Olson, a notorious pedophile who'd raped and murdered eleven children. At Kingston Penitentiary in Ontario, Levin spent a number of hours trying to penetrate the man's personality and motivations.

In Washington's state prison at Walla Walla, Levin had interviewed Kenneth Bianchi, one of the notorious "Hillside Stranglers." Bianchi and his cousin took the lives of ten young women in the Los Angeles area during the late seventies. Seeking seclusion, Bianchi moved to Washington but couldn't stop his homicidal urges. He raped and strangled two more women. Found guilty, he avoided the death penalty by agreeing to testify in the trial of his cousin.

After naming several others he had contacted, Levin continued. "It's not always easy to get access to serial killers." Many of them are on death row and waiting for the long process of appeals. Because condemned convicts have a self-serving interest in getting their convictions overturned, or at least avoiding execution, it is not unexpected that they would resort to lying. For Levin's analytical purposes, killers' stories laced with deception would be of little value.

Some of the more cunning men on death row would never consent to being interviewed by a behavior analyst for fear they might say or do something damaging to their appeals. There would be no reason to expect Cesar Barone to be any different.

Steinke sought to make it clear that his purpose in bringing Levin to Hillsboro was to persuade the jury to save Barone's life for the purpose of studying him in prison. The goal of understanding what drove him, and perhaps discovering ways to prevent such crimes, would be far more valuable to society, the defender argued, than simply carrying out a vengeful execution. If Barone refused to see Levin or other researchers because of his need to spend his energies on trying to avoid execution, his value for study would be diminished. The attorney asked Levin if more value could be found in a killer serving a life sentence than in one waging a daily battle to stay alive. Maybe the jury would see the distinction between how a convict on death row might react versus one sentenced to life in prison.

Levin helped. He said that the serial killers who are lifers are more likely to talk candidly and openly about their crimes. People on death row are always thinking about how to avoid execution.

Having driven home that point, Steinke shifted to another. "How common is serial murder?"

"Well, it's really rare," Levin answered. He estimated that approximately 20 serial killers each year account for no more than 200 victims. To some observers, that sounded like a lot of murdered people. Levin quickly explained that he wasn't being callous and acknowledged that the figure of 200 victims is far too many. The purpose of his study, he said, was to reduce the prevalence of serial murder. To put the numbers in perspective, he compared the 200 victims of serial killers to the 24,000 who die annually by the hands of murderers. But the serial killings, he pointed out, get most of the headlines. Levin stressed the importance of understanding the phenomenon.

"Is there impact disproportionate on society compared to other homicides?"

Steinke's question gave a great deal of latitude for a subjective answer. Some behavioral scientists might have answered by emphasizing the intense fear that serial killers cause in the public. Because so many of them are able to move invisibly in society, striking at random, everyone feels vulnerable. Ted Bundy was a perfect example of that problem. So was John Wayne Gacy, Chicago's stalker of young boys and men, and even David Berkowitz, New York's "Son of Sam."

Levin's answer agreed with the general consensus about fear. Serial murder, he said, usually hits front-page headlines and the top story on the eleven o'clock news, which exacerbates the terror that sweeps over the public. "You know," he commented, "people are scared to death anyway, and they're desperate when it comes to trying to resolve this problem of increasing crime." Levin's use of the term "scared to death" contained unintentional irony, in view of the death of Betty Williams, for which Barone had not yet been convicted when the professor testified. The expert witness agreed that serial murder is out of proportion to its prevalence.

Some observers wondered just how Levin would define a serial killer. The expert wasn't asked the question, so did not address it. Most scientists studying the problem agree that it might reasonably be defined as an individual who, over a period of time, murders three or more victims. The problem lies in trying to find characteristics linking them together, a cohesive pattern that might lead to predictability. There are some obvious similarities. The great majority of serial killers are white, male, of average intelligence, and are often loners. But those are too general to be of much help. Scientists like Levin hope to sort out more specific traits to use in studies.

Some studies are aimed at trying to determine the early backgrounds of serial killers. Were they abused, unloved children? Products of broken homes? How many of them suffered brain injuries somewhere along the way? And what motivates them? Defense attorneys frequently present evidence of horrific childhood abuse of men who became killers. One such case was Larry Eyler, who was convicted and sentenced to death in Illinois for killing a fifteen-year-old boy. Suspected of twenty other murders, he later offered to reveal what he knew about them in exchange for a commutation to life in prison. The state refused. In Eyler's trial, the defender revealed shocking details of savage abuse inflicted on the child by an alcoholic father and two stepfathers. In a California case, James Gregory Marlow received death penalties for killing two young women after sexually molesting them. He had the help of his girlfriend, who also sits on death row. As a child Marlow was neglected, beaten, and sexually abused by a male relative. His own mother seduced him and injected him with cocaine when the boy was thirteen.

Another factor with which analysts wrestle is the age at which killers start. Statistics show that murder is being committed by increasingly younger perpetrators. Adding more dimension to that picture, Levin expressed an interesting concept by saying, "I believe that serial killing gives us an opportunity to look at mainstream America. . . . Yes, it's very extreme, but a lot of what motivates serial killers also motivates kids in the inner cities and kids in small towns who are going out on a Saturday night and, for the thrill, for the excitement, bashing people, assaulting people." He bolstered the theory with some statistics, concluding that the homicide rate has gone up 124 percent since 1984 for fourteen-year-old boys.

Nearly all serious studies of serial murder stress the killers' need for control. Some analysts focus on sexual control. More commonly, though, they see murderers seeking the ultimate control, power over life and death. Jack Levin's view agreed, almost verbatim, with Saul Stolzberg's statement that "the perpetrator operates in a world of power, control, and domination."

On that theme Levin said, "What I found is that many serial killers are motivated by this excessive need for power and dominance and control. That's why they are so sadistic. That explains a lot of why they carry out sexual assaults. They enjoy squeezing the last gasp of breath from their dying victims. They love hearing their victims scream. That's why they do it. They feel superior." Some observers had no trouble placing Cesar Barone in the dead center of that mental picture.

Levin continued on that point for several minutes, winding it up with his pragmatic observation about contempo-

rary misspent youth. "So what they do is . . . go out on a
Saturday night. I think twenty or thirty years ago, they
would have stolen hubcaps. Now they go out looking for
someone to assault or maybe murder, go out in a group
and sometimes with a knife . . . (or) firearms." Again, it
was easy for listeners to visualize a long-haired youth
named Jimmy Rode slipping into the homes of vulnerable
elderly women to exercise power and control over them
with brutal force.

Steinke asked, "Dr. Levin, within that rare group that
you have described, how does Cesar Barone fit?"

Barone had puzzled investigators who spent months trying to solve a string of apparently unrelated murders. By
being inconsistent, he'd avoided the classic serial killer pattern that often leads to capture. Levin recognized the
anomalous behavior and explained its importance as related
to Barone. "We would like serial killers to be consistent,
so they're predictable, and, you know, they're not always
as consistent as we would like them to be. But I can tell
you this. The overwhelming majority of serial killers kill
strangers. They don't kill people they know. Apparently,
Barone did both. The overwhelming majority of serial killers either have a partner or they kill by themselves. Apparently, Barone did both. Once he used a partner, and then
for the other four he did them alone. Most serial killers
don't also become serial rapists. I mean, they either murder
their victims or they don't murder their victims. But Barone
did both . . . The only pattern that I can see is that Barone
killed women, and that's very common, and especially older
women, again very common."

One of the things that evidently appealed to Cesar Barone was the helplessness of the women he victimized. Some
critics would call it cowardice. Levin saw it more objec-
tively, pointing out that serial killers often target their victims based on vulnerability. Prostitutes, he noted, are
especially attractive targets. Of course, he was right. Two
hundred miles north of Barone's bloody trail, "The Green
River Killer" had left the bodies of hookers scattered for
miles over a period of years, and hadn't yet been caught.
The savaged remains of four prostitutes turned up during
the mid-eighties in North Portland, Barone's stomping

grounds, and investigators worked diligently to link them to the Green River case, but never proved it.

Not all murdered prostitutes are women. In Southern California, men and boys willing to sell their sexual services began vanishing in the early seventies. Randy Steven Kraft cruised bars and highways looking for young male victims and is believed to have killed 67 of them between 1972 and 1983. Kraft was convicted of 16 murders, which sent him to California's death row at San Quentin. New reports recently revealed that Kraft organized a routine in the prison exercise yard, joining three other men each day for a game of bridge. His partners included Lawrence Bittaker, who used pliers on the nipples of at least five young women he killed in the back of a van, and Bill Bonin, who lured boys into his car and left their mutilated bodies alongside freeways, thus being dubbed "The Freeway Killer." The card games were interrupted early in 1996 when Bonin died by lethal injection.

Serial killers, some experts think, are divided between sociopaths and psychopaths. Sociopaths, it has been said, know what they are doing is wrong, but they don't care. Psychopaths, on the other hand, may not understand the difference between right and wrong, so they suffer no guilt or pains of conscience. Jack Levin calls them confused and disorganized, and says that they are easily captured because they're not methodical or careful. He testified, "They kill to prevent earthquakes. You know, they hear the voice of demons or maybe even God, they think, telling them what to do."

But Cesar Barone, he said, was neither. "He didn't talk to dogs and he didn't hallucinate. He's not out of touch with reality. In fact, my guess is that he knows exactly what he's doing and he chooses to do it." The expert reemphasized that Barone did not demonstrate the organization with which some serial killers operate. "I mean, he didn't try to dump the bodies. He didn't restrain the victims. He didn't do anything that you would expect an organized serial killer to do."

Levin added, "So you know, in almost every count, when talking about whether he used a partner or not, whether he's a serial killer or not, whether he targets strangers or not, or whether he's organized or disorganized, he doesn't fit any patterns. He is very rare among a rare breed. He didn't do anything that you would expect an organized serial killer to do. . . . I haven't seen too many like Barone, I'll tell you."

The importance of organized preparation by serial killers was expressed by California's "Night Stalker," Richard Ramirez, who set off a wave of shivering panic in the late eighties during a prolonged rampage that left thirteen people dead. He reportedly said, "To be a good killer you have to plan things out carefully. You've got to be prepared in every way when the moment comes to strike; you cannot hesitate."

Even though Cesar Barone didn't appear to fit any of the patterns, his defense attorney argued that he might be worth studying. Steinke asked Jack Levin if that very nonconformity made Barone a particularly valuable research object. Levin said he thought so, and would like to have the opportunity to understand Barone. "And by the way, that's another thing. . . . It's hard to find a serial killer who uses a gun. Barone did, at least in a couple of cases, as I understand it. Why would a serial killer use a firearm? I mean, that only robs him of his greatest pleasure, that is, exalting in his victim's misery, causing that kind of suffering with his own hand. I know this is disgusting, but it's the physical contact that most serial killers enjoy so much. They're having fun at our expense. But Barone used a firearm . . . not consistently, of course. . . . It's just not like most serial killers."

Steinke wanted to know if Levin would like to be personally involved in research involving Barone. The professor said he certainly would. But he hadn't yet interviewed Barone, and wasn't sure the timing would be right to do so very soon. Levin explained. "You know, he has a vested interest in lying. . . . He wants to save himself from execution. And just like other serial killers on death row . . . they're not going to be very candid."

Barone, like all serial killers, could have stopped at any time, but he didn't. Scientists agree on the importance of understanding why killers seek more victims after the first one. Stanford University psychology professor David Rosenhan told author Dennis McDougal, "The first murder is like a good meal. A truly memorable meal. The kind you can shut your eyes and remember for years afterward. All the other murders stem from that first one, like you or me trying to recapture that perfect dinner we experienced once in a little Parisian cafe. But we never recapture it."

Richard Ramirez, the "Night Stalker," according to a writer, expressed the same thought. "For a true killer, a good murder is like a good meal: you want to make it last and get the most out of it."

Jack Levin didn't compare the blood lust to a meal, but agreed on the importance of knowing why killers strike more than once. It would take intensive research to find the answers. He commented, "We're in the dark ages . . . we need to understand where this horrible thing comes from so we can prevent it."

Griffith Steinke formulated his next questions to reinforce the need for more research on the subject, with the hope the jury would see Barone as a prime candidate for study.

"Do you need research subjects alive for more than a few years?"

Yes, Levin said, comparing it to the quest for a cure to cancer. He said that eventually science would make a breakthrough. Levin hoped it would be soon. "I'd like to have a sample of subjects around to study when we do come up with some breakthrough ideas."

After winding down by underscoring the extreme importance of additional study, Steinke turned the witness over to Bob Hermann.

The prosecutor first wanted to know when the professor had initially learned of Cesar Barone. Levin recalled that it had happened recently because he associated it with the timing of being interviewed by *People* magazine about Jeffrey Dahmer's death. Hermann asked if Levin had been interested in studying several killers from the Pacific Northwest, including Dayton Leroy Rogers, Westley Allan Dodd, and Jerome Brudos. Levin had heard of them, but hadn't studied them in detail.

"Did you interview Danny Rolling, the Gainesville [Florida] serial killer?

"No."

_ "You wrote a book about him, though, right?"

"Yes I did. But there were other people who interviewed him, and I was able to use those interviews."

"Mr. Rolling is on death row, isn't he?"

"Yes."

"Is it your position that anybody who is on death row just really doesn't satisfy your requirements?"

"No, no. That would be ridiculous." Levin explained that he was talking about guys who have a vested interest in saving themselves.

Hermann got an agreement from Levin that Cesar Barone is "pathological in his lying." The prosecutor asked, "What guarantee can you give us . . . that Mr. Barone is ever going to give you a straight answer to any of your questions?"

"I have absolutely no guarantee of that."

"In reaching your conclusion that you'd like to study him, did you take into consideration the potential danger to inmates, guards, barbers, bakers, so forth, that will be coming into contact with Mr. Barone over the next years?"

"I did. I understand what you're saying, and it isn't easy for me either." Levin expressed hope that Barone would be kept under close custody or in isolation. "I can tell you this. People could have said the same thing about Jeffrey Dahmer, and let me point out that he was the one that was murdered. Because the truth is, serial killers are not well liked by other inmates. They're at the bottom of the status hierarchy in most prisons, and their lives are on the line. What I'm saying is, it's more likely that he's going to be murdered in prison, and I won't get the chance to study him."

The last few exchanges were more in the way of pleasantries, and Steinke had no re-direct questions. The witness stepped down.

Jack Levin's testimony wound down the penalty phase of Cesar Barone's first murder trial, for killing Martha Bryant.

In the second trial, no experts, or any witnesses, were called for the penalty phase of the Woodman, Schmidt, and Williams murders. On December 5, 1995, one day after Cesar Barone's thirty-fifth birthday, the jury returned with recommendations for two more death penalties. Judge McElligott later made the sentences official.

In the study of serial killers, so many questions remain unanswered. For example, what are the effects of violence and gore dished out so liberally in motion pictures and on television? When the horrors of killer-cannibal Jeffrey Dahmer, who admitted to killing sixteen young men, became known to the public, it was revealed that he owned videotapes of his favorite movies, *The Exorcist, Exorcist II: The Heretic, Hellraiser,* and *Hellbound: Hellraiser II.* Ted Bundy blamed pornography for his crimes. John Wayne Gacy typed a long list of things he regarded as important in his life, titled "Bio Review." In it he identified the television show *Unsolved Mysteries* as one of his favorites. Among movies he liked was *GoodFellas,* which in 1990 graphically depicted murder in the world of organized crime. Richard Ramirez studied *The Satanic Bible* and declared himself a believer in it.

Questions far outnumber answers. The potential for learning what makes killers tick is an unplowed field. Until science finds ways to explore the human mind with technology rather than subjective interviews, it may remain that way.

At the close of the Oregon trials, authorities transported Cesar Barone to a cell in death row in the state prison at Salem. Whether or not he submits to behavior analysis remains to be seen. More than likely, he will spend most of his time seeking to have the verdicts overturned, or preparing to defend himself against murder charges in Florida.

Epilogue

Officials in Florida didn't wait long to extradite Cesar Barone. He returned to his home state on January 8, 1996, to face charges of murdering Alice Stock over sixteen years earlier.

There was no homecoming party. His sister, Debbie, expressed her familial affection for him, saying, "I would never turn my back on him."

Barone's father, though, maintained a cold distance. "I haven't spoken to my son in fifteen years," he said, and chose not to offer any more details.

It wasn't a matter of dragging a screaming, resisting prisoner across country against his will. On the contrary, Barone hastened the move by filing a formal request for the transfer. The sooner the better, he said. "My catalyst is Florida," he told a reporter, "getting this case off my back. I think it's going to work this time." He wouldn't even be facing the charges, he complained, except that Broward County authorities just wanted "to get on the bandwagon." Acquittal in Florida, Barone said, would give him the momentum to return to Oregon, force appeals courts to overturn those four murder convictions and lead to ultimate exoneration, which he confidently said would happen as soon as he could get a fair jury.

Strategically, the request to be returned to Florida was a shrewd one. He submitted the paperwork just prior to the outset of his final trial in Hillsboro, and Broward County authorities received it on October 10, 1995. By law, officials had 180 days, from date of receipt, to begin trial proceedings in Florida. Barone complained that he'd actually initiated the request in September and immediately filed a motion to dismiss the charges because he'd been denied his constitutional rights to a speedy trial. After a judge ruled against that motion, Barone lodged an appeal in early April 1996, on the very day jury selection for his trial was scheduled to start. The trial was postponed.

During his years of participating in the legal maneuvers of his trials, Barone had learned a few things about the law. He filed the Florida appeal himself. But the judge appointed an attorney to process it correctly, saying Barone, "doesn't know that much."

In any case, after a series of hearings, the trial was repeatedly postponed. Finally, with the matter still somewhere in the convoluted pipeline of appeals, Florida authorities decided to ship Barone back to Oregon State Penitentiary until final resolution of the matter.

Meanwhile, on Oregon's death row, an inmate decided he'd had enough of the appeals nonsense. Douglas "the Animal" Wright, the tough bodybuilder, wrote to a friend, "Some dudes prefer life to death. But not me. I'd just as soon get the whole thing over with. I hate prison, I hate noise, petty rules. . . . I've got so much anger and hatred inside me . . ."

Refusing any legal maneuvers, Wright demanded to be executed. At one minute after midnight, Friday morning, September 6, 1996, he lay strapped on a gurney, hands and fingers taped so he couldn't flex his muscles to work the needle out of his arm. He looked through the blinds that had just been raised between the execution room and the visitors' gallery. A woman sat there, in a wheelchair. Her son had died when Wright fired three bullets into his brain. The mother and the convict locked eyes. His mouth formed two words. "I'm sorry."

Someone gave a signal, and the lethal chemicals poured through tubes. By five minutes after midnight, his chest stopped rising and falling.

Oregon had finally reopened the door to capital punishment, closed for thirty-four years.

Cesar Barone arrived back on death row one day later.

Prosecutor Roger Hanlon cautioned a writer not to put too much stock in the resumption of implementing the death penalty. "Don't confuse execution of a man who re-

fused all appeals with finally sending one to his death who
fights it all the way." He's no doubt correct. But Oregon
voters still support the death penalty three to one.

In Hillsboro, Sergeant Tom Robinson remains at the
head of his group of detectives, continually expanding their
investigations of theft in the county's growing high-tech industry, plus the ongoing violent crimes that come with spiraling population. His personal accomplishments are
exemplified by a plaque on the wall of his second-story
office. Lettered in gold on a blue background, enclosed by
an oak frame, and presented to him by the Washington
County law Enforcement Council, it reads, . . . SERGEANT
TOM ROBINSON, FOR HIS OUTSTANDING LEADERSHIP AND
CONTRIBUTION.

Lieutenant Lila Ashenbrenner accepted a promotion to
captain.
Sergeant Mark Christy, over in Cornelius, grinned with
pride when the Veterans of Foreign Wars, Forest Grove
Post, handed him a Law Enforcement Award plaque en-
graved with his name and the words, IN GRATEFUL RECOGNI-
TION OF UNYIELDING ADHERENCE TO THE HIGHEST IDEALS OF
LAW ENFORCEMENT IN MAINTAINING, PRESERVING, AND PRO-
TECTING THE LAWFUL RIGHTS OF ALL CITIZENS. 1996. It hangs
right next to his plaque naming him CORNELIUS POLICE DE-
PARTMENT EMPLOYEE OF THE YEAR, 1994.

Detective Michael O'Connell stood in front of more than
300 people to accept Washington County's bestowal of its
highest honor, a Bronze Medal of Honor for an outstanding
act or conspicuous service in the line of duty. He was recognized specifically for his determination and performance in
bringing Cesar F. Barone to justice.

Sergeant Cleo Howell of the WCSO, who also worked
on the investigation, received a Bronze Medal of Honor,
for his twenty years of outstanding service.

The impact of Judge Michael McElligott's oversight in
not swearing in the jury remains to be seen. Appeals courts

will give it due consideration and make a ruling, but they are not usually in a hurry.

McElligott's words still resounded in the memory of everyone involved in Martha Bryant's life and the trial which convicted her killer. "We still have people changing their lives because of what happened in October 1992, both in terms of the conduct of the defendant and its impact on society."

About forty paces east of the sight where Martha Bryant was abducted from her stalled Volkswagen, a rectangular granite marker was placed by her friends from the Tuality maternity ward. Flush with the grassy strip between the sidewalk and Cornell Road, a few feet from a flowering cherry tree planted to memorialize the slain midwife, the marker is engraved with these words:

> In Memory of MARTHA BRYANT
> We planted this tree
> to express our sorrow and rage at those
>   Who took a kind and loving
>   Midwife
>   From tomorrow
> A beautiful tree to grow and flower
> in place of memories of
> the last hour
>   So that Martha's peace and strength
>   Endure
>   We'll carry her spirit with us
>   To hold the future.

Etched into the stone, on the right side of the plaque are a pair of open hands, held apart, symbolically "catching" a baby.

⬡ ONYX

HAUNTING TRUE-CRIME

☐ **FINAL JUSTICE by Steven Naifeh and Gregory White Smith.** This shocking book exposes the behind-the-scenes true story of how Cullen Davis, heir to a legendary Texas dynasty of oil and money, used his power and wealth to protect himself from charges of murder. Filled with pulsating courtroom dramas, this book will change the way you think about the American justice system forever. (405137—$5.99)

☐ **MORMON MURDERS: A True Story of Greed, Forgery, Deceit, and Death by Steven Naifeh and Gregory White Smith.** The Salt Lake City car bomb murders that rocked the foundations of the Mormon Church. Exclusive interviews and secret documents reconstruct the most riveting tale of God and greed ever exposed. "Compelling, un-put-downable ... a first-rate true-crime thriller!"—*Detroit Free Press* (401522—$6.99)

☐ **POISONED DREAMS** *A True Story of Murder, Money, and Family Secrets* **by A. W. Gray.** A shattering account that gives us a glimpse into the lifestyles and sins of the Texas rich and famous. True crime at its most powerful and most revealing. **"A jewel—must reading!"**—*Jack Olsen* (405064—$5.99)

☐ **LETHAL SHADOW by Stephen G. Michaud.** With 8 pages of graphic photos! When U.S. Secret Service agents arrested Mike DeBardeleben, they thought they had captured the most cunning counterfeiter ever to elude them for years. Little did they know that they had also captured a sadistic sex slayer. (405307—$5.99)

*Prices slightly higher in Canada

Buy them at your local bookstore or use this convenient coupon for ordering.

PENGUIN USA
P.O. Box 999 — Dept. #17109
Bergenfield, New Jersey 07621

Please send me the books I have checked above.
I am enclosing $_____ (please add $2.00 to cover postage and handling). Send check or money order (no cash or C.O.D.'s) or charge by Mastercard or VISA (with a $15.00 minimum). Prices and numbers are subject to change without notice.

Card #_____ Exp. Date _____
Signature_____
Name_____
Address_____
City _____ State _____ Zip Code _____

For faster service when ordering by credit card call 1-800-253-6476

Allow a minimum of 4-6 weeks for delivery. This offer is subject to change without notice.

🅓 SIGNET   🅔 ONYX

INCREDIBLE—BUT TRUE CRIME

☐ **SLEEP MY CHILD, FOREVER The Riveting True Story of a Mother Who Murdered Her Own Children by John Coston.** Without evidence of any kind, physical or medical, Detective Sergeant Joseph Burgoon of the St. Louis homicide division, slowly unraveled a labyrinth of deceptions and lies to reveal Ellen Boehm as a cold-blooded killer who couldn't wait to collect on the large insurance policies she had secretly taken out on her children.
(403355—$5.99)

☐ **PRECIOUS VICTIMS: *A True Story of Motherly Love and Murder* by Don W. Weber and Charles Bosworth, Jr.** Who would believe a mother would kill her two-week-old baby? Here is the terrifying story of the twisted hate that seethed below the surface of a seemingly normal family. (171845—$5.99)

☐ **EVERY MOTHER'S NIGHTMARE by Charles Bosworth. With 8 pages of photos.** When Jude Govreau's teenage daughter and Mari Winzen's three-year-old son are found hideously slain, the two mothers join in a fierce resolve to see the killer brought to justice. This is the riveting story of what happens when mother love turns to hating the guilty—and becomes a force greater than the law and the lawless combined.
(405374—$5.99)

☐ **THE DREAMS OF ADA by Robert Mayer.** A true story of murder, obsession and a small town. . . . "An outstanding book . . . the strange twists and turns of the case are more compelling than the finest mystery novel."—
The New Mexican
(169816—$5.99)

*Prices slightly higher in Canada

Buy them at your local bookstore or use this convenient coupon for ordering.

PENGUIN USA
P.O. Box 999 — Dept. #17109
Bergenfield, New Jersey 07621

Please send me the books I have checked above.
I am enclosing $_____ (please add $2.00 to cover postage and handling). Send check or money order (no cash or C.O.D.'s) or charge by Mastercard or VISA (with a $15.00 minimum). Prices and numbers are subject to change without notice.

Card #_____ Exp. Date _____
Signature_____
Name_____
Address_____
City _____ State _____ Zip Code _____

For faster service when ordering by credit card call **1-800-253-6476**

Allow a minimum of 4-6 weeks for delivery. This offer is subject to change without notice.

Ⓢ SIGNET   Ⓞ ONYX

SHOCKING TRUE-CRIME

☐ **DONNIE BRASCO My Undercover Life In the Mafia A True Story by FBI Agent Joseph D. Pistone with Richard Woodley. The National Best-seller!** Posing as jewel thief "Donnie Brasco," Joseph D. Pistone carried out the most audacious sting operation ever. Now his unforgettable eyewitness account brings to pulsing life the entire world of wiseguys and draws a chilling picture of what the Mafia is, does, and means in America today. **"Courageous and extraordinary"**—*New York Times Book Review*   (192575—$6.99)

☐ **KILLING SEASON The Unsolved Case of New England's Deadliest Serial Killer by Carlton Smith.** With in-depth research and eye-opening new testimony, this enthralling true-crime masterpiece is the story of the horrifying victimization of women, their vicious murders, and shocking official impotence. (405463—$5.99)

☐ **CHAIN OF EVIDENCE A True Story of Law Enforcement and One Woman's Bravery by Michael Detroit.** This thrilling, true account of a woman undercover police officer who infiltrated the Hell's Angels in Orange County, California, reveals as never before the dangerous risks and the exciting triumph of a law enforcement operation over a far-reaching crime network.   (404629—$5.99)

☐ **DEADLY THRILLS The True Story of Chicago's Most Shocking Killer by Jaye Slade Fletcher. With 8 pages of photos.** Here is the startling true account of a "boy-next-door" electrician whose twisted desires produced unspeakable havoc in the Chicago area. This incredible but all-too-real journey will take you into the heart of Robin Gecht, a monstrously evil man who ritually mutilated his victims and subjected their bodies to shocking acts of sexual violation.   (406257—$5.99)

*Prices slightly higher in Canada

Buy them at your local bookstore or use this convenient coupon for ordering.

PENGUIN USA
P.O. Box 999 — Dept. #17109
Bergenfield, New Jersey 07621

Please send me the books I have checked above.
I am enclosing $_____ (please add $2.00 to cover postage and handling). Send check or money order (no cash or C.O.D.'s) or charge by Mastercard or VISA (with a $15.00 minimum). Prices and numbers are subject to change without notice.

Card #_____ Exp. Date _____
Signature_____
Name_____
Address_____
City _____ State _____ Zip Code _____

For faster service when ordering by credit card call **1-800-253-6476**

Allow a minimum of 4-6 weeks for delivery. This offer is subject to change without notice.

① SIGNET   ⑧ ONYX

UNFORGETTABLE TRUE CRIME STORIES

☐ **WHO WILL CRY FOR STACI?** *The True Crime Story of a Grieving Father's Quest for Justice* **by Milton J. Shapiro with Marvin Weinstein.** With 8 pages of photos. On an October afternoon in 1982, ten-year-old Staci Weinstein was found savagely beaten and shot to death in her bedroom. From the moment he'd discovered his daughter's battered and abused body, Marvin vowed that Staci's killers would get their due punishment. This is the gripping account of one man's relentless crusade for justice.   (406044—$5.99)

☐ **A STRANGER IN THE FAMILY** *A True Story of Murder, Madness, and Unconditional Love* **by Steven Naifeh and Gregory White Smith.** Handsome, charming, straight-arrow son of a perfect all-American family, Richard Daniel Starrett was the dangerous visitor for too many unlucky young women in Georgia and South Carolina in the late 1980s. Answering "for sale" ads in the classifieds, he was a buyer hunting for victims, not bargains, and he paid in grim coin: rape, kidnapping, murder. "A powerful and perceptive study."—*Publishers Weekly*   (406222—$6.99)

☐ **BLOOD LEGACY** *A True Story of Family Betrayal and Murder* **by Judith Reitman.** With 8 pages of photos. For five months the putrid body of Robert Caris lay undisturbed in the attic of the home in elegant Southhampton, Long Island, until stunned police brought it out. The killer: the victim's wife, Arlene. Her defense: years of abuse at the hands of her husband—or so she claimed. This harrowing account probes the dark heart of a murderer as it unforgettably reveals a violently dysfunctional family.   (406516—$5.99)

Prices slightly higher in Canada

Buy them at your local bookstore or use this convenient coupon for ordering.

PENGUIN USA
P.O. Box 999 — Dept. #17109
Bergenfield, New Jersey 07621

Please send me the books I have checked above.
I am enclosing $_____ (please add $2.00 to cover postage and handling). Send check or money order (no cash or C.O.D.'s) or charge by Mastercard or VISA (with a $15.00 minimum). Prices and numbers are subject to change without notice.

Card #_____ Exp. Date _____
Signature_____
Name_____
Address_____
City _____ State _____ Zip Code _____

For faster service when ordering by credit card call **1-800-253-6476**

Allow a minimum of 4-6 weeks for delivery. This offer is subject to change without notice.

Ⓢ SIGNET   Ⓞ ONYX

RIVETING TRUE CRIME

☐ **TILL MURDER DO US PART by Ernest Volkman and John Cummings.** This page-turning true story is at once a riveting behind-the-scenes account of a notorious crime and a heart-wrenching portrait of a family victimized and torn apart by an abusive father. (404297—$5.50)

☐ **FATAL CHARM by Carlton Smith.** Randy Roth . . . was hardworking, morally firm, did not drink or do drugs, and kept himself in superb physical condition. Even better, he was courteous and kind—a perfect gentleman. When his second wife died on a hiking trip, it seemed a tragic accident. But when wife number four drowned on a boating outing, suspicions mounted. (404165—$4.99)

☐ **TO DIE FOR by Joyce Maynard.** The shocking story of a young woman who seduced her sixteen-year-old lover into committing the cold-blooded murder of her husband. "A powerful novel of murder and sexual obsession . . . chilling."—*Newark Star-Ledger* (173279—$5.99)

☐ **MURDERER WITH A BADGE by Edward Humes.** "Fascinating . . . a superbly crafted chronicle of one of the most complex, enigmatic criminals in memory . . . far stronger and more compelling than most crime fiction."—*Kirkus Reviews* (404025—$5.99)

*Prices slightly higher in Canada

Buy them at your local bookstore or use this convenient coupon for ordering.

PENGUIN USA
P.O. Box 999 — Dept. #17109
Bergenfield, New Jersey 07621

Please send me the books I have checked above.
I am enclosing $_____ (please add $2.00 to cover postage and handling). Send check or money order (no cash or C.O.D.'s) or charge by Mastercard or VISA (with a $15.00 minimum). Prices and numbers are subject to change without notice.

Card #_____ Exp. Date _____
Signature_____
Name_____
Address_____
City _____ State _____ Zip Code _____

For faster service when ordering by credit card call **1-800-253-6476**

Allow a minimum of 4-6 weeks for delivery. This offer is subject to change without notice.